Theatre, Opera and Consciousness

General Editor:
Daniel Meyer-Dinkgräfe

Theatre, Opera and Consciousness
History and Current Debates

Daniel Meyer-Dinkgräfe

Amsterdam - New York, NY 2013

Cover image created by Brigitte Abt-Harrer

Cover design by Aart Jan Bergshoeff

The paper on which this book is printed meets the requirements of "ISO 9706:1994, Information and documentation - Paper for documents - Requirements for permanence".

ISBN: 978-90-420-3663-5
ISSN: 1573-2193
E-Book ISBN: 978-94-012-0929-8
E-book ISSN: 1879-6044
© Editions Rodopi B.V., Amsterdam - New York, NY 2013
Printed in the Netherlands

Contents

Acknowledgments

Some of the material in this book is based on earlier versions of published work: case study four in Chapter One is revised from the 2009 "Body against Boundaries: Consciousness in Raimund Hoghe's Choreography". In *Consciousness, Theatre, Literature and the Arts 2009*, ed. Daniel Meyer-Dinkgräfe, 155-158. Newcastle: Cambridge Scholars Publishing. Chapter Two on Consciousness and ethics is revised from the 2010 "The Ethical Dimension of Theatre". In *Ethical Encounters: Boundaries of Theatre, Performance and Philosophy*, eds. Daniel Meyer-Dinkgräfe and Dan Watt, 135-153. Newcastle: Cambridge Scholars Publishing. An earlier and shorter version of Chapter Four is in press with Palgrave in Jade Rosina McCutcheon and Barbara Sellers-Young (eds), *Embodied Consciousness: Technologies of Performance*, in the chapter entitled "Embodied consciousness: warm-up and cool-down". "Opera and spirituality", and "Spiritual aspects of operatic singing" are based on "Opera and Spirituality", *Performance and Spirituality* 2:1 (2011), 38-59. Online at http://www.utdl.edu/ojs/index.php/pas/article/viewFile/3/3; and "Spiritual Aspects of Operatic Singing: Klaus Florian Vogt". *Performance and Spirituality* 3:1 (2012), 71-94. http://www.utdl.edu/ojs/index.php/pas/article/viewFile/49/18, respectively. I would like to thank Harry Youtt and Per Brask for their very insightful comments on a draft of this book.

Introduction

The *Consciousness, Literature and the Arts* research context, 2000-2013

Thirteen years have passed since the launch of the referred web journal *Consciousness, Literature and the Arts*, and with it the publication of more than 150 original articles that relate aspects of theatre, literature and the arts to aspects researched in consciousness studies. Eight years have passed since the launch of two book series in 2005, *Theatre and Consciousness* with Intellect (three titles published so far) and *Consciousness, Literature and the Arts* with Rodopi (thirty-one titles published so far). Eight years have passed since the launch, in 2005, of the biannual international conferences on *Consciousness, Theatre, Literature and the Arts*, which so far have attracted 250 different delegates from more than thirty countries across the world. It is therefore time to reassess the achievements of the field .

Consciousness studies as a discipline was launched in 1994 by the Center for Consciousness Studies at the University of Arizona in Tucson, USA, funded by the Fetzer Institute. The *Journal for Consciousness Studies* was founded in 1994, the *Association for the Scientific Study of Consciousness* in 1996, with its journal, *Consciousness and Cognition*. The British Psychological Society approved two consciousness-related sections in 1997: *Consciousness and Experiential Psychology* and *Transpersonal Psychology*. The discipline of consciousness studies provides an umbrella for a range of individual disciplines that have studied, in their own ways, how we think, feel and act, why we think, feel and act as we do, and what it feels like to think, feel and act as we do. The contributing disciplines are philosophy, neuroscience, cognitive sciences and psychology, and physical and biological sciences. Thus it is likely that a large percentage of departments, institutes or schools representing these disciplines in many universities world-wide will have some contribution to consciousness studies to offer. In some cases such contribution is implicit, for example when departments of philosophy emphasise the research interest of one or more staff members in *philosophy of mind*. In other cases such contribution is explicit, for example in the case of the Sackler Centre for Consciousness Science at the University of Sussex. In the context of those disciplines, consciousness studies cannot be anything else than mainstream: well-established in academia across the world.

The list of constituent disciplines that make up consciousness studies is complemented by two further lists of academic fields that contribute to it: one focuses on *experiential approaches* to consciousness not covered explicitly within the disciplines mentioned so far, and encompassing the following: meditation, contemplation and mysticism; hypnosis; other altered states of consciousness; transpersonal and humanistic psychology; psychoanalysis and psychotherapy; lucid dreaming; anomalous experiences; and parapsychology. From this list, psychoanalysis and psychotherapy are without doubt mainstream, whereas the remaining ones could be classified as either niche (transpersonal and humanistic psychology, altered states of consciousness, parapsychology, and hypnosis), or emerging (meditation, contemplation and mysticism, lucid dreaming, and anomalous experiences).

The second list, under the heading *culture and humanities* encompasses the fields that may also contribute to the understanding of consciousness, but which predominantly benefit from the findings of consciousness studies in the understanding of the contents specific to them. The sub-headings here are: literature and hermeneutics; art and aesthetics; music; religion; mythology; sociology; anthropology; information technology; ethics and legal studies; and education. From this list, only mythology might be placed into the niche category, while the others are squarely mainstream.

Consciousness studies, then, can be understood as a useful umbrella for predominantly mainstream disciplines, with some niche and some emerging contributions, that study consciousness, defined as how we think, feel and act, why we think, feel and act as we do, and what it feels like to think, feel and act as we do. The arts and humanities disciplines contribute to this understanding to some extent, but to a larger extent the arts and humanities benefit from the insights of other disciplines under the umbrella of consciousness studies in developing the understanding and knowledge specific to their own disciplines.

For the remainder of this section I want to explore further what precisely this means for the discipline of theatre studies, by listing the questions that research into phenomena of theatre have addressed against a consciousness studies (CS) background.

As far as topics are concerned, the range covers essays on specific dramatists, specific plays, issues to do with the actor, the reception process, specific practitioners, specific non-Western theatre aesthetics, and a selection of points of contact of theatre with other fields of the arts or sciences. Dramatists analysed in relation to consciousness studies include Beckett, Crimp, Genet, Ionesco, Pinter, Pirandello, Stoppard, Shakespeare and Soyinka, as well as the question, in general, as to how to understand the dramatist's inspiration. Emphasis has been placed on the following plays: *The Balcony* (Genet), *Crave* (Sarah Kane), *Hamlet*, *Macbeth* and *Much Ado About Nothing* (Shakespeare), *A Mouthful of Birds* (Caryl Churchill), *Oedipus Rex* (Sophocles), *Rhinocéros* (Ionesco), *Happy Days* (Beckett) and Peter Brook's adaptation and production of *The Mahabharata*. In general terms, the question has been addressed as to how different plays reflect human consciousness.

With regard to the actor, the range of topics of enquiry has been equally broad. Issues covered include the relation of the actor to Lecoq's neutral mask, to the mask in non-Western contexts, and to the marionette. The actor has been considered as shaman, or as urban shaman. The actor's experience has been analysed empirically, on the basis of questionnaires. The actor's emotional involvement has been studied both from the conventional Western contexts of Diderot and Stanislavsky, and from the perspective of Indian theatre aesthetics. The actor's presence has been the topic of one essay and one full-length book. Mnouchkine's concept of *state*, and Grotowski's of *translumination* have been discussed. *Stage fright* or *performance anxiety* was studied in an AHRC-funded project, and there have been nine publications on different aspects of actor training, ranging from the science of acting via Buddhism to Decroux.

With regard to the reception of theatre, issues covered include the development of models to explain the impact of scenography on the spectator, the senses in performance, the possibility and explanation of a sixth sense, and implications of autobiographical spectatorship.

Non-Western theatre aesthetics have been discussed in the contexts of Indian *Kudiyattam* and consciousness, breathing and consciousness and Balinese and Noh masks and consciousness, in addition to a reassessment, against a consciousness studies perspective, of the concept of *rasa*, central to Indian performance aesthetics.

Practitioners at the centre of the debates have been Artaud, including a reassessment of his so-called, or alleged, mental illness, Michael Chekhov (here the categories blur with those of actor training), John Cage and Richard Foreman, dancer Raimund Hoghe and voice trainer Catherine Fitzmaurice.

Finally, theatre has been identified as having been exposed to a range of points of contact with other arts or sciences, or concepts deriving not specifically from within theatre itself. Thus, discussions have included the relation of theatre in the conventional Western context and the Japanese form of Butoh, as well as forms of intermediality. Ethical implications of theatre have been discussed in terms of consciousness studies, and theatre has been related to magic and conjuring. The concept of motherhood has been analysed in relation to theatre and consciousness; the role of robots in and for theatre has been raised in the context of the topical debate on posthuman developments. Further discussions from the perspective of consciousness studies include the function theatre can play in dealing with terrorism, the relation of theatre and consciousness to ritual, postmodernism, the sacred, and spirituality. Finally, consciousness studies has added a further dimension to the question of whether a universal language of theatre is possible in the first place, and if so, what it may be, how to achieve it and what its impacts are. Finally, consciousness studies has been able to deepen the debate about the concept of utopian performatives.

All these studies have been published in the *Consciousness, Literature and the Arts* venues (journal, book series, and conference proceedings). It is interesting to note that outside of this cluster of venues, emphasis has been on the senses (one book), the relation between aspects of the theatre and neuroscience (two books, 2010 and 2011 with Routledge and McFarland, respectively), and cognitive science (three books in 2001, 2006 and 2007 with Princeton and

Routledge), and a book series (Cognitive Studies in Literature and Performance) with Palgrave launched in 2008 with five titles related to theatre so far. To date the *Journal of Consciousness Studies* has not published on drama and theatre specifically, but on dance, prose literature and poetry, and fine arts. Overall, then, the considerable majority of work on drama and theatre over the last ten years has been published in the context of *Consciousness, Literature and the Arts.* The approaches reflect the full scope of the field of consciousness studies, not limited to cognitive science and neuroscience.

The table below summarises the questions and issues, identifies the format (book, journal article, book chapter) and the author and year of publication—full details can be found in the bibliography.

Table 1: Publications on Consciousness, Literature and the Arts

Question / Issue	Format	Reference
The use of an asterisk (*) denotes a publication outside of the *Consciousness, Literature and the Arts* cluster of publications.		
The Dramatist		
What inspires the dramatist to write a play?	Book chapter	Meyer-Dinkgräfe 2005
The sacred in *Strindberg*	Book	Malekin 2010
Beckett	Journal article	Favorini 2006
Beckett	Journal article	Sion 2006
Crimp	Book chapter	Angelaki 2007
Genet	Book chapter	Haney 2008
Genet	Journal article	Lavery and Yarrow 2004
Ionesco	Book chapter	Haney 2008
Ionesco	Journal article	Runde 2007
Ionesco	Book chapter	Angelaki 2007
Pinter	Book chapter	Haney 2008
Pinter	Book chapter	Angelaki 2007
Pirandello	Book chapter	Haney 2008
Stoppard	Book chapter	Haney 2008

Question / Issue	Format	Reference
Soyinka	Book chapter	Haney 2008
*Shakespeare and cognitive science	Book	Crane 2001
The Play		
How do different plays reflect human consciousness?	Book chapter	Meyer-Dinkgräfe 2005
The Balcony	Journal article	Boyko-Head 2002
Crave	Book chapter	Mangold 2007
Hamlet	Journal article	Bray 2009
Hamlet	Journal article	Jones 2007
Happy Days	Journal article	Conde 2007
Macbeth	Journal article	Larrass 2000
Mahabharata	Journal article	Mower 2010
A Mouthful of Birds	Journal article	Nutten 2001
Much Ado	Journal article	Bird 2005
Oedipus Rex	Journal article	Fairchild 2002
Rhinoceros	Journal article	Haney 2010
The Actor		
and Lecoq's neutral mask	Book chapter	Hopkinson 2007
and the marionette	Book chapter	Meyer-Dinkgräfe 2005
and the mask	Book chapter	Coldiron 2006
*and Noh and Balinese masks	Book	Coldiron 2004
as shaman	Book chapter	McCutcheon 2006
as urban shaman	Book chapter	Pienaar 2007
The Actor's emotional involvement	Book chapter	Meyer-Dinkgräfe 2005
Experience	Book chapter	Hetzler 2009
Presence	Book chapter	Meyer-Dinkgräfe 2005
Presence	Book	Power 2008

Question / Issue	Format	Reference
State	Book chapter	Meyer-Dinkgräfe 2005
Training	Book	McCutcheon 2008
Training	Journal article	Brask 2003
Training	Journal article	Brask 2006
Training	Journal article	Daboo 2007
Training	Journal article	Mower 2009
training	Book chapter	Meyer-Dinkgräfe 2007
Training	Journal article	Weiss 2000
Training	Journal article	Weiss 2006
Training	Book chapter	Kogan and Pierpoint 2006
translumination	Book chapter	Meyer-Dinkgräfe 2005
self	Book chapter	Bockler 2006
stage fright	Journal article	Meyer-Dinkgräfe 2006
Reception		
The impact of scenography on the spectator	Book chapter	Meyer-Dinkgräfe 2005
The senses in performance	Book chapter	Meyer-Dinkgräfe 2005
*The senses in performance	Book	Banes and Lepecki 2006
The sixth sense in performance	Book chapter	Meyer-Dinkgräfe 2005
Autobiographical spectatorship	Journal article	Freeman 2001
Indian Performance Aesthetics		
Kudiyattam	Book	Madhavan 2010
Breath and performance	Book	Nair 2007

Question / Issue	Format	Reference
A reassessment of the concept of *rasa*	Book chapter	Meyer-Dinkgräfe 2005
The Pashyanti project	Journal article	Malekin and Yarrow 2000
Practitioners		
Artaud	Book chapter	Meyer-Dinkgräfe 2005
Artaud	Journal article	Meyer-Dinkgräfe 2005
Michael Chekov	Book	Ashperger 2008
Cage and Foreman	Journal article	Majzels 2008
Raimund Hoghe	Book chapter	Meyer-Dinkgräfe 2007
Catherine Fitzmaurice	Book chapter	Morgan 2006
Theatre and ….		
Breath	Journal article	Fitzmaurice 2000
Breath	Journal article	Sellers-Young 2002
Butoh	Journal article	Robbins 2003
cognitive science	Journal article	Pierce 2004
*cognitive science	Book	McConachie and Hart 2006
*cognitive science	Book	Blair 2007
*cognitive science	Book	McConachie 2008
*cognitive science	Book	Cook 2010
*cognitive science	Book	Stevenson 2010
*cognitive science	Book	Lutterbie 2011
*cognitive science	Book	Tribble 2011
ethics	Journal article	Meyer-Dinkgräfe 2010
intermediality	Book chapter	Collard 2009
Magic	Book chapter	Mangan 2007
Motherhood	Journal article	Piper 2006
*neuroscience	Book	diBenedetto 2010
*neuroscience	Book	Pizzato 2011

Question / Issue	Format	Reference
postmodernism	Book chapter	Meyer-Dinkgräfe 2005
postmodernism	Journal article	Creely 2007
Ritual	Book chapter	Meyer-Dinkgräfe 2005
Robots	Journal article	Ramsay 2003
spirituality	Book	Hammer 2010
Spirituality	Journal article	Weiss 2006
Terrorism	Journal article	Meyer-Dinkgräfe 2003
the performance site	Book chapter	Ozturk 2006
the sacred	Book	Yarrow 2008
the sacred	Journal article	McCutcheon 2001
universal language	Book chapter	Meyer-Dinkgräfe 2005
utopian performatives	Book chapter	Meyer-Dinkgräfe 2005
Artists' reflections		
	Journal article	Adalian 2000
	Journal article	Bonshek 2004
	Book chapter	Munro 2006

Subjectivity, spirituality and the *Vedanta* model of consciousness

Theatre has been, and is certain to remain, fascinating for people to engage in as participants, spectators and commentators/critics. One of the major reasons why this is so is that theatre is predominantly a deeply subjective, personal experience for all involved in its production and reception. Indeed, as many of the articles and book chapters relating theatre to consciousness studies published so far have demonstrated, the very subjective nature of theatre is what aligns it so closely with desirable altered states of consciousness and experiences of spirituality.

This very reason of fascination is also what makes its study particularly challenging, because the ways we acquire knowledge are still dominated by a paradigm of science explicitly intent on excluding the subjective as potentially interfering with an objective, scientific approach to gaining knowledge. First-person approaches to consciousness in consciousness studies have gained prominence for the last ten to twelve years. The subjective element of consciousness studies does not simply capture subjective input as data conversion; it honours the processes of individual minds in the exercise of conscious activity.

It is against this background that in this book I widen my analysis of aspects of the theatre to increasingly subjective areas of first-person experience in the context of a dimension of consciousness studies that has been increasingly of interest to researchers over the past eight to nine years: *spirituality*, as a sound, reliable and verifiable category of experience that must be understood beyond its conventional use in the context of religion. This focus of my argument allows me to go beyond science, and it is this focus that makes my argument distinctive and unique.

In order to be able to do justice to the subjective nature of theatre and its relation to spirituality, I need to engage the support of a model of consciousness that encompasses those areas. Hence a model that is based on Western science, even science that cautiously welcomes first person approaches, and that is prepared merely to consider the possibility that the subjective and the spiritual might exist, is too limited for the purposes of my argument in this book. What I need is a model of consciousness that is more comprehensive in providing a diversified palette of colours for the analysis of consciousness. The model I need must include the subjective and spirituality as fully equal aspects of consciousness, and it must offer appropriate terminology for describing, contextualising and explaining subjective experiences and experiences of spirituality.

The model of consciousness that meets those specific criteria best has been developed on the basis of Indian *Vedanta* philosophy in the late Maharishi Mahesh Yogi's reassessment as *Vedic Science*. This model of consciousness will remain central to the material covered in this book. Below is therefore a survey of the major components of the model.

States of consciousness

At the centre of the *Vedanta* model of consciousness are distinct states of consciousness, each with its own range of experiential and physiological characteristics. Humans share the experience of three conventional states of consciousness, waking, dreaming and sleeping. The sleep state is devoid of immediate experience: we know, on waking up, that we must have been asleep, and we can gauge whether we feel rested after sleep or not, and depending on this, with hindsight we consider our sleep to have been "good, restful, deep etc.", or "heavy, restless, superficial etc.". The dream state occurs during sleep, and the range of potential experiences we encounter in the dream state of consciousness is much wider; all sensory perceptions can be aroused in dreams: we can dream in a wide panoply of colours or in black and white, and shifts can occur between them back and forth within seconds. We can hear, touch, taste and smell in our dreams. When we wake up after sleeping we may remember that we have had dreams, and we may have more or less vivid recollections of the contents of dreams; often, memory of dream contents seems to melt away almost tangibly as we attempt recollection. The waking state of consciousness is distinctly separate from sleep and dream, as in it we actively live our lives (while typically we cannot control the nature of sleep and the contents of dreams actively, or at least fully).

The relation of states of consciousness to each other

According to the *Vedanta* model of consciousness, several layers make up the levels of experience characteristic of the waking state of consciousness. They can be imagined as six concentric circles around a core. The six levels are senses, desire, mind, intellect, ego, and feeling (together with emotions and intuition). The core is pure consciousness. The further away the respective circles are positioned in relation to the core, the more expressed, more concrete and more manifest, or tangible, they are. In reverse, each subtler level, closer to the core, encompasses the less subtle levels further away from the core. For example, intuition is capable of grasping events, processes and occurrences not only on its own level, but also on those of ego, intellect, mind, desire and senses. In reverse, however, the mind, for example, is not able to make sense of the contents of the intellect, ego, feelings, emotions and intuition. In contrast to conventional Western science, feelings and emotions are distinct levels of consciousness.

Intuition is regarded in the *Vedanta* model of consciousness as a level of consciousness as well, as an actual phenomenon rather than an unexplainable artefact. The drawing below provides a survey of the levels of consciousness in the waking state:

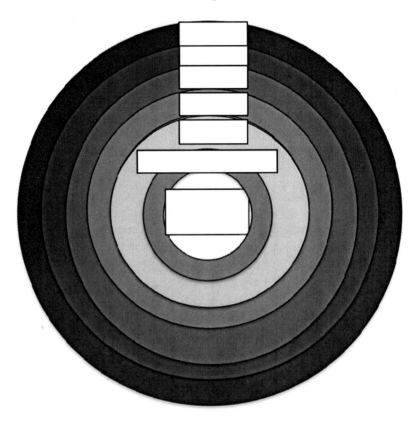

Higher states of consciousness

Pure consciousness is a fourth state of consciousness, and serves as the basis for the six expressed levels of consciousness characteristic of the waking state of consciousness. Pure consciousness is also at the basis of the states of sleep and dream. It can be experienced either on its own, or together with waking, dream or sleep. Experienced on its own, it is a state of consciousness that is devoid of any contents otherwise associated with the senses, desire, mind, intellect, ego, or intuition, feeling or emotion. A person experiencing pure consciousness on its own is not aware of anything other than consciousness itself. The experience of pure consciousness together with waking or dreaming or sleep is characteristic of higher states of consciousness as defined in the *Vedanta* model of consciousness.

A fifth state of consciousness is characterised by the co-existence of waking, or dreaming, or sleeping, and pure consciousness. In cosmic consciousness, the level of pure consciousness, which is never overshadowed in daily experience by the activities and experiences of the individual psyche, becomes a 'stable internal frame of reference from which changing phases of sleep, dreaming, and waking life are silently *witnessed* or observed' (Alexander and Boyer 1989: 342). The experience of this state of consciousness entails a detached self-awareness, enabling the person to "look down upon" him-or herself (the waking, dreaming and sleeping states of consciousness) from a position "on high" (pure consciousness). By explaining such a spiritual experience as normal characteristics of this fifth state of consciousness, the *Vedanta* model of consciousness is at an advantage over Western science that will have methodological problems in addressing such experiences.

In the fifth state of consciousness, the field of pure consciousness is permanently experienced together with waking, or dreaming, or sleeping. This level of functioning is maintained in the sixth state of consciousness and 'combined with the maximum value of perception of the environment. Perception and feeling reach their most sublime levels' (Alexander and Boyer 1989: 355).

The final level of human development is called *unity consciousness*. In this state of consciousness, 'the highest value of self-referral is experienced' (Alexander and Boyer 1989: 359). The field of pure consciousness is directly perceived as located at every point in creation, and thus 'every point in creation is raised to the (...) status' of pure consciousness. 'The gap between the relative and absolute aspects of life (...) is fully eliminated' (Alexander and Boyer 1989: 360). The experiencer experiences himself and his entire environment in terms of his own nature, which he experiences to be pure consciousness. The table below provides a survey of states of consciousness. For further discussion and examples of experiences of higher states of consciousness, see (Meyer-Dinkgräfe 2005: 24-29).

Table 2: States of consciousness

	State of consciousness	Experience of pure consciousness	Mode of Perception
1	Waking	Absent	Conventional
2	Dreaming	Absent	Absent (interior)
3	Sleep	Absent	Absent
4	Pure consciousness	Present	Absent
5	Cosmic consciousness	Present	Witnessing
6	Refined cosmic consciousness	Present	Refined
7	Unity consciousness	Present	Unified

According to the *Vedanta* model of consciousness, the highest state of consciousness, unity consciousness, is the same as *moksha*, enlightenment. The development of consciousness towards the attainment and permanent experience of *moksha* is the purpose of human life.

The *Vedanta* model of consciousness meets the criteria that I developed earlier as requirements a model must fulfil in order to be able to account meaningfully for subjectivity and spirituality in the context of theatre and opera. Pure consciousness at the basis of consciousness is pure subjectivity; higher states of consciousness are states of spirituality, and pure consciousness, as the basis of higher states of consciousness, is thus also the basis of spirituality. As the source of the expressed levels of consciousness (feelings, emotion and intuition, ego, intellect, mind, desire, senses), pure consciousness is all-encompassing.

The activities central to Western science are located predominantly on the level of the intellect. While insights gained in science are interesting, important and accurate within this specific framework of the intellect, those insights are also limited by that very framework. To the extent that science is restricted to the intellect, it remains limited in its comprehension, by definition, of aspects of the ego, the intuition, feeling, and emotion, and pure consciousness, and that limitation can even take the shape of doubting or denying the existence of those seemingly incomprehensible subtler levels. A good example for those limitations is Bruce McConachie's work (2008). His deliberations on cognitive science in relation to theatre are excellent within the strictures he chooses to impose upon himself in selecting the Western scientific approach of which cognitive science is an integral part. The limitations are apparent when McConachie dismisses as "bad science" those areas that science is just not able to grasp—not due to any individual's deficiencies, but by definition of science as an activity of the intellect. In this context I maintain that much of what I have argued so far and what I argue in this book about the relationship between theatre and consciousness can serve as the basis for science: my argument can be revised in the form of hypotheses, which can then be operationalized to serve as the basis for scientific experiments to test the hypotheses.

Given that pure consciousness as pure subjectivity and the basis of spirituality in higher states of consciousness is central to my argument in this book, it is important to discuss further the nature of pure consciousness. According to the *Vedanta* model of consciousness, pure consciousness must be understood as the unmanifest, unexpressed source of all creation, animate and inanimate.

Principles of pure consciousness
While the experience of pure consciousness is devoid of any contents otherwise characteristic of the experience of waking, dream and sleep states and higher states of consciousness (1,2,3 and 5,6,7 in table (2) above, page 24), there is an unmanifest dynamic within pure consciousness which is responsible for the emanation of all creation from within pure consciousness. Different angles or perspectives on this dynamic allow easier comprehension. According to the first perspective, within pure consciousness, there are four active and interactive components or agents: unity (*samhita*), the experiencing, observing or knowing component or the subject (*rishi*), the object of experience, observation and knowledge (*chhandas*) and the process of experiencing, observing and knowing (*devata*). These four components interact with each other, and each specific interaction leads to a specific part in the process of the emergence of creation from within the field of pure consciousness. The specificity of interaction lies in the originator of interaction, and the target. Thus, for example, if the *rishi* component of pure consciousness originates interaction with the target of the component of *samhita*, the aspect of creation results that is described in the *Vedic* text of *Sama Veda*.

It is possible to establish further detail with regard to the processes involved in the emergence of creation from this interaction of the components that are active within pure consciousness. The activity within pure consciousness creates a universal, cosmic sound, captured in the first letter (A), of the first word (AGNI) of the major *Vedic* text, *Rig Veda*. There is gap between the first letter and the second letter, A and G. The sound of the A collapses into the gap, representing a movement from fullness and infinity to the limitation of a minute point. This process is called *Pradhvamsa Abhava*. The point is a point of all possibilities, called *Atyanta Abhava*. What happens in the gap, the interaction of *samhita*, *rishi*, *devata* and *chhandas* discussed above, provides structure to the emergence from the gap. The structuring dynamics of what happens in the gap are referred to as *Anyonya Abhava*. The mechanics by which a sound emerges from the point value of the gap, i.e. the emergence of the following sound, is called *Prag Abhava* (adapted from Nader 1995: 34).

Contents and scope
Against the background of the *Vedanta* model of consciousness that I have introduced above, in my 2005 book *Theatre and Consciousness: Explanatory Scope and Future Potential* I came to the conclusion that this particular model of consciousness allows better understanding of

- the artist's creative inspiration;
- the depiction of desirable higher states of consciousness in drama, such as spiritual visions;
- the concept of dual consciousness central to the approaches to acting developed by Diderot, Stanislavsky, Meyerhold, Brecht and Strasberg;
- reception processes in the theatre;
- various concepts of theatre (studies), many based, initially, on direct experience, such as "language of nature" (Artaud), "universal language of the theatre", ritual, postmodernism, and *utopian performatives*.

Based on the findings of the 2005 book and the knowledge disseminated since then in the *CLA* journal, the *CTLA* conferences and the book series with Intellect and Rodopi, as well as recent work specifically on cognitive science in relation to theatre outside of the

CLA / CTLA body of publications, in this book I write about further aspects of theatre and consciousness in Part One, followed by an exploration of the relationship between opera and consciousness in Part Two.

Specifically, in Part One I develop a new approach to history within the context of the model of consciousness based in Indian *Vedanta* philosophy, and explore the implications of that new approach to theatre history. Initially I demonstrate how a non-teleological and non-causal understanding of history in general and theatre history in particular can be developed within the *Vedanta* model of consciousness. In a second stage I begin to discuss the ways in which the same model of consciousness is also able to provide the framework for a causal analysis of why one epoch in theatre history follows the preceding one by necessity.

Four examples illustrate this new approach to theatre history in further detail. In the first example I apply the *Vedanta* model of consciousness to a specific kind of dramatic text (biographical plays about famous artists within contemporary British drama). The main purpose of this case study is to provide an explanation for the emergence and success of this genre of play within the context of the approach to theatre history developed in Chapter One. The second example discusses the way in which a specific phenomenon of consciousness, *synaesthesia*, is dealt with in a range of plays. The third example moves from dramatic text to performance, considering the relationship of consciousness to the relevance of story-telling for 21st century updates of plays and opera productions. The fourth example expands the discussion of performance beyond theatre and opera to dance with a consideration of Raimund Hoghe's choreography from a consciousness studies perspective.

In the remaining chapters of Part One of the book I discuss important implications of that new approach to theatre history. Chapter Two takes the discussion from dramatic and performance writing to the work of the actor and director with a reassessment of ethical implications of theatre, acting and directing. Chapter Three widens the perspective to non-Western theatre and performance contexts in its reassessment of the role of the teacher, or *guru*, for the actor. Much of the evidence in this chapter is based on subjective and anecdotal evidence, demonstrating the importance of this approach to my argument. Chapter Four tightens the focus further on the actor:

warm-up and in particular cool-down have been considered as important for the actor's artistic achievement and personal well-being only relatively recently—the *Vedanta* model of consciousness provides an explanatory framework for their importance and on that basis I discuss a range of practical approaches to enhancing especially cool-down.

In Part Two I introduce my thinking about the relationship between opera and consciousness. Chapter Five provides a general survey of this relationship, framed in terms of spirituality as one specific dimension of consciousness. Chapter Six discusses the singer in terms of spirituality, with specific reference to Klaus Florian Vogt. Chapter Seven focuses on operatic conducting, with reference to a range of extraordinary experiences reported by conductors in relation to their art, and special attention to three conductors in three separate case studies: Peter Schneider, Karen Kamensek and Sir Roger Norrington. In chapters Six and Seven, the subjective element of consciousness studies comes to the fore in the use of interviews, with Vogt, Schneider, Kamensek and Norrington; this approach honours the processes of individual minds in the exercise of conscious activity. It also serves to relate myself as researcher/writer/critic directly to the source of the data (that is, the interview or conversation) so that the generation of a study of consciousness comes in the form of a dialogue in which two minds are intermingling. The effect of the subjective approach to consciousness studies is sometimes like panning for gold in a narrative that does not intentionally isolate it because it does not know what it is looking for. In fact what it is searching for is only later discovered when the data is reviewed. The subjective, as I use it in my interviews, captures the technique's true essence, the embodiment of emotion, also the embodiment of wisdom. The interview structure becomes the embodied source of discovery and insight. This structure has been overlooked by scientific study which tends to dismiss it as anecdotal and not replicable. What science fails to recognize in its dismissal of the subjective is that the subjective often becomes the source of scientific insight and contributes the seeds of future scientific exploration. Thus, my emphasis on subjectivity and spirituality in the context of consciousness studies develops, in effect, a new perspective on theatre and opera.

PART ONE: THEATRE AND CONSCIOUSNESS

Chapter One

Consciousness and Western Theatre History: Theory and Examples

In this chapter I develop a new approach to history within the context of the model of consciousness based in Indian *Vedanta* philosophy, and explore the implications of that new approach to theatre history. Initially I demonstrate how a non-teleological and non-causal understanding of history in general and theatre history in particular can be developed within the *Vedanta* model of consciousness. In a second stage I begin to discuss the ways in which the same model of consciousness is also able to provide the framework for a causal analysis of why one epoch in theatre history follows the preceding one by necessity.

Schiller's concept of universal history
I take as my point of departure Schiller's understanding of, and aims for, history. He developed the concept of *universal history*, for which the historian selects from the past, as the material to work with, historical data that have an essential, irrefutable and easily traceable influence on the way the world is today. The nature of those data is such that there are many uncertainties and many gaps. The result of this is that on the basis of such data alone, world history could not develop beyond an aggregate of fragments. Philosophical reason comes into play at this point: it seeks to combine the fragments with the help of artificial linking elements, thus raising the aggregate to a system, a wholeness connected by reason. The historian takes from his own human nature the innate tendency to unify in this way, and

transposes such unifying principles on to the data of history. Aware that this image of unity exists only in his mind (it does not necessarily exist in real life), he keeps checking the data of history against this unifying principle, finds many instances that support the teleological principle of world history, and as many that refute it. However, as long as there are missing links (which will be forever), the question is ultimately undecided, and the opinion wins that has to offer reason the highest level of satisfaction and the heart the highest level of bliss (1972: 332). I develop *linking elements* to lift the fragments of theatre history to the level of a system, a wholeness connected by reason. Those linking elements are the qualities of pure consciousness discussed in the previous section for the non-causal, non-teleological first part of this chapter, and the sequence of creation within pure consciousness for the second part of this chapter, in which the causality of theatre history is central to my argument

History and time: non-teleological and non-causal approach

If we understand history as the sequence of changes of human conditions of life, insofar as we can reconstruct them through interpretation of documents, the fundamental importance of the concept of time for any understanding of history is evident. In the context of *Vedanta*, time is eternal, as described by Maharishi Mahesh Yogi:

> The eternity of the eternal life of absolute Being is conceived in terms of innumerable lives of the Divine Mother, a single one of whose lives encompasses a thousand life spans of Lord Shiva. One life of Lord Shiva covers the time of a thousand life spans of Lord Vishnu. One life of Lord Vishnu equals the duration of a thousand life spans of Brahma, the Creator. A single life span of Brahma is conceived in terms of one hundred years of Brahma; each year of Brahma comprises 12 months of Brahma, and each month comprises thirty days of Brahma. One day of Brahma is called a Kalpa. One Kalpa is equal to the time of fourteen Manus. The time of one Manu is called a Manvantara. One Manvantara equals seventy-one Chaturyugis. One Chaturyugi comprises the totals pan of four Yugas, i.e. Sat-yuga, Treta-yuga, Dvapara-yuga, and Kali-yuga. The span of the Yugas is conceived in terms of the duration of Sat-yuga. Thus the span of Treta-yuga is equal to three quarters of that of Sat-yuga; the span of Dvapara-yuga is half of that of Sat-yuga, and the span of Kali-yuga on quarter that of Sat-yuga. The span of Kali-yuga equals 432,000 years of man's life. (1969: 253-4)

Based on this idea of time, according to *Vedanta*, the emphasis of history is on the importance of events, not on chronology. For this reason, in the first part of this chapter, I discuss the history of Western theatre in terms of indicators of "importance of events". This is a non-chronological approach to theatre history in so far as although I discuss the development in time from the Greeks through to the present, I do not seek to uncover and reveal answers to questions as to why one distinct epoch followed the other by some inner necessity. In this approach, the qualities of pure consciousness form the linking elements that allow me to raise the aggregate of data available about theatre history "to a system and to a wholeness connected by reason", taking my cue from Schiller's understanding of, and aims for, history. I elaborate the context of this cue later on in this introduction. The linking element for this non-chronological approach is formed by the principles of creation that reside within pure consciousness.

In the context of the *Vedanta* model of consciousness, not only are the principle for the development of creation and the processes that are involved in expressing this principle inherent in pure consciousness (as discussed above): principles for all possible qualities of creation are equally inherent in pure consciousness. Some of these relate to the interactions of *samhita, rishi, devata* and *chhandas*, and to the bodies of knowledge that emerge from the various interactions, captured in the *Vedic* texts that in turn capture those bodies of knowledge. Each *Vedic* text is associated with a predominant quality, or unmanifest principle. While time is not a feature at the level of pure consciousness, it becomes a major factor once pure consciousness has emerged into manifestation, and any manifest phenomenon that can accrue a history over a specific duration of time will need to express all predominant qualities or unmanifest principles as a prerequisite to be able to serve as a conduit for pure consciousness not only to express itself fully, but also for pure consciousness to find back to itself through its expression. Within the *Vedanta* model of consciousness, repeated alternation of the experience of pure consciousness and the ordinary waking state of consciousness is the technique that will lead to the development of higher states of consciousness. Each of these qualities of pure consciousness, listed below, has the potential of serving as a vehicle for human consciousness to experience pure consciousness. In this first part of this chapter, I discuss theatre history against the background of those qualities.

Rig Veda	holistic
Sama Veda	flowing wakefulness
Yajur Veda	offering and creating
Atharva Veda	reverberating wholeness
Sthapatya	Veda establishing
Dhanurveda	invincible, progressive
Gandharvaveda	integrating, harmonising
Shiksha	expressing
Kalpa	transforming
Vyakarana	expanding
Nirukta	self-referral
Chhandas	measuring, quantifying
Jyotish	all-knowing
Nyaya	distinguishing and deciding
Vaisheshika	specifying
Samkhya	enumerating
Yoga	unifying
Karma Mimamsa	analysing
Vedanta	I-ness (the Transcendent)
Ayur-Veda	balancing
Smriti	memory
Purana	ancient, eternal
Itihasa	blossoming
Brahmana	structuring
Aranyaka	stirring
Upanishad	transcending

Theatre history and time: non-teleological and non-causal approach

In the first part of this chapter, the aim is to identify, as the principle of linking data of the past, the relationship of characteristics of pure consciousness and major trends and characteristics of distinct epochs or phases in theatre history. The brushstrokes are intentionally very broad, to allow a broad picture to emerge relatively quickly. Details can be filled in at any level to the extent required.

Greek tragedy develops from an emphasis on characters as representatives of universal conflict and reconciliation of dramatic conflict in an all-encompassing principle (Aeschylus) via emphasis on individual, complex, psychologically motivated characters (Sophocles), to further development of the realistic exploration of the character's psychological motivation (Euripides). At the same time, there is development from the assumption of a higher than human law behind events (Aeschylus and Sophocles) to the position that chance rules the world and the initially higher beings, the gods, are less concerned with moral values than humans (Euripides). There is, finally, a tendency to question increasingly the validity of the status quo (Euripides and the comedies by Aristophanes and Menander). The characteristics of pure consciousness expressed in these developments are flowing wakefulness (universal view of humans and gods, the existence of a higher than human law behind events), invincible, integrating and harmonising (reconciliation of dramatic conflict), and analysing (detailed depiction of character as well as the observation at the basis of comedy)

Drama in Rome is characterised by further development from the inside (such as universal contexts and reconciliation) to the outside (such as realistic psychology and the rule of chance), with a focus in Seneca's plays on violence and horror on stage (they had been confined to messenger reports in their Greek counterparts), and a preoccupation with magic, death, and the super-human world of ghosts. Performing arts in Rome developed further from performances based on scripted literary drama to spectacles on a grand scale, such as gladiatorial contests. The characteristics of pure consciousness expressed in drama and performance across Roman times here are expanding, expressing, and dynamic creativity.

Across the Middle Ages, drama and its performance were related predominantly to the Christian Church, as religious drama and later deviations from it in the process of secularisation. The purpose of religious drama was to reveal, to churchgoers unable to read, God's ordering of existence as revealed in the Bible, in legends about biblical figures and saints, writings of the Church Fathers, and collections of sermons. An eternal order sees human virtue rewarded and punishes vice. This corresponds to the beginnings of Greek tragedy with its emphasis, albeit in pre-Christian terms, on universal contexts. Secularisation in the Middle Ages brought with it a development of comedy, with farces pointing to human imperfection, and emphasis on human levels of power in comparison to one divine rule. The Middle Ages thus reflect, on their own terms, the development in Greece and Rome from inside to outside, from humans guided by divine providence to life lived at random, and by chance. The characteristics of pure consciousness dominating the Middle Ages range from the reverberating wholeness, unifying, and integrating at the height of Christian religious drama to diagnosing, enumerating, unfolding, analysing and measuring in the later process of secularisation.

In the Renaissance, Greece and Rome were literally re-discovered, and focus shifted from the Christian emphasis on the afterlife dominant in the Middle Ages towards a concern for the worth of humans in the here and now. It is the time of Leonardo da Vinci, Michelangelo, Raphael, Luther, Henry VIII, Thomas More, Elizabeth I, and Shakespeare and his contemporaries. The Renaissance is dominated by the characteristics of pure consciousness of establishing, memory and synthesizing, with additional aspects of unfolding and omnipresence.

Neoclassicism launches a series of movements across the arts, and thus also relevant for drama and theatre, in which one major epoch reacts directly against the decline of the preceding epoch by developing new ideals and ideas specifically in relation to the preceding ones. In neoclassical drama, the emphasis was on verisimilitude, i.e., reality in the sense that events were depicted as they could happen in real life. Fantasy and the supernatural, rife in late Renaissance drama, were avoided, the use of soliloquy or chorus was discouraged: protagonists could reveal their innermost thoughts to trusted companions instead. Death, violence, battles and crowd scenes were placed offstage. The plays had to reveal an ideal moral pattern. Tragedy, like its Greek model, depicted characters from the ruling classes, based on history or myth, with an unhappy ending and written in a poetic style. Comedy, equally like its Greek model, depicted middle or lower class characters, focused on domestic and private affairs, led to happy endings and used everyday speech. In England, witty and satirical Restoration Comedy gave way, following accusation that theatre did not meet its own declared purpose of teaching and pleasing, to sentimental comedy with its more conservative moral outlook. The purpose of comedy changed as well, not seeking to arouse laughter or ridicule, but to arouse noble sentiments. In terms of qualities of pure consciousness, the neoclassical period is characterised by the qualities of invincibility, analysis, stirring, structuring and unfolding.

The Romantic period followed Neoclassicism. In classical music, there are composers such as Schumann, Schubert, Weber, Liszt, Chopin, and Mendelssohn-Bartholdy. The field of painting is represented by Friedrich, Turner, Blake and Delacroix. In poetry, there are Keats, Shelley, Byron, Wordsworth, Coleridge, Goethe and Schiller. Dramatic work comes from many of those poets, sometimes intended for the stage, sometimes for reading. The Romantic age is characterised by radical idealism, an emphasis on feeling, faith in the visionary imagination, and the infinity of existence. Despite the emphasis on feeling, reason was still needed to prevent the imagination from descending into the absurd. Subjectivity was therefore not paramount: artists had to include elements in their work that transcended the individual. Romantic artists found inspiration in being alone and in landscapes; many held pantheistic views, and resorted to traditional myths, legends and folklore to deal with the supernatural, with the grotesque and the abnormal. The characteristics of the Romantic period in terms of characteristics of pure consciousness are integrating, flowing wakefulness, dynamic creativity, self-referral and balancing,

In reaction to the deterioration of Romantic drama in the form of melodrama, realism developed, and naturalism took realism even further. Socio-political conditions, such as urbanisation, the industrial revolution and the wave of disillusionment resulting from it, and philosophical influences best summarised under the heading of materialism (Darwin, Compte, Marx), paved the way for first scenic, then dramatic realism in the theatre. Stanislavski's approach to acting took note of this development. The characteristics of the realism and naturalism in terms of characteristics of pure consciousness are expressing, establishing, expanding, specifying, enumerating, analysing, diagnosing and structuring.

With hindsight, the development of drama from Greece to Rome represents one sub-cycle, from universal to human concerns, from literary to spectacular, and from feminine intuitive to masculine extrovert. The Middle Ages represent a further such cycle, with comparable phases. With the onset of the Renaissance, the nature of the cycles changes: each phase of a cycle now represents an epoch in itself, with an inward-looking, feminine Renaissance, followed by an extrovert, masculine period of Neoclassicism, followed by an inward-looking, feminine Romantic period, followed by an extrovert, masculine period of realism and naturalism. The cycles are comparable with regard to their phases, (emerging at a high level of sophistication and deteriorating in the course of time), and with regard to their characteristics (such as masculine, feminine, introvert and extrovert), but it would not be appropriate to suggest that the cycles are mere repetitions of the same. Rather, in each cycle, the characteristics and phases receive further refinement and elaboration, building on their respective predecessors.

With the beginning of the 20th century, the development is no longer linear in the sense that one distinct cycle (epoch) follows the preceding distinct cycle, with only a little of time overlap. Instead, much more short-lived cycles emerge and disappear very quickly and with many instances of several existing at the same time. They all exist on a fluid scale whose opposing poles can be defined in terms of whether the play is realistic or non-realistic. Approaches to acting and directing have developed in relation to these fast-changing approaches to writing and, increasingly, devising for the theatre. Performance, performance art, and postdramatic theatre are some of the most recent developments, which also include theatre of the absurd, neo-romantic theatre, epic drama and the related developments launched by Brecht, theatre of cruelty, Dadaist theatre, Bauhaus, expressionist theatre, surrealism, political theatre, poetic drama, and drawing room plays. These movements usually each originate in one specific country but spread across countries through direct contact of artists involved with them.

After the Second World War, the number of distinct movements has not gone down, but despite the development of globalisation, the differentiation limited within individual countries has increased. For example, immediately after the Second World War, British theatre continued the drawing room drama of Coward and Rattigan, while German theatre was dominated by documentary drama. The wave of biographical plays about famous artists has been characteristic of British drama since 1979, while it has not featured at all as prominently in Germany, France or the USA. In turn boulevard comedy has been a major player in terms of audiences (not so much dramatic or literary criticism) in Germany since the 1950s, while it does not feature at all in the UK and is a minor form in France. In-yer-face theatre was characteristic of British 1990s theatre, while it merely surfaced in the indigenous writing of other countries.

On increasingly smaller scales of the dimension of time, then, the cycles have appeared, disappeared, reappeared, mingled, overlapped, coexisted and interacted in a multitude of ways. A cycle that lasted several centuries in the case of Greece and Rome, or the Middle Ages, may be limited now to a number of years.

History and time: teleological and causal approach
My argument across both parts of this chapter is placed within current debates in historiography. Predominantly, academics in general history and the history of specific disciplines, have used the terms of *world history*, *global history* and *universal history* synonymously. Geyer and Bright, writing in 1995 note that "the main current of social science scholarship and of historiography" is "anti-universalist" (1036), and leading theatre historian Postlewait is cautious regarding historians, including theatre historians, who "attend almost exclusively to individual events" (2009: 10) or who "champion a reigning idea, derived from this or that theory. All events are illustrations of that theory, which defines the context and controls the interpretation" (10). Postlewait considers both approaches as limited because "the isolationist gives us events that supposedly explain themselves; the universalist gives us events as formulaic illustrations of a system or theory" (10).

More recently, there have been endeavours to re-assess the concepts and methodologies of *world history* and *global history* (Osterhammel 2009), which have already led to significant increase in our knowledge of human past and present. Osterhammel, for example, does not engage in conventional historical practice of teleologically narrating nationalisation, modernisation and globalisation or standardisation, but he first registers and notes the changes across the world, and then he asks whether they share a common direction (Fahrmeir 2009). World history approaches history differently, and this approach leads to a significant change in our evaluation of the future. The re-assessment of the significance of *world history* is not limited to general history: in 2010, a project on global theatre histories was launched, whose explicit aim is to "investigate the emergence of theatre as a global phenomenon against the background of imperial expansion and modernization in the late 19th and 20th centuries" (Balme 2011).

In contrast to the concepts of *world history* and *global history*, so far the concept of *universal history* has not been reassessed, either in the context of general history or the history of specific disciplines. However, in view of the relevance of the insights gained in the case of Osterhammel's world history approach, and the expected insights of the global theatre histories project (insights that must be assumed to be at the basis of the decision of the Deutsche Forschungsgemeinschaft to fund the project), it is logical to argue that a re-assessment of the concept of *universal history* will prove as important.

My argument in this book addresses this need for a re-assessment of the concept of *universal history*. It does so in the context of the specific discipline of theatre studies, and thus theatre history. *Universal theatre history* serves as a paradigm and model for other disciplines and history in general. The *universal* approach I develop in this book places particular emphasis on the subjective nature of theatre, which has been explicitly problematic for theatre scholars, especially in cultural and epistemological contexts where the scholarship sought, or was expected, to emulate hard science. To date a universal history of theatre has not yet been developed, and its development will be my original contribution to the field of theatre studies.

Writing in 1995, Geyer and Bright use the terms and related concepts of *world history* and *universal history* as synonyms. I challenge the appropriateness of using the terms of *world history*, *global history* and *universal history* as synonyms. This challenge leads to hypothesis (1): *World history, global history and universal history are expressions for three different concepts that need to be discussed on their own terms, but not as interchangeable synonyms.* On the basis of this differentiation of terms and related concepts, I turn to *universal history* and note Geyer and Bright's argument that *universal history* had been, for many decades, predominantly considered among historians, as "an illegitimate, unprofessional, and therefore foolish enterprise. It was for dilettantes" (1034). I challenge this position, arguing for a re-assessment of the concept of *universal history*. This challenge leads to hypothesis (2): a reassessment of the concept of *universal history* will significantly enhance our knowledge of history, in general, and in relation to specific disciplines. Challenge and hypothesis (2) are supported by Geyer and Bright's recognition that there has been a resurgence of *world history* over the last few years:

> [i]t is still a hesitant and fledgling historiography, which remains mired in the old, unsure of its scholarly status, and with a tendency to service existing knowledge rather than create new knowledge. But a start has been made, and its impetus comes from many places, a great diversity of scholars, and a variety of disciplines. (1038)

In this section, I develop a history of Western theatre that is equally based on the *Vedanta* model of consciousness but which also takes account of chronology in the sense that I seek to develop reasons why one epoch or form follows the other by necessity. This approach is interested in causality and teleology. The linking elements (Schiller) are different from the qualities of pure consciousness employed as linking elements for the development of the non-chronological, non-causal and non-teleological approach: *Vedanta* proposes that creation moves from the infinity of pure consciousness to all possible forms of creation, animate and inanimate, as expressions of pure consciousness, and back, or onwards, to the state of pure consciousness at the origin. This movement from infinity to all aspects of finite creation back to infinity is reflected in the Sanskrit alphabet at the centre of *Vedic* texts. [a] is pure sound, not yet formed, oscillating at infinite speed between infinity of pure consciousness and expressed value of the sound. As pure consciousness becomes aware of its dual nature, it becomes aware of its unity—only by experiencing duality can unity be recognised as such. Awareness of unity causes bliss, expressed by [a:]. Realising its own nature as unity through the experience of duality, pure consciousness develops the will or desire to return to unity (which it has apparently, but not really, "lost" in the process of realising its unity by way of the experience of duality). This will or desire is expressed through the sound of [i]. This desire increases, represented by [i:].

Pure consciousness was able to realise its unity by creating duality. This is a general principle: pure consciousness creates in order to recognise. This is [u], the opening of the eyes. The process of recognition is an indication of a certain degree of ignorance, given that pure consciousness has apparently forgotten that it is both subject and object (unity). It needs the duality of subject and object to find out more about either, but this process comes at the expense of developing a lack of unity, expressed by [u:]. The further sounds of the Sanskrit alphabet, in particular the consonants, represent manifest creation. "Once entirely produced, the cosmos can only end in cosmic resorption, by returning to its divine source" (Padoux 1992: 305).

Theatre history and time: teleological and causal approach

It is possible, as demonstrated above, to discuss the history of theatre in terms of qualities of pure consciousness as a non-causal principle, highlighting the importance of events rather than development in time. The same qualities of pure consciousness can serve to develop, as a further linking principle, an explanation of why one phase followed the other, at least from the Greek origins of Western theatre to the onset of the multiplicity of theatre movements at the beginning of the 20th century. The clue to this lies in the sequence of the major characteristic of each cycle identified above. In the course of time, the holistic nature of creation leads to the flowing wakefulness of Greek theatre, just as *Sama Veda* develops from *Rig Veda*. From *Sama Veda* develops *Yajur Veda*, from flowing wakefulness develops dynamic creativity, and from Greek theatre develops Roman theatre, which has dynamic creativity as its major characteristic. *Yajur Veda* develops into *Atharva Veda*, dynamic creativity develops into reverberating wholeness, and Roman theatre develops into the theatre of the Middle Ages, which has reverberating wholeness as its main characteristic. *Atharva Veda* develops into *Sthapatya Veda*, reverberating wholeness develops into the quality of establishing, and the theatre of the Middle Ages develops into that of the Renaissance, whose main characteristic is establishing. *Sthapatya Veda* develops into *Dhanur-Veda*, the quality of pure consciousness changes from establishing to invincible, and in theatre history, the Renaissance develops into the Neoclassical age, whose major characteristic in terms of qualities of pure consciousness is being invincible. *Dhanur-Veda* develops into *Gandharva Veda*, the invincible quality changes to an integrating characteristic, and neoclassical theatre develops to the Romantic age, whose main characteristic is integrating. Finally, *Gandharva Veda* develops towards *Shiksha*, the integrating quality develops into the expressing one, and theatre of the Romantic age develops into theatre of realism and naturalism, whose major quality is expressing.

Thus the development of movements and epochs, in the history of theatre across time is not at all arbitrary, but follows universal principles of development embedded in pure consciousness. Since the beginning of the 20th century, developments in theatre history have moved faster and faster, with movements overlapping. It is still possible to relate specific movements to specific qualities of pure consciousness, and it will be possible to demonstrate that each shorter-lived movement finds its specific place in the timeline of theatre history by necessity just as the longer-lived movements from the Greeks to realism and naturalism.

Elaborating on this, however, would lead into much detail and merit a further book in its own right. Instead, I want to provide four examples from most recent theatre and performance history. The first example considers the high number of biographical plays about famous artists written and performed in England since 1978 from a consciousness studies perspective. I demonstrate, with reference to Peter Shaffer's *Amadeus*, how the artist's consciousness is shown in the play, and I argue that the reason for the surge in numbers is related to the phenomenon of self-reflexivity. Pure consciousness is entirely self-reflexive, and all creation emerges from this self-reflexivity. Over the past thirty-five years, many academic disciplines have (re-) discovered self-reflexivity as a major component in their subject-matter, and many dramatists engage in writing plays about other artists to find out more about themselves as artists.

Example one. Consciousness and drama: English biographical plays about famous artists

Introduction

The first example focuses on plays written and performed in Britain since 1979 that have as their major character a famous artist. This means that the artist character in the plays in this genre, was alive once, or, in some cases, is still alive, and was and is famous, well-known to an audience; "artist" is further defined as a representative of any branch of the arts, i.e., not merely a fine artist, but also a musician, composer, conductor, actor, director, scenographer, etc. Between 1900 and 1977, about eighty plays were written and produced in the UK whose main character is a famous artist, compared to well over 500 such plays in the much shorter time period of 1978-2013. In this example, I introduce three levels of classification of biographical plays about famous artists: the use of historical reality in the dramatized reality, i.e., the level of historical accuracy or authenticity; second, the function of the artist character within the play's plot, or the focus of the plays; and third, the constellation of characters around the central artist character. I discuss one play in particular, Peter Shaffer's 1979 *Amadeus*, as an example for the genre, to demonstrate how the artist character's consciousness is presented in the play, and proceed to develop an explanation, against a consciousness studies background, for the emergence and persistence of the genre. Throughout, I differentiate two distinct phases of this genre, the one from 1979 to 2004, and the other from 2004 to the present.

Authenticity
The biographical plays about famous artists can be placed on a sliding scale that measures the degree to which dramatists make use of *historical reality* in the *dramatized reality*. One pole will indicate a play that takes very much of *historical reality* into *dramatized reality* . Such a play can be said to be most authentic. *Authentic* here means the orientation of the *dramatized* to the *historical* reality. The opposite pole indicates plays that are least authentic: plays for which the dramatists took the life of a historical artist merely as an inspiration for a play about an artist. The artist characters in such plays do not even carry the names of their historical sources.

A high degree of authenticity can be found in one person-shows about historical artists which constitute a compilation of excerpts from letters, diaries, or autobiographies of the artist whose life is dramatized in that play. There is, for example, the 90-minute *Tynan* by Richard Nelson with Colin Chambers, serving as a star vehicle for the late Corin Redgrave in 2005, who played Kenneth Tynan (1927-1980), renowned British theatre critic. One member of a famous double act, Stan Laurel (1890-1965), is at the centre of the one man show written and performed by Bob Kingdom: *Stan Laurel: Please Stand Up* (2008). Anton Burge wrote *Whatever Happened to the Cotton Dress Girl*, a one-woman show about Bette Davis (1908-1989). Its production in 2008 coincided with her centenary. Comedian Eric Morecambe (1926-1984) is at the centre of the one-man show *Morecambe* by Tim Whitnall (2009). It premiered at the Edinburgh

Fringe and made its way to London's West End. The twist in the one person show *Jiggery Pokery* (2009) is that the central character, comedian Charles Hawtrey (1914-1988), was played by a woman, Amanda Lawrence (who also wrote the play and plays another fifty-odd characters in it as well). William Somerset Maugham (1874-1965) is the character at the centre of the 2010 one man show *Mr Maugham at Home* by Anthony Curtis.

The middle ground between high and low levels of authenticity is represented by those plays that set authentically drawn artist characters in situations they are known not to have encountered in their real lives. *Master Class* by David Pownall (1983), for example, imagines a meeting of Stalin (1878-1953) with composers Prokofiev (1891-1953) and Shostakovich (1906-1975) in the Kremlin. Brian Stewart takes a look at the mysterious circumstances of Marilyn Monroe's death at the age of 36 in 1962 in his 2005 play *Marilyn: Case # 81128*. The play juxtaposes the assumed events in the five hours after her death with information about her life held together by the device of showing her in her psychoanalysis sessions with her analyst Ralph Greenson. At the centre of *Monkey's Uncle* by David Lewis (2005) is the French writer of farce, Georges Feydeau (1862-1921), who is subjected to two acts of farce in the manner he excelled at writing. In a twist on the genre and the historicity of the characters, in the third act the current writer (Lewis) finds himself in Feydeau's position, all other characters are transformed to their 21st century counterparts, and the play reaches its farcical climax in this context.

Apparently, Terence Rattigan (1911-1977) once met Joe Orton (1933-1967) for lunch in 1964, and congratulated him on the achievement of *Entertaining Mr Sloane* in a letter. In *Joe and I*, by Laurie Slade (2005), Rattigan encounters Orton in more depth, and their relationship is put into special relief by the appearances of and comments by Oscar Wilde (1854-1900). Drury Pifer's *Strindberg in Hollywood* places historical artists, August Strindberg (1849-1912) and his wife Siri von Essen (1850-1912) into a 21st century context. The comedy imagines how the Hollywood of today would deal with Strindberg's *Dance of Death*. In 2009, Roy Smiles wrote *Kurt and Sid*, about Kurt Cobain (1967-1994) and Sid Vicious (1957-1979). On the night of Cobain's suicide, Cobain receives a visit from Vicious, not quite sure whether it is an impersonator, or a ghost of his own troubled imagination. In the 1970s, Greta Garbo (1905-1990) visited

Donegal, Ireland. Frank McGuinness uses this event to develop a new fiction, making Garbo, as he puts it, "the catalyst that changes everyone's lives within the play." (2010)

The opposite pole indicates plays that are least authentic: plays for which the dramatists took the life of a historical artist as an inspiration for a play about an artist. Tom Kempinski's *Duet for One* (1981), about a violinist suffering from Multiple Sclerosis, was inspired by the similar case of cellist Jacqueline du Pré (1945-1987). In Ronald Harwood's *The Dresser*, the central artist character is Sir, an old actor-manager. Since the author was, early on in his career, dresser to one of the last actor-managers, Sir Donald Wolfit, Harwood might have created the character of Sir with Wolfit in mind. Harwood was at pains to emphasize, however, that "Sir is not Wolfit. Norman's [the dresser of the title] relationship with Sir is not mine with Wolfit. Her ladyship [Sir's wife in the play] is quite unlike Rosalind Iden (Lady Wolfit)." (9)

Function and focus

Apart from the level of authenticity presented in biographical plays about famous artists, another criterion of classification is the function of the artist characters within the plays. The historical artist characters serve the function to exemplify a wider issue. In Christopher Hampton's *Tales from Hollywood* (1983), for example, Bertolt Brecht (1898-1956) and Thomas Mann (1875-1955) and Heinrich Mann (1871-1950) represent, among others, those artists who emigrated from Germany to Hollywood during the Second World War. Brecht tries hard to use his time in Hollywood as much as possible to change the world through theatre. Thomas Mann is able to perceive the suffering of those remaining behind in Germany and tries to help, albeit ineffectually in his elitist-intellectual ways. The character of Heinrich Mann serves to emphasize the general feeling of loneliness of all the emigrants in a foreign country. Together, these artist characters exemplify the issues of political inefficiency and cowardice of the emigrant artists and intellectuals: "The intellectual is inefficient; politics and society overpower him, which is to a large degree his own fault" (Westecker). Dusty Hughes' *Futurists* (1986) shows the artistic-intellectual life of Russia in 1921, only a few years after the revolution. Among the play's characters are Mayakovsky, Anna Akhmatova, Osip Mandelstam, Alexander Blok, Kolia Gumilyov, Lili

Brik and Maxim Gorki. Those artist characters mirror the unrest of their time. Different groupings of the artists try to develop the form of art most suitable to express the revolution, with its fundamental changes of inner and outer lives.

Master Class represents middle ground between biographical plays about famous artists that focus on the artists for the artist's sake and those in which the artist characters serve a more general function. The artist characters in *Master Class*, Prokofiev and Shostakovich, demonstrate that art cannot be prescribed and purpose-made to serve an ultimately un-artistic goal. In that sense, art and artists are independent, in this case of dictator Stalin's moods: the play is set in 1948, in a Kremlin antechamber. Stalin has summoned the two composers to explain to them personally (assisted by culture secretary Andrej Zhdanov) what correct and good Soviet music should be like. Apart from focusing on the political implications of the (fictional) encounter of the four main characters, Pownall manages to present the composers' suffering and their abilities of maintaining their personal dignities and artistic integrities under duress.

In contrast to plays in which the artist characters function as representatives of wider issues that the dramatist can debate by making use of these representative characters, many biographical plays about famous artists focus on the artist characters exclusively for their own, biographical, sake. Examples are Edna O'Brien's *Virginia* (1981) and Stephen MacDonald's *Not About Heroes* (1983), and indeed the majority of plays in the 2005-2013 period.

Constellations

A third criterion for differentiating among biographical plays about famous artists is the constellation of characters within the plays. Some plays show artists mainly among themselves, such as Mozart and Salieri in Shaffer's *Amadeus* (1979), Prokofiev and Shostakovich in *Master Class*, poets Owen and Sassoon in *Not About Heroes* and Alice B. Toklas and Gertrude Stein in Wells's *Gertrude Stein and a Companion* (1985). More recently, in 2005, three Pre-Raphaelites are put under the microscope in Gregory Murphy's *The Countess*: they are John Ruskin, his wife Effie, and painter Millais. In 2010, Jack Shepherd wrote *Demi-Monde: The Half-World of William Morris*. Bonnie Greer was inspired by a brief reference in a TV documentary about Monroe's time in New York about her becoming friends with

Ella Fitzgerald (1917-1996). *Marilyn and Ella* started off as a radio play, followed by a 2006 version for the Edinburgh Fringe and matured to a full length play in 2008. Personal relationships of a male protagonist with the women in his life were at the centre of the 1999 *Larkin with Women* by Ben Brown, revived in 2006. The same is true for the 2006 *My Matisse* by Howard Ginsberg. The play about poet Larkin is structured around dialogue with the three women in his life, while Ginsberg's play focuses on monologues of the seven women in painter Matisse's life.

Other plays present a wider picture, placing a central artist character amongst several other characters, not necessarily including other artists. Alan Plater wrote *Sweet William* for Northern Broadsides in 2005. The play is set in a pub after a performance of *Henry V*. Apart from Shakespeare himself, the characters in the play are the usual punters at the pub, many of whom have served as inspiration for characters in Shakespeare's plays. *Tosca's Kiss* by Kenneth Jupp (2006) focuses on the writer Rebecca West (1892-1983) and her relationship with American judge Francis Biddle at the Nuremberg trials. The frame for the plot is provided by West reading from her book based on her reports on the trials for the *Daily Telegraph* newspaper. Apart from the personal relationship between West and Biddle, Jupp is interested in the character of Hjalmar Schacht, director of the Reichsbank until 1939 and in that position in charge of providing the funds for Germany's rearmament prior to World War II. While the central character in Carol Ann Duffy's *Casanova* (2007) is Casanova and thus not an artist, this female Casanova serves as inspiration to some of Voltaire's philosophy and to Mozart's *Don Giovanni*. In *Afterlife* (2008) Michael Frayn returns to two major areas that have characterized his work so far: real-life people—as in *Copenhagen* (physicists Niels Bohr and Werner Heisenberg) and *Democracy* (German politicians, most notably Willy Brandt), and the theatre itself—as in his farce *Noises Off* and *Look Look*. The central character of *Afterlife* is German stage director Max Reinhardt (1873-1943). Frayn's play adopts the characteristics of a morality play, especially *Everyman*, a reference to the play that became a landmark production for Reinhardt: it has been revived annually in Salzburg with a star-studded cast to this day. *Afterlife* is also written in the kind of verse characteristic of *Everyman*. London Evening Standard critic Nicholas de Jongh turned his pen to playwrighting in *Plague over*

England. His central artist character is actor Sir John Gielgud (1904-2000), whose humiliation in 1953, when he was arrested and fined for soliciting in a public lavatory, serves as the starting point for de Jongh to analyse 1950s British homophobia.

Adversity versus genius

Over the period 1979-2004, many biographical plays about famous artists shared ways in which the artist characters were presented. In the majority of plays from that period, the dramatists placed the main artist character(s) in an adverse situation. Adversity takes different shapes, inward (e.g., mental illness) or outward (a personal enemy, or an anonymous power, such as war). Against the background of such adverse forces, the artist characters tend to come across as flawed human beings. Here are examples from the plays at the centre of the 2005 book. In *Amadeus*, Mozart is subjected to Salieri's higher social power; the composers Prokofiev and Shostakovich suffer from Stalin's political power (*Masterclass*); the poets Owen and Sassoon in *Not About Heroes* face the anonymous power of the First World War. Virginia Woolf, in *Virginia* struggles against her own mental illness. *Piaf* (Pam Gems, 1978) and *No Regrets* (Vanessa Drucker, 1981) show how Edith Piaf copes with adverse situations in her life. Stephanie Abrahams in *Duet for One* has to cope with her MS, and Sir in *The Dresser* just as Miss Helen in *The Road to Mecca* (Athol Fugard, 1985) have to deal with their age. It is striking that for the period 2005-2013, showing the artist characters in explicitly adverse situations is no longer central to the biographical plays about famous artists.

Modes of identification

The pattern of demonstrating the artist characters' artistic and moral integrity and strength against the backdrop of adversity, identified as characteristic for a large number of biographical plays about famous artists 1979-2004, can be explored further in the context of its impact on the reader / spectator. I discuss such impact on the reader or spectator in terms of concepts of identification developed by Jauß: he developed a heuristic differentiation of further possible forms of literary identification. His point of departure is identification with the hero in literature. The forms of identification he proposes are associative, admiring, sympathetic, cathartic and ironic. For our purposes, the last four are most important. Admiring identification is the aesthetic attitude that is formed in view of the perfection of an ideal. It is beyond any differentiation between tragic or comic impact, because the admiration of a hero, saint or sage does not, usually, result from tragic movement or comic relief. Rather, admiration demands that the aesthetic object, by its very perfection, takes expectation towards an ideal and thus triggers surprise that does not end when the novelty factor is lost (Jauß 1977: 231-2). Jauß differentiates between genuine admiration as the genuine striving of the soul, which is led to admiration through those things it considers beautiful (1977: 232) and mere imitation as an activity, which tries to copy the original, by close observation. The admired ideal of a hero can, according to Jauß, be transformed to an unattainable ideal, or it can be reduced to become the object or trigger of daydreams. Sympathetic identification reduces the distance between recipient and admired hero. The recipient will be moved by the hero's suffering and this leads to solidarity with him or her (1977: 237).

Cathartic identification is the aesthetic attitude described already by Aristotle, which transposes the spectators from the real interests and emotional complexities of their lifeworld into the world of the suffering or threatened hero, in order to effect, through tragic movement or comic relief a freeing up of their minds (1977: 244). Ironic identification, finally, is that level of aesthetic reception on which a predictable identification is developed only to be treated ironically afterwards or negated entirely (1977: 250). Such means of identification are used to arouse the recipient's aesthetic and moral reflexion. Applied to the biographical plays about famous artists 1979-2004, the argument is that for a large number of these plays, any idolising admiration for the artist character that may have existed prior to reading or watching the play is broken. At the same time, most plays take care to provide good insights into the artists' genius and their artistic integrity in the face of the adversity. The impact on the reader or spectator is that admiring identification builds. With the relatively smaller number of the *adversity versus genius* pattern in biographical plays about famous artists in the time period 2005-2013, the context of the various dimensions of identification are no longer appropriate for their discussion either.

Peter Shaffer's Amadeus *(1979)*

Peter Shaffer's *Amadeus* received its opening night on 2 November 1979 on the Olivier Stage of the National Theatre, London. The text of this production was published by André Deutsch in 1980. For the Broadway transfer, which opened at the Broadhurst Theatre on 17 December 1980, Shaffer revised the text, published by Penguin and, further revised, in an American edition of Shaffer's collected plays. Richard Adams published yet another version in the Longman Study Texts series. In his introduction he writes: "Since then [1981] Peter Shaffer has reworked the text yet again (...) and has restored certain details (...) that were originally included in version one but dropped from version two" (1984, xii). In this section I quote the Adams version. Since my focus is the theatre version of the play, I do not refer to the film version, for which Shaffer wrote the screen play.

Composer Antonio Salieri (1750-1825), contemporary of Mozart (1756-1791), is the main character of Shaffer's play and serves as its narrator. The plot begins in 1823: the audience encounters old Salieri, who addresses them as collective confessor, in order to present them with his last composition, entitled *The Death of Mozart, or Did I do it*? Old Salieri metamorphoses into young Salieri, both played by the same actor, who presents to the spectators short episodes from the years 1781-1791. The episodes show how Salieri first meets Mozart, how he envies him, schemes against him, drives him into financial ruin and thus contributes intentionally to Mozart's untimely death. All throughout, young Salieri comments the action from old Salieri's perspective. The play ends in 1823, with Salieri's unsuccessful suicide attempt.

Wolfgang Amadeus Mozart died on 5 December 1791. The cause of death is unclear and is still subject to controversial debates among historians of music and medicine (Greither 1967). According to some historical sources, Mozart is said to have claimed, shortly before his death, that Salieri poisoned him. This rumour is supported by the further rumour that old Salieri is supposed to have accused himself, in a state of dementia, of having poisoned Mozart (Novello 1829/1959). Shaffer clearly took up those rumours as the starting point of his play; however, in the play Salieri kills Mozart not through literal poison, but he drives him to death by scheming against him.

The individual events of that scheming are historically accurate. In the first plot against Mozart, Salieri manages to prevent Mozart getting a position as music tutor of a member of the Emperor's family. A letter from Mozart to his father demonstrates that Mozart wanted the position. It is historical fact that Salieri got the job instead. Shaffer takes up the historical material and shapes it to serve his purpose: in *Amadeus* it is Salieri who dissuades the Emperor from hiring Mozart; instead, he recommends Herr Sommer to be appointed. Thus the spectator is left with the impression that Mozart did not get the position due to Salieri's direct interference.

The second plot against Mozart relates to Mozart's opera *The Marriage of Figaro*. Historical sources confirm that opera director Rosenberg censured the ballet in Mozart's opera, under the pretext that the Emperor had forbidden the use of ballet in opera altogether. Shaffer adds Salieri's involvement in this: in the play, it is Salieri who suggests to Rosenberg the possibility of demanding that the ballet in *Figaro* be cut. Following historical sources, the Emperor then watches the dress rehearsal, realises the idiocy of having the singers and chorus onstage dancing without music and insists that the ballet be reinstated with its music. Shaffer uses this development further in involving Salieri: when Mozart is distraught at the censorship and accuses Salieri of being involved, Salieri in turn denies involvement and promises Mozart to intervene on his behalf with the Emperor by asking him to attend the dress rehearsal. He does nothing of the sort and is dismayed when the Emperor does attend. Mozart, of course, believes the Emperor came due to Salieri's help and is grateful to Salieri and ashamed, at the same time, for having suspected him of malice.

The opera *The Marriage of Figaro* ran for only nine performances. The Duschek family, friends of Mozart, were afraid that broad machinations were going on to ruin Figaro and that Salieri and his followers would do everything they could to prevent the opera becoming a success (Hutchins 1976: 83). Shaffer takes up this historically documented rumour and has his Salieri confirm to the audience: "I saw to it through the person of the resentful Director that in the entire year Figaro was played only nine times!"(70). Historically, Salieri's involvement was merely rumour, as suggested by Paumgartner, who points out that *Cosa Rara*, an opera by Martin, was much more successful with Vienna audiences than *Figaro* (Paumgartner 1949: 359).

Documents prove that Mozart became successor of Gluck as Royal and Imperial Court Composer on 7 December 1787. Shaffer takes this event up in the play. He changes the title to chamber composer. Historical sources confirm that Mozart received an annual salary of 200 florins, a pittance compared with Gluck's 2,000 florins. In *Amadeus* it is Salieri who suggests this miserly salary for Mozart to the Emperor. Salieri's intervention on this occasion is not documented in historical sources. Some contemporary music historians question whether the sum of 200 florins, although much lower than Gluck's salary, was a pittance. Hutchings, for example, argues that 200 florins was eight times the amount Mozart would have received for an opera and the duties of the post consisted mainly in composing dance music for the court balls, something Mozart would have done very quickly and easily (1976: 86).

Perhaps the most important and decisive intrigue against Mozart relates to Mozart's closeness to the freemasons. Shaffer's Salieri suggests to Mozart to include Masonic material in the opera he is composing for Schikaneder's popular theatre (*The Magic Flute*). Mozart happily accepts this idea and Salieri achieves his aim: the freemasons, represented in *Amadeus* by Baron van Swieten, are outraged, they feel betrayed and will no longer support Mozart financially, as they had done before. There is no historical evidence of Salieri influencing Mozart to use Masonic material in the opera. Shaffer was aware of the comparatively large degree of poetic licence:

> I, of course, took certain obvious liberties with this part of the story. I have no reason whatever to believe that the Masons actually repudiated Mozart, or that Baron van Swieten announced that he should never speak to him again. Nevertheless, Masonic displeasure over The Magic Flute constitutes one of the most persistent rumours attached to the Mozartian legend. (1982: xvii)

Salieri's final intrigue against Mozart that Shaffer selects from the historical sources relates to the documented masked messenger who visited Mozart on behalf of Count Walsegg and commissioned a requiem from him. In the play, Mozart tells Salieri about this figure that comes to haunt him day and night; due to his advanced ill health, he is no longer certain whether it is real or part of his feverish imagination. Salieri makes use of Mozart confiding in him thus. In the first version of the play, Salieri initially sends his servant disguised as the masked messenger and only when the servant refuses to continue does Salieri put on the mask himself. In the second and third versions, however, Salieri disguises himself as the messenger right from the beginning and haunts Mozart.

So sum up, Shaffer picks up historically documented material, including rumours and uses it, modifies it and interprets it in such a way that Salieri appears as the origin and driving force of machinations against Mozart. Such modifications serve to guide the audience's relation to Mozart in the course of the play. Up until publication of Hildesheimer's biography of Mozart (1977), Mozart was idealised, even idolised, in society and in literature (Gruber 1985). Shaffer's way of presenting Mozart breaks with this idolising mode, causing controversial debate in the wake of the opening night of *Amadeus* (Thomsen and Brandstetter 1982: 196). At the basis of such controversy were passages in the text in which Mozart behaves in a childish manner and uses drastic language. Here, for example, is Mozart's first appearance in the play. He is in the library of Countess Waldstädten and believes that he is alone in the room with Constanze Weber. Salieri is hiding in a large armchair, unknown to them. Mozart and Constanze play cat and mouse:

> MOZART: I'm going to bite you in half with my fangs-wangs! My little Stanzerl-wanzerl banzerl!
>
> CONSTANZE: Stop it, Wolferl! Ssh!
>
> *She giggles delightedly, lying prone beneath him.*
>
> MOZART: You're trembling...I think you're frightened of puss-wuss! ... I think you're scared to death! (*Intimately*) I think you're going to shit yourself. (*She squeals, but is not really shocked*). In a moment it's going to be on the floor!
>
> CONSTANZE: Sh! Someone'll hear you!
>
> *He imitates a noise of a fart.*
>
> MOZART: All nasty and smelly on the floor.
>
> CONSTANZE: No!
>
> MOZART: Here it comes now. I can hear it coming! ... O what a melancholy note! Something's dropping from your boat. (17)

Some critics were as shocked as Salieri to be faced with such a Mozart. Peter Hall, who directed the first production of *Amadeus*, was aware that Shaffer's way of writing Mozart was potentially problematic, as demonstrated in the following entry in his diary:

> I must be careful that Simon [Callow] does not act Mozart too coarsely, despite the oafishness in the part. Mozart admired grace and precision in everything. For instance, he hated pianists who waved their heads about when they performed. His awfulness in the play must therefore be delicate. (1983: 462)

Thomsen and Brandstetter pointed to an inconsistency in the way Shaffer chose to characterise Mozart in the play: Mozart would hardly have behaved as badly at court when he knew he was in the company of the courtiers, because he had been exposed to appropriate behaviour in the courts across Europe since early childhood (1982, 208). It is important to remember, here and throughout the discussion that follows, that all we see of Mozart in the play is presented through Salieri's eyes, and we may not be able to trust the Mozart we thus encounter as being "real". Spectators or readers used to the mode of idealising or idolising Mozart may well feel appalled when faced with Shaffer's Mozart in *Amadeus*. In Iser's terminology, by threatening the ideal of Mozart for the spectators, an empty space has been created which the spectator needs to fill. Against the background of the broken ideal, in the course of the play, Salieri as commentator of the play's events causes further modifications and distortions of the spectator's expectations. This device gives the play overall an epic character. Old Salieri tells the spectators about his complex relationship with Mozart over the years of 1781-1791, so that the majority of the plot is a retrospective. Salieri metamorphoses into his younger self, takes part in the remembered action and comments on this action from Old Salieri's perspective. In the first few scenes that introduce Salieri's memory, the spectator learns about the court in 1781, the most important courtiers, such as Strack, van Swieten, opera director Rosenberg, the Emperor and Salieri himself, his two spies and finally Mozart. Salieri often addresses the spectators directly, thus involving them in the action. Old Salieri's comments continue throughout the play, in different dramatic forms: the action on stage might freeze at an appropriate moment for Salieri to address the spectators. When Salieri has finished his comment, the retrospective action continues. Stage directions such as "without emphasis Mozart freezes his movements and Salieri takes one easy step forward to make a fluent aside" (26) indicate the beginning of such a comment from the future. In other cases, the action on the stage continues while Salieri comments on it.

In his first speech to the audience, Old Salieri announces what is to follow, his memories, in the form of a composition his entitled *The Death of Mozart, or Did I Do It?* The outcome of the action that is to follow, Mozart's death, is thus known. The audience at this stage also knows that Salieri accused himself of having murdered Mozart. The spectator will develop some tense expectation as to the real outcome of the play, since Salieri puts his claim of having poisoned Mozart into question: "Did I Do It?" This tension is enhanced by the position Salieri puts the spectators in: he declares his memory a confession, with the audience as collective confessor. Usually, people only need to confess their sins. It is thus sins the audience expects to hear from confessing Salieri.

The Death of Mozart is presented and commented on from Old Salieri's perspective. It is his confession. After any idealizing or idolizing attitude of the audience towards Mozart is broken in their first encounter with him as childish and drastic Mozart in the library of Baroness Waldtstädten, Salieri hears Mozart's music for the first time and his extreme reaction to this music culminates in the exclamation: "It seemed to me I had heard a voice of God" (20). It is divine music, but it is created by a human being "whose own voice I had also heard—and it was the voice of an obscene child" (20). While the audiences' first encounter with Mozart rocks their ideal image of the great composer, Salieri's full appreciation of the divine quality of Mozart's music appears to counter any breaking of the ideal / idol. Such an oscillation between showing Mozart as a flawed human being and pointing to the divine quality of his music is repeated several times throughout the play. Salieri studies some further compositions by Mozart and qualifies them as "the productions of a precocious youngster" (21).

Salieri queries whether the overwhelming impression of the Serenade for thirteen wind instruments KV 361, which he considered divine, could have been a one-off. This doubt weakens the initial impression that Mozart's music is that of genius. Mozart's first audience with the Emperor plays further with the ambiguity of talent and genius: after listening to it only once, Mozart repeats a simple march of welcome, composed by Salieri, from memory and brilliantly changes it, in no time at all, into the famous tune of Figaro's aria *non piu andrai* from *The Marriage of Figaro*. The audience can only admire this expression of genius. The very same scene, however, shows beyond doubt that Mozart's ways of behaving at court are not within the expectations, even if he is not as obscene as he was in the Baroness's library. Later scenes confirm that Mozart's extravagant life is irritating to the courtiers, as is his relaxed way of talking.

Mozart enthusiastically talks about his ideas for a new opera, *The Abduction from the Seraglio*, which is about love. When Salieri comments that opera hardly deals with any other topic than love, Mozart interrupts: "I mean manly love, Signore. Not male sopranos screeching. Or stupid couples rolling their eyes. All that absurd Italian rubbish" (25). Mozart says all this in the presence of the Emperor and, to make it worse, in the presence of Salieri and Kapellmeister Bonno, who are both Italians and could well take offence. Some scenes of the first act show Mozart drunk and rough in his manners at court. Salieri's spies report to him rumours that Mozart is unfaithful to his wife. All those scenes serve to demolish for the spectator any ideal image of Mozart they may have held before. Then, however, Salieri and through him the spectator, has a look at Mozart's original scores. Salieri now grasps the full extent of Mozart's genius: "I was staring through the cage of those meticulous ink strokes at an absolute beauty" (48-9). Salieri recognises that Mozart writes his scores without any corrections: "What was evident was that Mozart was simply transcribing music (...) completely finished in his head. And finished as most music is never finished." (48) The stage directions show how Salieri's words in this passage are interwoven with excerpts from Mozart's music, which the audience hears as indicated: Salieri opens the folder with the scores and leafs through it.

> Music sounds instantly, faintly in the theatre as his eye falls on the first page. It is the opening of the 29th Symphony in A Major. Over the music, reading it (...) He looks up from the manuscript at the Audience: the music abruptly stops (...) He resumes looking at the music. Immediately the Sinfonia Concertante for Violin and Viola sounds faintly. (48)

The spectators understand that the music they can hear is the music Salieri reads in the scores. Even Mozart's music is thus presented from Salieri's perspective, through Salieri's ear. Only after this decisive event is it clear for both Salieri and the audience that Mozart's music is an expression of genius. It is now that Salieri starts his machinations against Mozart, which I discussed at the beginning of this section in their relation to historically documented facts, rumours and poetic licence. It is also now that the way the audience relates to Mozart changes. Any initial reference to Mozart's genius was severely undermined by showing a range of human flaws. Only at the end of the first act does the full extent of Mozart's genius become obvious to Salieri and through him to the spectator. In the second act Shaffer further emphasises the contrast between Mozart's genius, expressed in his music and his suffering. This suffering throughout is caused by Salieri's machinations. The audience is led to feel sympathy for Mozart: each of the discussed machinations is followed by a brief scene showing Mozart's reaction. Mozart blames himself when he does not get the post as Princess Elizabeth's music teacher: "It's my own fault. My father always writes I should be more obedient. Know my place." (55) Mozart bursts out in anger when opera director Rosenberg censors the dance in act three of *The Marriage of Figaro* and tears out the relevant pages from the score. His words are quite drastic:

> You shit-pot ... Woppy, foppy, wet-arsed, Italian-loving, shit-pot ... [*Screeching after him*] Count Orsini-Rosenshit! ... Rosencunt! ... Rosenbugger! ... I'll hold a rehearsal! You'll see! The emperor will come! You'll see! You'll see! You'll see! [*He throws down his score in a storm of hysterical rage*] (64)

The impact of this outburst on the spectator's relation to Mozart is different here, however, to the impact of similar obscene language in act one. Mozart is shown in a situation in which he is helpless. An important part of his opera has been censored, cut. There are only two days left until the opening night and because for Mozart the music that he has composed for the opera is perfect, he cannot simply change anything or compose anything in addition to what is there. Mozart's screaming in this context is the result of utter helplessness and leads to the audience feeling pity or compassion for Mozart, who has been humiliated, has been turned into what the stage directions call a "shrieking little man" (64). Mozart is outraged when *Figaro* gets only nine performances (70) and full of despair when the freemasons distance themselves from him (89).

Any compassion that spectators will develop towards Mozart is enhanced by Salieri's behaviour towards Mozart. Salieri not only causes Mozart's suffering, but also ingratiates himself with Mozart by pretending, repeatedly, to help him. In this context, the death of Mozart's father Leopold takes on particular importance. Leopold's death means for Mozart the loss of a guardian: "How will I go now? (...) In the world. There is no one else. No one who understands the wickedness around. I can't see it!" (72) Salieri has confessed to the audience that from now on he wants to focus his machinations more on Mozart the person, because it would not be too difficult for him to ruin any possible success of Mozart's future operas after he has seen to it that *Figaro* failed. Now he sees his chance in Leopold Mozart's death and presents himself as a surrogate father to Mozart: "Wolfgang. My dear Wolfgang. Don't accuse yourself. Lean upon me, if you care to... Lean upon me." (72) If Mozart accepts Salieri as a father figure, by implication he must now regard Salieri as his guardian against the evil of the world. Salieri exploits Mozart's trust by suggesting to him to use Masonic ideas in his *Magic Flute*. The audience's compassion with Mozart is strengthened considerably by encountering Salieri's repeated meanness towards his innocent victim.

Mozart's suffering extends to his marriage. Constanze reproaches Mozart because of their poverty. Mozart is able to pacify his wife and a scene follows which is reminiscent of the one in the first act on which Salieri had eavesdropped. The passage makes clear to the audience that despite suffering and poverty, Mozart and Constanze are still in love with each other:

MOZART: [*insistent: like a child*] Come on - do it. Let's do it. 'Poppy'

They play a private game, gradually doing it faster, on their knees

CONSTANZE: Poppy.
MOZART: [*changing it*] Pappy
CONSTANZE: [*copying*] Pappy
MOZART: Pappa.
CONSTANZE: Pappa
MOZART: Pappa-pappa!
CONSTANZE: Pappa-pappa!

MOZART: Pappa-pappa-pappa-pappa!
CONSTANZE: Pappa-pappa-pappa-pappa!

They rub noses

TOGETHER: Pappa-pappa-pappa-pappa! Pappa-pappa-pappa-pappa!
(84)

This idyllic scene, reminiscent of the exchange between Papageno and Papagena, the earthy lovers in *The Magic Flute*, is broken immediately: Constanze screams, Mozart is worried, both characters freeze and the audience finds out via Salieri's spies that Constanze had given premature birth to a baby boy. The spies comment on the events in a way that supports the compassion aroused already by the events themselves: they say that the poor boy should be pitied, having been born into such poverty and to a father who was hardly more than a baby himself (84-5).

Shaffer guides the audience's compassion for Mozart by appealing to two basic human experiences all spectators share: suffering and love. Mozart's musical genius is never in doubt: on the contrary, throughout act two Salieri further comments on Mozart's music: *Figaro* moves Salieri to tears and he concludes that the very form of opera had been created for Mozart. Salieri believes to see Leopold Mozart in the Commendatore of Mozart's *Don Giovanni* and recognises: "We were both ordinary men, he and I. Yet he from the ordinary created legends—and I from legends created only the ordinary." (73) For Salieri, Dorabella and Fiordiligi in *Cosi fan Tutte* become incarnations of Aloysia and Constanze Weber: "two average girls turned to divinities: their sounds of surrender sweeter than the psalms in heaven." (73) Whenever Salieri comments on those operas, as well as on *The Magic Flute* and the *Requiem*, music from those compositions are played in the theatre, again serving to enhance the spectators' awareness of Mozart's musical genius.

While the spectator's conventional views of Mozart prior to watching *Amadeus* may well attribute to Mozart the position of genius, far distant from ordinary humans, such distance is initially reduced by the way the play presents all of Mozart's human faults. The unattainable, distant genius has come closer, has become human. This proximity of the spectators to the character of Mozart may be charged with surprise, rejection, or disappointment. However, in the course of act two, such feelings towards Mozart are replaced by compassion, which in turn brings Mozart even closer to the audience. Genius becomes comprehensible, at least to a certain degree. Compassion for the fellow human being, which the audience increasingly comes to feel for Mozart, in turn increases the impact his music can have on them. Human being and genius are no longer separated. The conventional idealising, idolising view of Mozart is gradually replaced by recognition and appreciation of Mozart's musical genius, avoiding, however, the idealising and idolising components of the conventional Mozart image. Mozart the man is now seen as innocent and naïve, in part child-like (rather than childish) in his behaviour and strong in his expressions, living his daily life on the basis of the same spontaneity and intuition that form the source of his genius and his music. Mozart the man dies at the end of *Amadeus*. His genius survives in his music. In this sense, Mozart's essence, his music, survives all of Salieri's machinations.

Shaffer employs two further strategies in guiding the audience in their relation to Mozart and Salieri: one relates to the two characters in *Amadeus* representing two distinct views on the ways artists work; the second relates to Salieri's relation to God. Salieri is a talented technician, while Mozart is an intuitive genius (Huber and Zapf 1984: 303-4). Salieri recognises this difference and declares himself the patron saint of mediocrity (101) and repeatedly comments on his worth as a composer: "I regret that my invention in love, as in art, has always been limited." (54); "I was to be bricked up in Fame (…) but for work I knew to be absolutely worthless" (98). Mozart, on the other hand, composes intuitively; he has completed his compositions fully in his mind before writing them down:

> MOZART: Tell the emperor the opera's finished.
> STRACK: Finished?
> MOZART: Right here in my noddle. The rest's just scribbling. (61)

Salieri sees this in Mozart's scores, which do not show any corrections. This in turn demonstrates Salieri's own mediocrity to himself:

> Tonight at an inn somewhere in this city stands a giggling child who can put on paper, without actually setting down his billiard cue, casual notes which turn my most considered ones into lifeless scratches. (49)

The phrase "most considered" confirms that composing means hard work for Salieri, whereas Salieri feels that Mozart composes without any effort. The contrast between Mozart and Salieri extends beyond music to everyday life: Mozart's way of behaving comes across as equally intuitive, he is well-meaning, naïve and, as he himself admits, not able to recognise and ward off the evil of the world. Salieri's behaviour is guided by his intellect rather than his intuition. He knows precisely what he wants: fame. At the beginning of the play he tells the audience: "I wanted fame. No to deceive you. I wanted to blaze like a comet, across the firmament of Europe. Yet only in one special way. Music" (7-8). When it comes to his machinations, Salieri is as decided in his approach. The contrast between intuition and intellect exists on both levels of music and daily life. The characters' language helps to demonstrate the contrast: Salieri's language is often courtly, formal, always very precise, a kind of "verbal wizardry" (Hinden 1982: 60). Mozart's language, in contrast, is more lively and more spontaneous and even Salieri finds passages like the following fascinating:

> ... That's why opera is important, Baron. Because it's realer than any play! A dramatic poet would have to put all those thoughts down one after another to represent this second of time. The composer can put them all down at once and still make us hear each one of them. Astonishing device: a vocal quartet! (More and more excited)... I tell you I want to write a finale lasting half an hour! A quartet becoming a quintet becoming a sextet. On and on, wider and wider—all sounds multiplying and rising together—and the together making a sound entirely new! ... I bet you that's how God hears the world. Millions of sounds ascending at once and mixing in His ear to become an unending music, unimaginable to us. (To Salieri) That's our job! That's our job, we composers: combining the inner minds of him and him and him and her and her—the thoughts of chambermaids and Court Composers—and turn the audience into God. (60)

Against the background of Salieri's talent, the audience further realises Mozart's genius as a composer.

Salieri imagines God as an old man staring at the world with merchants' eyes: "Those eyes made bargains, real and irreversible: "You give me so—I'll give you so! No more. No less"" (8). Thus Salieri at the age of sixteen makes a bargain with God:

Signore, let me be a Composer. Grant me sufficient Fame to enjoy it.
In return, I will live with virtue. I will be chaste. I will strive to better
the lot of my fellows. And I will honour you with much music all the
days of my life!" As I said Amen, I saw his eyes flare. [As "God"]
"Bene. Go forth, Antonio. Serve Me and Mankind - and you will be
blessed!" ... "Grazie!" I called back. "I am Your Servant for life!" (8).

Salieri thus expects that God will reveal Himself to Salieri through the
music Salieri will be able to compose through God's grace. But it is
not in his own music that Salieri one day hears the voice of God, but
in Mozart's music. Salieri's jealousy and envy in *Amadeus* are based
on Salieri's insight that it is in Mozart's music and not his own music
that God's voice is heard on earth. All Salieri's virtuous life, led to
gain God's grace in the form of fame through music, was in vain.
Now that God has not maintained his side of the bargain, Salieri
declares himself God's enemy:

Dio Ingiusto. You are the enemy. I name Thee now: Nemico Eterno.
And this I swear: To my last breath I shall block you on earth, as far
as I am able. [He glares at his God. To audience] What use, after all, is
Man, if not to teach God his lessons? (50)

Salieri fights God by destroying God's voice on earth, Mozart.
Although Salieri reaches his goal physically (Mozart dies), Salieri has
to live for many years after Mozart's death to find that his own
success means, in effect, his defeat, because Mozart's divine quality,
his music, does not die. Through Mozart, Salieri fights God. While
Mozart's music survives, Salieri's music is forgotten in his own
lifetime. Realizing this, Salieri realises God's victory.

To summarise: the play offers the spectator numerous points of
identification, often relating to basic human needs, such as love,
suffering and compassion. Mozart is shown as a genius not completely
distant to the spectators, but close to them, because they can identify
with him, with his love and suffering; they can develop compassion
with him, which brings him closer to them. They can understand
Mozart's initially irritating behaviour and they can participate in his
ultimate triumph through his music, which survives Salieri's
machinations and Mozart's physical death. Any conventional, pre-
Amadeus Mozart ideal or idol that the spectators may have brought
with them to the performance of *Amadeus* is broken and replaced by
an image of Mozart that does not cover up human flaws, but helps to

understand them and in which Mozart's genius is emphasised in many ways, not least in relating it to God. In terms of consciousness, the play sets masculine intellect against feminine intuition, with the latter gaining the upper hand in the long run.

The tribute play and its relatives

Some biographical plays about famous artists of the 1979-2004 period, were found to deviate from the general pattern characteristic of these kinds of plays of that period: they are characterized by the very lack of any specific problems, let alone any tendency towards critical reflection of the lives of the artists at their centre. Timothy West, who played the part of conductor Sir Thomas Beecham in *Beecham* by Caryl Brahms and Ned Sherrin (1979) described the particular nature of this play thus:

> *Beecham* is not really a play at all. It is a portrait, an affectionate portrait, a celebration, if you like, of a distinctive man. I don't think there would have been any reason to do it at all had it not been for the fact that Beecham is largely regarded by a lot of people as just a fund of funny stories, and he was that, of course, a very witty man, but he also had an extraordinary love and interest in, and passionate regard for, the welfare of music. (1985)

In more recent times, such plays, which West calls an affectionate portrait or a celebration, have been referred to as *tribute plays* by the newspapers' theatre critics. Thus, Maxwell comments on *Whatever Happened to the Cotton Dress Girl* (the one-woman show by Anton Burge about Bette Davis) that while the play 'fills us in on Davis's biographical details (…) dramaturgically, (…) not much is going on (…) So this loving, well-researched tribute show never quite makes a case for its existence. And Wilcox? A good actor. But, sorry, she's no Bette Davis' (2008). Brian Logan suggests that Whitnall's *Morecambe* is a good example of a tribute play, feeding the public need for nostalgia without seeking to address deeper levels or to convey messages. Logan also refers to *Jiggery Pokery* as a tribute play (2009). Another example is *Sophie Tucker's One Night Stand* (2005), which Chris Burgess wrote as a vehicle for his wife, Sue Kelvin. The play is about the vaudeville star Sophie Tucker (1884-1966); according to Thompson in the *Evening Standard*, the play highlights Tucker the icon, and does not get to the depths of Tucker the 'real human being', avoiding analysis of vulnerability, fear and conflict in her life. Burgess took up the friendship of Marlene Dietrich (1901-1992) and Noel Coward (1899-1973) in his play *Lunch with Marlene* (2008). While the first half of the performance started off with the frame of Dietrich seeking advice from Coward about her autobiography—a device allowing both characters to reminisce about their lives, the second half consisted of the actors, Frank Barrie and Kate O'Mara, singing about twenty of their characters' most famous songs.

Comedy about comedians
Critical reaction to a good number of funny plays about famous comedians written and performed between 2005-2013 has been similarly ambiguous, showing some disappointment that the plays did not go deep enough. *Pete & Me* (2005) by Tim Marriott is about comedian Peter Cook (1937-1995), focusing on the hours after his 1972 comeback with Dudley Moore (1935-2002). He finds himself berated by his American producer for being drunk, and attempts to seduce the ASM to be able to get hold of the booze she has hidden at the producer's request. They are discovered in the shower by Cook's girlfriend. *Pete and Dud: Come Again* (2006) by Chris Bartlett and Nick Awde is also about Peter Cook and Dudley Moore. The framing device in this play is a 1982 TV talk show, complete with a Terry Wogan-like host, and with the audience serving as the talk show audience. The interviewee is Dudley Moore, fresh from Hollywood fame with *Arthur*. The interview allows for flashbacks of the two characters' lives, and some of their most famous sketches. Roy Smiles is an author who has written more than one bio-play, with an emphasis on British comedians. *Ying Tong* (2005) is about Spike Milligan (1918-2002), the main creator of *The Goon Show*, which ran on BBC Home Service between 1951-1960. The other main goons, Peter Sellers (1925-1980) and Harry Secombe (1921-2001), also feature as characters in the play, which is set in a psychiatric hospital where Milligan was treated in 1960 for a nervous breakdown. Milligan, in turn, is also at the centre of the 2008 play *Surviving Spike* by Richard Harris, in a production that starred Michael Barrymore. The play is based on the memoirs of Norma Farnes, Milligan's agent, and she is the other character in this two-hander. Lyn Gardner commented in *The*

Guardian that the play's 'determination to concentrate on the man and not his work sells the latter short' (2008)

Long live Hollywood

The world of Hollywood film is at the centre of *Moonlight and Magnolias* by Ron Hutchinson (2007). The play's title quotes the working title of the film that became famous as *Gone with the Wind*. A comedy, the play focuses on the process of producer David O. Selznick (1902-1965) and director Victor Fleming (1889-1949) working with author Ben Hecht (1894-1964) on the script—a difficult endeavour given that Hecht has not read the novel. Adam Rolston's *A Sentimental Journey* (2009) is about another Hollywood great, Doris Day (b. 1922), in a play that combines scenes from her life with her own musical numbers, and those of some of her most famous co-stars, such as Frank Sinatra. Hollywood practices are also at the centre of *Rock* by Tim Fountain. This 2008 two-hander has agent Henry Willson (1911-1978) and actor Rock Hudson (1925-1985) as its characters. I already referred to Anton Burge's 2008 production of *Whatever Happened to the Cotton Dress Girl*, a one-woman show about Bette Davis (1908-1989).

VIP authors

After *Piaf*, which arguably, together with Shaffer's *Amadeus* launched the unstoppable wave of biographical plays about famous artists, Pam Gems's latest contribution to this genre has been *Mrs Pat* (2006) about the actress Mrs Patrick Campbell (1865-1940). The reviews suggest that the play covers a lot of material and five actors are stretched by having to play some twenty-four characters, including a young John Gielgud and most notably George Bernard Shaw (who wrote the part of Eliza in *Pygmalion* for Mrs Patrick Campbell). Perhaps this abundance of material, insufficiently subjected to a dramaturgical pruning, reflects the conditions of *Piaf*, where director Howard Davies spent a year with Gems finding the right format, contexts and characters for this play before rehearsals began (Davies 1985).

Ronald Harwood has written several biographical plays, possibly starting with *The Dresser* in 1980, and including composer Peter Warlock (*Poison Pen*, 1993), conductor Furtwängler (*Taking Sides*, 1996), and composer Gustav Mahler (*Mahler's Conversion*).

Collaboration (2008) places composer Richard Strauss and novelist Stefan Zweig under the threat of the Nazis in their collaboration on *Die Schweigsame Frau*.

Some established dramatists find it difficult to portray in their plays about famous artists precisely what is at the source of those artists' genius. An example is the depiction of T.S. Eliot (1888-1965) in *Tom and Viv* by Michael Hastings (1985), and similarly, the more recent *Afterlife* by Michael Frayn does not manage to get across what kind of person Max Reinhardt was, nor how he was able to achieve his considerable success and influence in theatre history.

The Giant (2007) attracted considerable critical attention because it was written by well-known actor Anthony Sher. Its main artist characters are Leonardo da Vinci (1452-1519) and Michelangelo (1475-1564). Billington's review in the *Guardian* was respectful: he concedes that it is better to "shoot at the stars than to aim low and miss", concedes that Sher "sets up an intriguing contrast between the young, fervently faithful Michelangelo and the mature, sceptical, inventive Leonardo", and that Sher "wrestles with the anguish of the artist" in his "ambitious" play that made for a "longish" evening (2007). Even the *New York Times* devoted a review to the play—which turned out to be twice as long as any of the UK reviews. Here, critic Matt Wolf mirrors Billington's view that the first act lacks suspense in more direct terms, calling it "murky" and "clunky". Conceding that "Sher is on to something in the nexus between desire and artistic inspiration", Wolf deplores, however, that both play and production "feel so compelled to overembellish at every turn" (2007).

Critical response to Timberlake Wertenbaker's *The Line* (2009) was equally ambiguous. The play focuses on the meetings between French painter and sculptor Edgar Degas (1834-1917) and Suzanne Valadon (1865-1938) from the 1880s to shortly before Degas' death in 1917. Billington called it a

> decent if somewhat undramatic work (…) In the end, the play poses an old question: is it worth sacrificing life to art. But, while Wertenbaker implies not, she also wants us to see Suzanne and Degas's house-keeper as women expected to sacrifice themselves to the male ego. (2009)

Billington also notes a structural problem: "Suzanne changes while Degas essentially doesn't" (2009). Critics highly praised Alan

Bennett's *The Habit of Art* (2009), which has a fictional meeting between poet W.H.Auden (1907-1973) and composer Benjamin Britten (1913-1976) at its centre. The plot works on multiple levels: a group of actors at the National Theatre in London are seen in a rehearsal, where, in the absence of the director, they run through the play they are working on (about the encounter between Auden and Britten) in the presence of the author and led by the stage manager. Much time of the performance is taken up by the frame of the rehearsal; this allows for much comedy, leaving the encounter between the two artists to the second act, and allowing perhaps too little space for sufficient depth in the debates around art to develop.

The principle found to dominate the first phase of biographical plays about famous artists, setting the artists' genius against adverse situations, is much less dominant 2005-2013, while the number of tribute plays is on the increase. Plays of the period 2005-2013 tend to be more rather than less authentic, and focus on the artist characters' lives more than taking those characters as representatives of wider issues. This development can be related to the additional insight that critics tend to point more frequently to overtly evident dramaturgical devices applied by the dramatists in their attempts to frame the plots. For example, in *Tosca's Kiss* Jupp has Rebecca West reading from her book based on her reports on the Nuremberg trials for the *Daily Telegraph* newspaper. We see the title character in Burgess's *Sophie Tucker's One Night Stand* after her death, in limbo reflecting on her past life. This device provides the opportunity for Kelvin and her co-star Russell Churney as Tucker's pianist to present the most famous of her songs. Another character in limbo after death, reflecting on his life, is James Dean in *James Dean is Dead (Long Live James Dean)* by Jackie Skarvellis (2007). A variation of this particular device is the actor Sir Henry Irving (1838-1905) facing a posthumous trial in *The Trial of Sir Henry Irving [Lately Deceased]* by Andrew Shepherd (2005). Irving has to convince a jury that his life as an actor was not wasted. I have already pointed out the devices in *Marilyn: Case # 81128* (Monroe's sessions of psychotherapy), *Pete and Dud: Come Again* (an imaginary talk show) and *Lunch with Marlene* (Marlene Dietrich seeking advice from Noel Coward about her autobiography). Of course such devices can also be found in the early phase of biographical plays about famous artists, but they are not usually highlighted by the critics because the substance of the plays was more weighty and thus worth writing about.

Why so many—still?

Why have there been so many biographical plays about famous artists over the past thirty years? It is possible to distinguish primarily outward motives and predominantly inward ones. It is a case of outward motivation if dramatists try, by writing their own biographical plays about artists, to imitate commercial successes such as *Amadeus* or *Piaf*. A few examples follow to suggest that such an attempt may not always work.

Michael Hastings' *Tom and Viv* (1985) is a play about poet T. S. Eliot's first marriage to Vivienne Haigh Wood. In a series of more or less short episodes, events from the years 1915, 1921, 1927, 1932, 1935, 1937 and 1947 are dramatized, based on some unauthorised biographies, and in particular Vivienne's brother Maurice Haigh Wood whom Hastings interviewed over a period of five months prior to Haigh-Wood's death. The majority of scenes shows Tom and Viv fighting each other, or shows conflicts between Tom and / or Viv with Viv's parents. Only one scene indicates some sort of harmony between Tom and Viv, which is evidenced in one of the biographies (Ackroyd 1984: 85). Eliot's genius as a poet is not evident anywhere in the play. Tom Wilkinson, who played Eliot in the first production of the play at the Royal Court in London, found that this lack made it more difficult for him to portray the famous poet on stage:

> I found one of the most frustrating problems of the play was that he [Eliot] is one of towering geniuses of the 20th century and there is no evidence in the play to suggest that he was anything other than a curious sort of pervert. (1985)

Hastings was not allowed to quote from Eliot's poetry, as Matthew Evans from Eliot's publishers, Faber and Faber, confirmed in a letter to the *Times Literary Supplement* (1984). Nevertheless, there is a scene in the play in which Viv explains to her (little interested) father a passage from *The Waste Land*, then still under the title of *He do the police in different voices*. She reads lines 108-114, Tom reads lines 115 and 116. In the published text of the play, the lines are printed as follows:

Under the firelight, under the brush her hair
Spread out in fiery points
Glowed into words, then would be savagely still.
My nerves are bad tonight. Yes, bad. Stay with me.
Speak to me. Why do you never speak?
Speak.
What are you thinking of? What thinking?
What?
I never know what you are thinking. Think.
I think we are in rats' alley
Where the dead men lost their bones. (78)

The arrangement of lines in *The Waste Land* does not correspond with that used in Hastings' play. 'Speak' and 'What?' originally belong to the end of the line above compared to where they have been placed by Hastings. Maybe this is merely an oversight of Hastings' publishers or the author himself, or an indication that Viv does not only provide a chaotic interpretation of the poem, but also distorts the meaning when reading it. No matter: if this passage could be quoted in Hastings' play despite the lack of permission, why not more, which could have helped to show Eliot's genius? Barber wrote in his review:

> ... the portrait of Eliot is shamefully inadequate, giving little impression of the supersubtle mind or the travelled sophisticate, and none whatever of the introspective torments and spiritual achievements of the greatest religious poet of the century. ... It is the old problem of presenting genius on stage. (1984)

In *Virginia*, Edna O'Brien managed quite well to portray Virginia Woolf's genius on stage. Virginia's love for Vita Sackville-West was introduced gently and poetically, and a three-page scene was enough to present a striking, but not revolting, impression of Virginia's mental imbalance. In the play, the language of the character Virginia is that of Virginia Woolf herself, taken from diaries and letters. In *Tom and Viv*, in contrast, Eliot's words are those of Hastings. If the author was not allowed to show Eliot's genius by quoting his poetry, why not use more of his linguistic characteristics? Wilkinson comments, based on his research for playing Eliot:

> Eliot was not an inarticulate person. You know, there was the problem that he spoke, I mean, maddeningly spoke, in sentences, in paragraphs, and if he was interrupted, he would stop at the interruption and then carry on. (1985)

Instead of long, complex sentences we get an Eliot speaking in short main clauses, as in the following passage:

> We met an old tutor of mine. Bertie Russell has a flat in Bury Street. He insisted we share it with him. It's a room behind the kitchen where he stores china. It's large enough for a single cot, and there's a davenport. Sometimes I sleep in a deckchair in the hall. (68)

The question arises whether *Tom and Viv* is indeed primarily about aspects in the life of a famous poet, or whether the quintessence of the play is better summarised in the words a female spectator addressed to actor Wilkinson:

> I don't want you to think that this play is about anything as grand as literary pretensions and all that. Forget about that, I say. I don't care if this play is called Bert and Deb or Dick and Sylv. This play is about one woman who loved one man to the exclusion of all others. And I want you to know this. Goodnight. (Hastings 1985, 47)

Thus *Tom and Viv* somehow comes across as a biographical play about a famous artist without the artist. Nevertheless the play was commercially successful, both in London and in New York.

In other attempts of jumping the bandwagon of successful plays, music tends to be important. The success of *Amadeus*, *Piaf*, *Master Class*, *No Regrets* and *Duet for One* depends to a good extent on the integration of music into the plot. Whereas in *Amadeus*, Mozart's and Salieri's compositions, and in *Duet for One* the playing of the violin can be heard from tape only, music in *Piaf*, *Master Class* and *No Regrets* was live. Howard Davies, who directed the first production of *Piaf*, comments thus: "I think that in the case of *Piaf*, and to a certain extent with *Amadeus*, in a very different way, it was shown that musical theatre was very popular, commercially successful" (1985).

In the mid-1980s, two plays were premiered in London that sought success on a similar basis: *Cafe Puccini* (Playscript 3024) premiered in the West End in 1986, and failed mainly because the production expected actors to sing Puccini arias, accompanied by four strings, piano, flute and accordion. Trained opera tenors have their problems with Calaf's aria *Nessun Dorma* from Puccini's *Turandot*. If an actor with some voice training attempts to sing this aria live on stage, it is, according to one critic, a laudable act of bravery, but "no one should have done this to him or to us!" (Colvin 1986: 21). The show closed after only forty-three performances. *After Aida* (Playscript 3017) is another example of a commercially intended but not successful play, dealing with the last phase of Giuseppe Verdi's career. *Times* critic Wardle wrote:

> There is no dramatic situation. The setting [the stalls of a theatre] is merely a playground where speakers can address us with memoirs, team up for brief scenes and rehearsals ... members retreat to the stalls to read newspapers or sit looking bored; a sight that leaves you wondering why you should be interested in a spectacle they cannot be bothered to look at. (1986)

The episodes of the play were interrupted at irregular intervals by excerpts of Verdi operas, sung by professionals from Welsh National Opera. The overall impression was chaotic and the production's commercial success remained modest at twenty-eight performances. The limited success of both plays suggests that it takes more to make a biographical play about a famous artist successful than using well-known and popular music. *Café Puccini* demonstrates, moreover, how important appropriate and adequate performance of music on stage is.

Commercial reasons may also be given for the large number of one-person shows about a famous artist. Their productions cost less, and unemployed actors can tour in shows they have compiled and perhaps also directed themselves. David Pownall, author of *Master Class* and several other plays about composers, acknowledges the commercial reasons behind one-person plays, but adds: "I love one man plays. As a writing exercise it is very exciting and good for me. You have to entertain with just one person on the stage" (1985).

There is a clear transition from the dramatist's outer to inner motivation when at least the beginning of the wave of biographical plays about a famous artist is related to the political climate of the late 1970s and 1980s, dominated in Britain by Margaret Thatcher's time in office as prime minister. Tom Wilkinson commented at the time:

> There are two Britains, and at the moment the Thatcherite kind of bully seems to have taken over the whole of people's lives, the whole of their thinking, and it is not surprising to me that people then turn towards poets. It is the exact antithesis of Thatcherite right wing brutalism. (1985)

Amanda Saunders, in charge of the National Theatre Platform Performances in the 1980s, which featured many short productions about famous artists, tried to explain the rising number of biographical plays about a famous artist with reference to dramatists' lacking originality (1985). This opinion points to a lack of inner motivation, as does her opinion that the observed tendency shows, ultimately, a shocking trend towards escapism:

> instead of using the form of drama to address ever more threatening current problems, instead of shaking spectators and readers, sensitising them and confronting them with solid alternatives, dramatists escaped into some safe past with artists who are anything other than down to earth (Saunders 1985).

Theatre critic Irving Wardle feels that many British dramatists who had, since the 1950s, placed their emphasis on subjects of their own experience and less on subjects from books, had now enough of writing "end of Britain" plays and were therefore turning towards artists as subjects for their plays (1985). Those opinions, voiced in the mid-1980s by theatre experts, are plausible, at least at first glance. The accusation, however, that dramatists writing about famous artists lack originality, would, strictly speaking, apply to many other plays that all depend on some outward source of inspiration. For example, David Pownall wrote a play about black actor Ira Aldridge after black actor Joseph Marcell had told him he thought he was an incarnation of Aldridge.

The predominant reason, however, is that dramatists feel the urge to write about fellow artists to find out more about themselves as artists. Writing these plays becomes a kind of self-referral process. Here is one example, Athol Fugard's *The Road to Mecca* (1985). The artist character in this play is Miss Helen, a widow seventy years of age, who lives in a small village in South Africa. After her husband's death Miss Helen started to create strange sculptures in her garden. The inside of her house changed as well: she placed numerous lamps and candles and painted the walls blue and golden. She is visited by Elsa, a young, energetic, politically active teacher from Cape Town. It turns out that the evening that is dramatized in the play gains special importance for Miss Helen: she also expects the visit of Marius, the village priest, who will ask her for a decision as to whether she wants to move into an old people's home or not. Elsa and Marius indirectly help Miss Helen to find herself and make her decision. The historical model for the character of Miss Helen was an old woman in New Bethesda, a small village in South Africa, who was considered slightly odd in her village because after her husband's death she started to produce strange sculptures and statues which were all standing around her house. After some fifteen years suddenly her creativity dried up. She grew depressive and paranoid, and finally committed suicide.

Fugard commented that writing this play "coincided with a need in me that I hadn't recognized, a curiosity about the genesis, nature and consequence of creative energy, my own" (Smith 1985). Three years later, with even more hindsight, Fugard wrote, on the occasion of a revival of the play in Berkeley, USA, that at the time of writing the play he had himself been preoccupied, as his main character, Miss, Helen, with fears of his artistic creativity drying up: "I've been frightened by that ... and I explored it because I needed to. I am now 55 years old and one of the great terrors of my life is the thought of my creativity drying up before my time has ended" (Berson 1988: 35). After having written the play, in which Miss Helen overcomes her own fears, Fugard wrote: "I must say that since embodying that personal terror in the character of Miss Helen I've found it easier to cope with it myself" (Smith).

The phenomenon of self-referral, or self-referentiality, itself has moved to the forefront of research projects and insights over the past thirty years in physics, mathematics, chemistry and the arts and humanities. It is a key feature of the aesthetics of the performative as developed by Erika Fischer-Lichte. The question why that interest in self-referral processes, the Performative turn, as Fischer-Lichte describes it, should have developed so markedly in that specific period of time can be answered with reference to the *Vedanta* model of consciousness I described in the introduction: there we saw that at the basis of all creation in the universe are the self-referral interactions within pure consciousness, the interactions of *samhita* with *rishi*, *devata*, and *chhandas*. The grassroots spirituality movement, which developed rapidly over the past thirty years (Forman 2004), means that millions of people world-wide are engaging, on a daily basis, in techniques that enliven the experience of pure consciousness. Such enlivenment, in turn, facilitates the experience of self-referral phenomena not only on the level of pure consciousness, the basis of creation, but beyond, on all expressed levels of creation, giving rise to insights in the academic disciplines, and to works of art that reflect the self-referral nature of creation.

Outlook

The wave of biographical plays about famous artists has now lasted for some thirty years. It coincides with (and may be causally related to) the movements of grassroots spirituality, the performative turn and the related aesthetics of the performative, as discussed in performance and theatre studies, and an increased interest in the study of consciousness and phenomena of self-referral or self-referentiality, across a wide range of disciplines. The wave of biographical plays about famous artists is thus not coincidental, but part of a complex pattern or tapestry. The major aspect that characterizes the development of such plays over the period 2005-2013 is the increase of the number of tribute plays as opposed to plays that want to convey a message. This development can be understood further in the context of a wave of nostalgia noted for the same time period across literatures and the arts, as demonstrated and concluded in a good number of the presentations of the *What Happens Now* conference at the University of Lincoln, July 2010, and the attempt, over the same time period, to redeem nostalgia from its bad name (Wilson 2005). The next few years will show whether the movement, within biographical plays about famous artists—away from message and towards tribute plays—continues, and whether it constitutes the beginning of the end of the movement—in parallel to other movements, even large epochs, which tend to start on a very high level of sophistication (*Amadeus* and *Piaf* in the context of biographical plays about famous artists), and continue on a high level for some time but then deteriorate, and become mediocre, until it is time for the next movement that again starts on a high level of sophistication.

Alternatively, the development towards tribute plays, if it continues, can be understood further in conceptual contexts that choose to consider "tribute" less in terms of nostalgia, but in terms of celebration. Such a shift would indicate a development from conflict in the clash of artist and adverse situation towards a mode of drama and performance that does not rely on conflict, at all, or at least to a much smaller extent, than other modes of drama and performance typically do. This could constitute a step in the development of drama and theatre in the direction of not merely enabling the experience of pure consciousness through dramatic and dramaturgical devices but to reflect pure consciousness even more on the level of contents, with the artist as exemplar.

Summary

To summarise the findings of this example: in writing about famous artists, dramatists are confronted, in their writing, with real, not imagined, people who are artists just as the dramatists are artists. In working on their sources in the process of preparing for, and writing the play, the dramatist must make decisions in terms of the level of authenticity they want to bring from their sources to the play. The dramatist must decide on the function and the focus of the artist characters, their constellations and relationships to other characters, and the relationship between any idolisation of the artist character in popular culture and the way the dramatist chooses to present the character in the play. In the example of *Amadeus*, Shaffer chose, on the one hand, to portray Mozart in such a way that any prior idolisation is likely to suffer, while, on the other hand, he ensured that Mozart is still regarded as a genius. By destroying false idolisation and making the character of Mozart more human, the dimension of his genius even rises. Dramatists writing about other real artists, rather than imagined ones, also need to decide whether to set their main artist character(s) against some form of adversity, or whether they decide, instead, in favour of a tribute play.

The dramatists' inspiration for writing plays about famous artists, and the appeal of such plays for audiences, has been explained, with this example, in terms of self-reflexivity. This phenomenon constitutes the essence of pure consciousness, and it is a characteristic of the *Zeitgeist* of the past thirty to forty years that self-reflexivity has been detected as influential in many academic disciplines, and that self-reflexivity has featured prominently in people's lives in general in the form of spiritual practices. Dramatists pick up on this development in writing about other artists as a means to find out more about themselves as artists.

Example two. Consciousness in drama: *synaesthesia*

Introduction

The second example focuses on a much smaller number of plays specifically dealing with a phenomenon of consciousness— *synaesthesia*. In this example, contemporary neuroscience serves as the major frame for the discussion, apart from a brief speculation about the deeper implications of *synaesthesia* in the context of spirituality. Comparison with the other examples demonstrates how much more complex an analysis of theatre in relation to consciousness is possible if the discussion is based on the *Vedanta* model of consciousness, which includes the perspective of science, but goes far beyond the restrictions of science.

Conventionally, the experiences of the senses are mediated by specific parts of the body: the nose enables smell, the buds on the tongue enable taste, the eyes enable seeing, the sensory buds on the body enable touch, and the ears enable hearing. In a minority of people, the stimulus that normally triggers only one specific sensory experience triggers a second or third, or even multiple sensory experiences. For example, some people see a specific colour that corresponds to a specific general sound, or a specific musical note. Some see a specific colour when they think of time units, when they hear specific parts of words, down to single letters, when they smell specific smells, or taste specific tastes. Further triggers for the experience of specific colours are pain, personalities, touch, temperatures, emotions, or orgasm. Other non-ordinary associations of sensory experience include touch triggering the hearing of sounds, smells triggering the experience of temperatures or of being touched, sounds triggering experiences of smells, tastes and temperatures, and tastes triggering the experience of sounds, temperatures, or touch. Taken together, such experiences are captured by the term *synaesthesia*.

According to Harrison and Baron-Cohen (1997) there are four categories of *synaesthesia*: (1) developmental *synaesthesia*—the term they use for naturally occurring *synaesthesia*, (2) acquired *synaesthesia*—caused by neurological dysfunction or other dramatic physical change, (3) drug-induced *synaesthesia*, and (4) metaphorical *synaesthesia* or pseudo-*synaesthesia* (Lambert 2010: 159)

Lambert further defines metaphorical or pseudo-*synaesthesia* as "cultural and literary manifestations as synesthetic metaphors in language, literary tropes and all deliberate artistic constructions employing the term "*synaesthesia*" to describe multisensory joinings" (160). In the first part of this example, I deal with the first three categories and the depiction of such states of consciousness in drama. In the second part I focus on metaphorical or pseudo-*synaesthesia*.

Synaesthesia as a neurological phenomenon
Until late into the 20th century, *synaesthesia* was not taken seriously by researchers in psychology, and explained away as the result of a hyperactive imagination, or attention-seeking, or memories of childhood when letters were written in bright colours, or the experiences of people under the influence of drugs, or metaphorical, as in "bitter cold" (Ramachandran and Hubbard 2001: 4).

In a seminal study published in 2001, Ramachandran and Hubbard conclude that "*synaesthesia* is a genuine perceptual phenomenon, not an effect based on memory associations from childhood or on vague metaphorical speech". They further identify the reason for *synaesthesia* as "hyperconnectivity" between the brain areas responsible for the two or more modes of perception that come together in *synaesthesia*. They seek to explain different intensities of synaesthetic experience with reference to cross-wiring or cross-activation at different stages of the processing of the sense perceptions. Pribram proposes, in contrast, that the mechanism that leads to *synaesthesia* is based on inhibitory rather than excitatory brain activity (2003: 76). Ramachandran and Hubbard also conclude that for one person his/her specific connections appear to remain stable across time; however, different people associate differently from each other: "A" might trigger "red" for one person, and "blue" for another (2003: 50). Shanon counters that argument with his earlier study in which he concluded that there are similarities of association across larger numbers of synaesthetes (Shanon 2003: 70). Responding to Shanon in 2003, Ramachandran and Hubbard acknowledge that there has been more evidence since Shanon's initial study (1982) supporting the suggestion of more regularity than hitherto assumed (78).

Shanon (2003) points out, and Hubbard and Ramachandran (2003) confirm with reference to further literature that psychedelic experiences induced by LSD or Ayahuasca often include those of *synaesthesia*, especially with reference to the experiences of colours in both that do not occur in "real life", that are not natural. Walsh (2009) found that there are more synaesthetes among meditators than among non-meditators, and that the intensity and duration of practice correlates with the intensity of synaesthetic experience. He concludes that it may be possible to cultivate synaesthetic experience through meditation, and that the findings of his study suggest that *synaesthesia* is within every person's potential, but not expressed in the majority of people. He cites ancient Buddhist texts that suggest that *synaesthesia* is characteristic of higher states of consciousness as experienced by a Buddha.

Among synaesthetes there is a significant number of creative people, such as artists, musicians and poets, compared with similar groups of people who are not synaesthetes. This finding has led to the assumption that *synaesthesia* is linked to creativity. Ward et al. found, however, that synaesthetes do not outperform others on cognitive aspects of creativity; they conclude that the tendency for synaesthetes to be engaged in the arts is related to the enhanced motivation that is likely to result from particularly rich experiences in relation to the practices of art due to the *synaesthesia*: a person with an interest in music will be more likely to engage in music if the experience of music is particularly rich due to the fact that they do not merely hear music but see or taste it was well (Ward et al. 2008: 135).

It should be noted that in addition to an increase in scientific-medical interest in, and published studies of *synaesthesia*, and perhaps triggered by that increase, there has been an increased interest in *synaesthesia* as a methodology, understood as an active process of

> consciously, voluntarily, adopting an exceptionally creative kind of attitude allowing for cross-modal sensitivity (…) The artwork, or the movie, or the ad, becomes the ground for joined perception or mixing of the senses and is no longer solely addressed at the eye (or the visually thinking mind), but at a multisensorial or polysensorial body. (Laine and Strauven 2009: 250).

Characters with synaesthesia in drama

Research suggests that there are two plays with characters who are explicitly living with *synaesthesia*. There are others in which characters report experiences that sound like *synaesthesia*, but the term itself is not used in the texts, nor do reviews refer to it. *Hey there boy with the bebop...* by Abi Bown was first performed in 2004. It was the first production for 12-16 year old audiences by Polka, a company founded in 1979 and dedicated to theatre for children. The play is set in a terraced street in Liverpool, and focuses on 12-year-old local girl Chantaye, and 13-year old Leo, who has moved to the street from London recently with his mother. He is terminally ill, suffering from a brain tumour that has affected his mobility; in addition, he experiences *synaesthesia*, which may or may not be related to the tumour.

The second time Chantaye and Leo meet, we get a first impression of his *synaesthesia*, when he suggests to Chantaye that she should smile more often, because "it makes angels dance about your ears" (2002: 37). Chantaye responds to this unexpected suggestion by touching her ears and looking surprised (37). He then tells her about further synaesthetic visual experiences, in response to Chantaye's question as to what things he can see from his bedroom window—she is of course referring to real "things", people and events that happen in the street that his window allows sight of. He takes this question as the opportunity to talk about his *synaesthesia*. The stage directions reveal that Leo's immediate response to Chantaye's question is physical: he "sits back in his chair, he takes a breath, there's a glint in his eye, he comes forward" (38). Then he builds up expectation: "Shall I tell you?" In response to Chantaye's "Yeah", he continues vaguely, "I can see so much, too much. Sometimes I see so much it hurts" (39). In the dialogue that follows, he reveals that he is not looking at something, but "things are there, I see them" (39). He explains that the things he sees, which are not real life objects such as Chantaye or the Coke can, are in the space around him. Leo then moves on to details and examples. He tells Chantaye that he can see the sound of her voice: when she is "narky", her voice looks like "shards of glass", "coloured triangles moving about" (39). However, when her voice is happy, he sees spots of colour with wings, which are the "angels" that "dance about her ears" (37).

Chantaye's responses shift from touching her ears when Leo first mentions the angels, to annoyance and a threat to leave, to actually picking up the thread of angels herself, when she says: "Go on, what else can you see? Angels? (She touches her ears)" (39). When he confirms, she smiles and "goes to the mirror, not sure if she's expected to see anything" (39). He associates the days of the week with colours: "Brown, Green, Yellow, Purple, Red, White,

Blue—there's a week for you". Chantaye still tries to find a rational explanation for Leo's experiences, suggesting that he colour-codes the days of the week. This is just the way he experiences the world. He can't explain this, but provides the technical name for it: "*Synaesthesia*. It's a 'syndrome of sensory-limbic hyper connection" (40).

His *synaesthesia* does not only associate colours with days of the week and with the sound of voices and music: in addition, he smells colours, and associates the smells with emotions: "Grey smells sort of brave, green smells happy" (40). Leo is both serious and playfully comical relating to his *synaesthesia*: when an exasperated Chantaye asks, in response to his revelation that green smells happy: "how can a cucumber smell happy?" Leo responds "I guess most cucumbers don't" (40). This comment is not only funny, but it reveals Chantaye's problem of grasping the nature of *synaesthesia*: she associates the abstract colour, which triggers the synaesthetic response independent of any object that might have that colour, with objects she normally associates with smells: "an orange smells like an orange", and she takes this association further to the cucumber example.

Leo is able to infer changes of mood from his synaesthetic impressions: when Chantaye is about to leave, he asks her whether she will come again. She feels trapped by that question, but does not say anything. Leo immediately follows his question with "I understand", explaining further: "Your angels have vanished" (41). The angels were a sign of her happiness; they vanished in response to Leo's question of whether she will come again, so he understands this to mean she might not.

Chantaye veers between scepticism and picking up on Leo's condition for the sake of playful banter. When she points out the house she lives in from his window, he says that it's a sad house, and pulls a sad face to support his words. Chantaye picks this up with "Don't tell me, the bricks smell miserable and there's no angels dancing round the chimney pots"; Leo rewards Chantaye's attempt to come his way with "Now you get the idea", and thus encouraged, Chantaye continues this line of conversation by asking "So what does my voice look like today?" Further emotional closeness develops as the dialogue progresses: Leo responds to Chantaye's question with "Sparkling, and your name...", to which Chantaye reacts by saying her name slowly, followed by Leo's "Tastes lemony, here (He points to his tongue)". This is as far as it can go for Chantaye, who ends this line of dialogue with "Daft, you" (47). The closeness that has developed between Leo and Chantaye, mediated to a good extent by the banter around his *synaesthesia*, allows Leo to tell Chantaye about his tumour. Commenting on Leo in a direct address to the audience, Chantaye says: "Whatever it was, in his head, it had stopped him dancing. But he could see his music and taste its sound, some days he said it almost made up for the fact it was killing him..." (48). The reference to "killing" suggests that Leo clearly associated the experiences of *synaesthesia* as an effect of the tumour.

Later, when Chantaye's mother disapproves of her seeing Leo and does not allow her out of the house, Chantaye tells the audience she has been thinking about Leo a lot, "I thought about Leo, stuck indoors, in his house, tasting the colour of sounds" (53). Other children in the street paint offensive graffiti about Chantaye and Leo on the wall. Chantaye gets the other children to go with her to the garage where they got the spray paint, to steal more paint to spray over the offensive graffiti; she shares her thoughts with the audience: "Just what colour was vengeance? Leo would know, he'd smell it, taste it. Red? Or was that just word association? I closed my eyes. (...)" (57). By now she has been thinking about Leo and his *synaesthesia* so much that she grasps more of it, and is able to differentiate between intellectual association (vengeance and red) and the intuitive nature of the synaesthetic experience. She closes her eyes to allow such intuition to affect her, to whatever extent possible, and indeed a few seconds later she comes up with "Yellow! It was yellow, like Wednesdays" (57).

When Leo plays the music he likes on a ghetto blaster, the music, according to the stage directions, "seems to flatten him against the yard wall. He's having visions". Leo teaches Chantaye to dance, and she later teaches her main mates, Trixie and Gary. The play ends with a reference to *synaesthesia*: Chantaye reads the final note that Leo has asked his mother to pass on to her: "P.S. Send your angels into overdrive" (60), a line that comes after the audience, according to the stage directions, has noticed that the curtains in Leo's room have been closed for the first time in the play, suggesting that he has passed away.

James Graham's *The Whisky Taster* premiered at the Bush Theatre in London on 26 January 2010, and was published by

Methuen Drama to coincide with the premiere. The play is set in a central London advertising agency. Malcolm is the line manager, Barney and Nicola, in their mid to late twenties, are working together on advertising projects; they are very successful because as a team they combine Nicola's eloquence when facing clients, with Barney's gift: he suffers from *synaesthesia* and the way he associates products with colours is apparently very successful with potential customers— at least it convinces the products' representatives. Barney is also hopelessly in love with Nicola, who does not love him; in fact she teases him, in what to her may appear to be a playful mode, but comes across to Barney and the audience as close to cruelty, about his physical appearance and his *synaesthesia*. Thus, less than two pages into the play, in response to his rather casual comment that he hates Mondays, she challenges him: "All right then, Picasso. Do it. What's Mondays?" (4). Vaguely, at first, he reveals, in a sequence of fragmented responses, that Mondays for him have a lilac colour and taste like Parma Violets. The colour is lilac only on Monday mornings, as the colour turns yellow and later green in the course of the day. Nicola knows that seeing specific colours can "send Barney funny", have an adverse effect on him, and she asks whether the white shirt she is wearing that day may have such an adverse effect. It has not, and anyway, Barney has ways of "sort of" controlling his experiences of *synaesthesia*: "By not... I just. Like I just try not to think about your short being. Lilac. I just try not to...*see* it. So that I don't start getting all of those...erm. Feeling. Things." (5)

The medical component comes in again when Nicola and Barney talk about the prospect that one of them might be selected, by way of promotion, to move to Mumbai. Nicola suggests that Barney would not be able to survive in the chaos of that city: "You'd have an eppy" (8), short for epileptic fit.

She is concerned about his behaviour in front of the important client, asking him "Don't be weird", explaining further: "Don't be the 'you' that's weird. Be the 'you' that's 'gifted'. Just today." (11) When he sips the vodka they are trying to develop a marketing campaign for, he comes up with the colours blue, silver and gold. This secures them the deal. Their line manager, Malcolm, who was with them during the event, is stunned, and asks Nicola how Barney does it. Nicola responds that she does not really know, and is hesitant to ask because she feels that it might hurt Barney. Malcolm realises, and Nicola confirms, that Barney is not even at full throttle when he releases his contract-clinching insights (21).

Nicola is in fact quite fascinated with Barney's *synaesthesia* and cannot stop herself asking him about it again and again, even though she also keeps checking herself when she has started yet another question, remembering, as it were, that it is bound to make Barney feel uncomfortable. But we learn in this way that January has the colour of "Ford Cortina Red. And it tastes like a, um...like a raspberry ice lolly. But with all the flavour sucked out, so almost just juice and it's cold and wet on my tongue and..." (26).

When the Whisky Taster of the play's title arrives, he wears a kilt, and this causes Barney acute discomfort. He stares at the kilt and has to steady himself, later he takes deep breaths and wipes his forehead. He grows increasingly unsteady and ultimately makes a faltering attempt of asking the Whisky Taster to take the kilt off—a request of course not quite understood by the Whisky Taster. Nicola tries to explain it to him, even making an attempt to say the word *synaesthesia*.

When Barney tastes the whisky, he tells the Whisky Taster that he tastes "A cat asleep in a bookshop...spring sunshine on white rocks...erm...molton iron crawling a steel floor...chemistry lesson in school...little nuggets of gold". In response to the Whisky Taster's quiet question "That's how you taste whisky?", Barney says, quieter, "That's how I ...taste. Everything". (48). He later reveals in more depth how much he suffers from his *synaesthesia*: "It hurts to feel these things when I do it. There's too many of them, that's why I try to keep it shut, there's just too many of them..." (55). The Whisky Taster later suggests to Barney that a gift, like his *synaesthesia*, is something that he has been given, not necessarily something he asked for or wanted. He asks him whether he has ever "just thought about...untying the bow. And letting it go?" (55). At the end of that scene the stage directions imply that Barney follows this advice: "*Beat. Colours start bleeding out across the room, as though escaping from the* **Whisky Taster***'s kilt. Only a little at first. And then more...* (56). Whereas the colours on set had been decidedly black and white so far, from the next scene onwards there are "many more colours around" (56).

An intense beam of white light when Barney kisses Nicola is later identified as the colour Barney associates with love. In the end he loses his job while Nicola calls off her wedding and gets promoted to the company's office near Mumbai in India.

Indirect references to synaesthesia
While Leo and Barney are the only characters I found in British drama that have got *synaesthesia* explicitly, there have been references to the symptoms of *synaesthesia* without knowledge of the term or concept. For example, for purposes of comedy, Bottom in Shakespeare's *A Midsummer Night's Dream* confuses text from 1 Corinthians 2:9 (But as it is written, Eye hath not seen, nor ear heard, neither have entered into the heart of man, the things which God hath prepared for them that love him) when he says:

> The eye
> of man hath not heard, the ear of man hath not
> seen, man's hand is not able to taste, his tongue
> to conceive, nor his heart to report, what my dream
> was. (Act IV Scene 1, 206-210)

Moran discusses the synaesthetic references in Shakespeare's *The Winter's Tale*, such as hearing and seeing in the Third Gentleman's "that which you hear you'll swear you see" (V.2.32-3), sight-taste in V.3: "Leontes speaks of the pain and pleasure of viewing Paulina's statue: "For this affliction has a taste as sweet / As any cordial comfort" (5.3.76–7)" (Moran 2005: 52), and touch-taste, when, Leontes exclaims "O, she's warm! / If this be magic, let it be an art / Lawful as eating" (V.3.209-11) once he has touched Hermione (Moran 2005: 53).

In *An Oak Tree* by Tim Crouch, premiered on 5 August 2005, *synaesthesia* also features indirectly, i.e., the term is not mentioned and the condition is not discussed as such. The play is about a father coming to terms with the death of his older daughter in a road traffic accident; the driver of the car that killed her is the second character in the play, a stage hypnotist. Boundaries of reality and hypnotic state are blurred in the play, and to drive this aspect home, the father is to be played by a different actor in each performance, without prior knowledge of the script or plot. In the third scene, both characters stand side by side and read from scripts, telling the audience what happened on the night of the accident. The father says that "that night has a colour, a touch and a sound." (2005: 35). Waiting for supper was blue, the father brushing against his wife Dawn while waiting was slate grey, they looked at their watches in yellow, their pulses raced in yellow, they phoned the piano teacher in brown, their stomachs knotted in green, the policeman walked up the path in red, they watched him approach in orange, he took off his hat at the door in gold (35), Dawn's knees gave way in white, the policeman spoke to them in silver, and pronounced two concrete blocks in black which he left in the father's chest (36).

Summary

This example serves to illustrate contemporary scientific understanding of a phenomenon of consciousness, the experience of *synaesthesia*, and to demonstrate how dramatists have made use of this phenomenon in their plays. The argument has been quite straight forward, and lacks the complexity and related depth of argument afforded, in comparison, by discussing phenomena of drama and theatre in the context of the *Vedanta* model of consciousness, in the other examples in this chapter and indeed throughout this book. In an attempt to add more food for thought here, therefore, I end this example with a speculation taken from the realm of spirituality.

A speculation

Let us assume that certain esoteric, or possibly political traditions subjected their followers voluntarily or involuntarily to practices and techniques intended to enhance the functioning of their senses beyond their natural limitations. Let us assume further that in the process of such training the trainees suffered considerably, leading to lasting mental and spiritual wounds, so strong that as a means of survival, the souls separated those wounds and shut them away. The people thus affected carried their wounds and split-off parts of their souls across reincarnations with the aim of healing the wounds and transforming the split-off parts of their souls to achieve full healing and reintegration. Being re-born as a synaesthete allows them to deal with those experiences from past lives, and to work towards healing and reintegration. Healing and transformation are strong powers of the arts, and for that reason, many synaesthetes engage in the arts, for the purposes of their own healing and transformation. It is also for the same reason and purpose that there are so many meditators among synaesthetes.

Example three. Consciousness and performance: the relevance of story-telling for 21st century updates of plays and opera productions

The first two examples of recent developments in drama and theatre, about biographical plays about famous artists and about plays dealing with *synaesthesia*, both fall into the category of "consciousness depicted in drama", and the first example addresses the issue of the dramatist's inspiration as well. These two categories were central to two chapters in my 2005 book. The third and fourth examples take the discussion from the play text to the performance dimension. In the third example I consider the role of storytelling in recent theatre and opera productions. With reference to Thomas Ostermeier's production of *Hedda Gabler* and a range of recent productions of Wagner's *Lohengrin* and *Tannhäuser,* I discuss storytelling in the context of Hayden White's concept of *narrative*, and argue that the *Vedanta* model of consciousness allows for a reinterpretation of the process of storytelling in such a way that it is no longer a process limited to the intellect, but allows access to subtler levels of consciousness.

For each production of a play or piece of music theatre such as opera, written and first performed in the past, independent of however wide or narrow a director wants to define the concept of *past*, the director needs to decide whether to locate the plot at the time and in the socio-political contexts suggested by the play, or whether to transpose it into the present time. The degree of transposition will determine whether the resulting production is best described or categorised as a version, or an adaptation, or whether it can do without such qualifying terminology. In this example I refer to a range of productions to argue that the critical success of a transposition of a play or opera into the present time depends on the kind of story such a transposed play or opera is able to tell. Thomas Ostermeier's 2005 production of Ibsen's *Hedda Gabler* at the Schaubühne in Berlin will serve as prime example for theatre, and a number of recent productions of Wagner operas will serve as examples for opera.

For the Schaubühne production of *Hedda Gabler*, which premiered on 26 October 2005, director Thomas Ostermeier selected the German translation of the play by Hinrich Schmidt-Henkel, a renowned translator of novels and plays, and frequent host, for radio, TV and theatre, of literary and cultural discussion events. The translation had been premiered at the Theater Basel in 2003. Ostermeier had premiered the Schmidt-Henkel translation of Ibsen's *A Doll's House* at the Schaubühne Berlin in 2002, and used Schmidt-Henkel's translation of *The Master Builder* for his production of the play in 2004 at the Vienna Burgtheater. In later years, Schmidt-Henkel translated *John Gabriel Borkman* (2005, Schauspielhaus Zürich, directed by Barbara Frey), *Rosmersholm* (2006, Staatstheater Nürnberg, directed by Stefan Otteni), and *An Enemy of the People* (2008, Theater St Gallen, directed by Martin Schulze). The dramaturg for Ostermeier's production of *Hedda Gabler*, German dramatist Marius Mayenburg, worked with the production team on further updating the text.

Mayenburg has an acute ear for the way contemporary Germans speak: his way of rendering Ibsen's text makes it as characteristic as possible of everyday German of the middle of the first decade of the 2nd millennium. This applies in particular to the characters' low key, understated responses to each other. When Hedda tells her husband that she is pregnant, he has his head in her lap. On hearing the news, he sits up and stares at Hedda in disbelief, takes his hands off her knees and moves away from her, uttering "Nee, oder?" "Nee" is a colloquial form of "Nein", "no", accompanied by an ever so slight shaking of the head. He moves away further from Hedda, while still looking at her. She does not react at all to his question. He turns his head away from her, and supports his left elbow on his knee and wipes his head with his left hand, accompanied by heavy sighs and a facial expression that demonstrates how deeply moved he is, close to tears. He briefly rests his chin in his hand, then turns again to Hedda, and stretches out his right hand to touch her belly. He turns away from her again with the words, again accompanied by tearful sighs: "Das gibt's doch nicht". [That's impossible!] Then he bursts out into a howl, crying, wipes his face, howls again, jumps up, and moves to open the glass patio doors that lead to the outdoors patio. There he howls again, longer, accompanied by further jumping and shaking of his arms. Hedda comments this with expressions of disbelief and says: "Gott, ich bring mich noch um. All das hier bringt mich noch um". [God, I'm going to kill myself. All this here is goin to kill me]

Juliane Tesman, Jørgen Tesman's aunt, has been transposed successfully into the 21st century as well. She is in her mid-sixties, and comes across as a representative of a middle class woman who has retired from a moderately successful career, perhaps as a teacher, and who now enjoys her retirement, by looking after people who need looking after, by reading her monthly fashion magazine to which she subscribes; she will also have her subscription to the local opera and theatre company, and participate, on an annual basis, in high-brow, educational trips to places of cultural interest, and have a good amount of lady-friends and acquaintances with similar socio-economic and educational profiles. She has selected for her visit to Tesman's house, on the return of the newly-weds from their lengthy honeymoon, a smart-casual outfit, of which the new hat is one integral part. It is not the kind of hat a woman without taste for fashion, or without money, would buy, and is thus not in itself ridiculous, or otherwise out of place in relation to her outfit, quite the contrary.

In comparison with productions in which the hat represents Aunt Juliane's somewhat desperate attempt to "fit in" and to impress Hedda, the context established in Ostermeier's production provides a new perspective on Hedda's spiteful comments on Aunt Juliane's hat as belonging to a servant: in the conventional scenario, where the hat is indeed somewhat out of place, Hedda responds instinctively to Juliane's weakness: she senses and lashes out at it. In the Ostermeier production, on the other hand, Hedda randomly selects the hat to comment on because Juliane left it behind. Had it not been the hat, she would have made her comment on any other item of her outfit. There is no weakness involved on Juliane's part, and her response is one of surprise rather than hurt, of wondering at Hedda's motivation for such unprovoked nastiness, rather than feeling sorry for herself.

In many productions of *Hedda Gabler*, Judge Brack is cast with an older actor, in view of Brack's seniority in social and professional position. In the Schaubühne production, Brack comes across as hardly much older than Tesman (the actor of Brack, Jörg Hartmann, is seven years older than the actor of Tesman, Lars Eidinger). The result is that the relationships between Brack and Hedda, and Brack and Tesman, are quite different than if an older actor had been cast as Brack. A younger Brack becomes a realistic rival to Tesman for Hedda's favours: it is more believable that Hedda could agree to an extra-marital relationship with a younger Brack than with an older Brack, and Brack's advances thus represent more of a temptation for Hedda. A younger Brack is attractive to her not only because he can talk cleverly, but also physically, and because in comparison with her husband, Brack has achieved so much more professionally, exudes so much more security, has so many more influential acquaintances, and is so much closer to the world Hedda grew up in as a general's daughter, than Tesman can ever hope for, even if he gains his professorship.

Thus Hedda's decision not to want to engage in an affair with Brack equally adds to the way this character is depicted in Ostermeier's production. In Brack she would have all the things she desired, and which she is so frustrated of not having with Tesman. However, she is also aware that Brack could have approached her for marriage before her marriage to Tesman, and did not: he was not interested in her as a wife, and may not be interested in any woman for marriage. He is interested in Hedda only (but very much so) as a mistress, without obligations and commitments, but with the added excitement of the forbidden, which as a judge he encounters on a daily basis, and which fascinates him. Hedda knows that for Brack she will be only one aspect of his life of pleasure without commitment, and she is determined not to stoop to that position of inferiority. Hedda enjoys her banters with Brack, where things are said in a witty, immediate response to a preceding statement of the other party, without the contents of the responses necessarily intended to be taken seriously by the other party, and not usually taken seriously either.

The way Katharina Schüttler's Hedda clearly tells Lövborg that hers is a marriage without love but also without betrayal, suggests that this is one of the few things she is convinced about: it is not the result of a vague, spoilt mood, not part of her banter with Brack. It is serious, it is one of very rare instances where Hedda does something because she has thought about it long and hard, and made that decision. Hedda does other things quite clearly without making a conscious decision: they just happen as immediate responses to various situations. Thus in an encounter with both Tesman and Lövborg in the same room, she invites Lövborg to sit, on the vast arrangement of sofas, very close to Tesman, and at a right angle to him. She then walks over to Tesman at a suitable point in the conversation and bends down and engages him in an extended French kiss that takes place at eye level for Lövborg, within inches of his own face. The actor playing Lövborg, Kay Bartholomäus Schulze, managed brilliantly, overall, to portray the just-about-dry alcoholic, ever so fragile in his abstinence, ever so prone to moods and depressions that might be considered as still part of the range of withdrawal symptoms, and ever so close to the relapse into full-blown alcoholism due to the mess of his personal life and his self-doubts about his abilities as an academic. He is recognised clearly as a genius by Thea Elvsted, who has served as his muse in inspiring the latest book, and by Tesman, who openly admits that he is nowhere as inspired and original in his own thinking. Lövborg, however, doubts his own abilities. Hedda also recognises the threat he poses to Tesman's career, and this plays one part in her on-the-spot decision to destroy the manuscript. In Ostermeier's contemporary version, however, it is not a printed text, but exists only on the hard drive of a laptop, without backup—so to destroy the manuscript, Hedda smashes the laptop with a hammer.

Lars Eidinger develops the image of a contemporary academic in his portrayal of Tesman. There are lots of books around the corners of the set, as well as stacks of paper. He matches Katharina Schüttler's Hedda in the conversational, everyday use of language, which has a limited range of ups and downs, and is thus close to monotonous; he comes across as really very much, and indeed romantically, in love with his Hedda. He sees her as a child, given that she is smaller than him, and younger, with eyes that do not reveal much of what is going on inside her, and attractive, pouting lips. Eidinger's Tesman is a modern man, full of feelings, and he cries on three occasions. There is the full outburst described above when Hedda tells him that she is pregnant; he also cries when he has beard that Lövborg is back and when he realises the threat that Lövborg might be to his own prospects of a professorship: Tesman may be a dreamer, stuck in his books and overall quite naïve, but he does realise that if Lövborg were to try to seal his comeback with an application for the professorship that Tesman is hoping to get, Tesman will have no chance in a competition with Lövborg. The third time we see Tesman cry is when Lövborg convincingly assures Tesman that he will not apply for the professorship, and that thus there is no more danger for Tesman to lose the prospects of his professional advancement and indeed future. The production's emphasis on the crying man, Tesman, comes at a time (first in 2005), when a study of audience response to the third part of the *Lord of the Rings* trilogy found that among the audiences in a wide range of countries in Europe and beyond, the highest percentage of men responding to the film with tears came from Germany.

For the final scene of *Hedda Gabler*, Ostermeier has a striking contemporary twist in store for his audience. The set design allows the audience to see into several rooms in the Tesman home at the same time, either directly, or indirectly through strategically placed mirrors. Tesman and Thea Elvsted are busy recreating late Lövborg's manuscript, with Brack in attendance: he is not merely observing, but is clearly interested in the work, and in observing how Tesman and Thea get closer to each other though their joint mission of restoring Lövborg's work of genius. This is the kind of work that Tesman excels at: he and Thea inspire each other. Hedda is an outsider in this scenario, nobody is interested in her any more, not even Brack. She moves into the room next door, in full view of the audience, takes out the pistol, looks at it, leans against the wall, puts the pistol to her temple and pulls the trigger. Her head slumps to her chest, blood pours from her head, she slowly sinks down along the wall to a sitting position, leaving a streak of blood on the wall. Her hand still holds the pistol. Thea, Tesman and Brack hear the sound of the shot. They hardly look up from their work. Tesman comments that Hedda is playing around with those pistols again, implying that she has done this before, and reminding the audience of an earlier scene where Hedda took aim at a vase of flowers and shot it to pieces. They continue their work, without bothering to go and see whether anything has happened to Hedda. She lies in her blood, dead, while the others carry on with their work on the manuscript. Tesman adds jokingly that perhaps Hedda has shot herself, and Brack comments that people just do not do such things. This phrase, at the end of the play, implies that Tesman's joke is poor.

The critical response to the production was overwhelmingly favourable. In many reviews, the most striking aspects of the story told by the production are re-told by the critics, as examples of the success of the play's transposition into the 21st century. Tesman's catch phrase "Ich glaub' das jetzt nicht" [I just don't believe this now] is noted, as is Hedda's terror at the combination of Tesman's red house shoes, Tesman's petit-bourgeouis homeliness, and his primordial scream of happiness at finding out that Hedda is pregnant (Tilmann 2005). Several reviews note Hedda's young age—the actress, Katharina Schüttler, was twenty-six when she first played

Hedda in 2005. Gardner in the *Guardian* calls her a "damaged child", a child-woman who is "trapped in her vast, minimalist, glass-walled apartment" (2008). Others comment on her fragile, slim body (Kohse 2005), referring to it as that of "a 14-year old" (Swann n.d.), and compare her young Hedda with the more mature nature of Hedda as portrayed by Isabelle Huppert or Corinna Kirchhoff (Tilmann 2005).

Hedda's physicality attracts further attention when Isherwood reports that she "does not stand if she can slouch, and does not slouch if she can drape herself across the long modular couch like a bored housecat" (2006). The feline nature of Schüttler's Hedda is equally central in a review that describes her first entrance thus: "We see this Hedda enter in her pyjamas with a naked midriff, looking just like one of today's sulky, pre-teen, sex kittens" (Swann n.d.). Bassett in *The Independent* writes in a similar vein: "A skinny little thing with a touch of feral cat about her—not fully domesticated—she looks skeletally fragile but sexually assured and surly" (2008). Charles Spencer in the *Telegraph* finds it amazing how not only the "spoilt young wife", but also the

> nerdish husband (…) the alcoholic genius and the manipulative lawyer seem just at home in the 21st century as they did in the 19th. This is still emphatically Ibsen's play but it also taps directly into the spirit of our own times—the moral equivocation, the curse of addiction, the sense of rootlessness, boredom and depression. (2008)

Tilmann emphasises that the way Katharina Schüttler says Hedda's phrase "I am so bored" implies that all her life has been boring so far, and that she does not expect any real change to that state of affairs. Bassett agrees that Schüttler's Hedda is "a horribly recognisable, 21st-century enfant terrible: materially indulged yet dissatisfied, already jaded and alarmingly amoral." (2008)

This Hedda, Tilmann continues, is as much a woman looking for greatness (and not recognising it in Lövborg's excessive nature) as a child that wishes for the moon (2005). Tilmann thus acknowledges an apparent reason for Hedda's inability to break out of her cage. While the Hedda of Ibsen's original was stuck because of the limitations society imposed on a woman in her time, Ostermeier's Hedda is stuck because she is small and cowardly. She has chosen security, she shuns risks and scandal because of her fear; in this insecurity she is representative of her generation, and it is indeed—

unnecessary—fear that is a major concern in the life of actress Katharina Schüttler: a life without fear is her highest dream (Böckem 2010). Spencer commends Kay Bartholomäus Schulze, whose Lövborg captures "all the agony and self-loathing of a reformed alcoholic falling spectacularly off the wagon" (2008).

Not all critics were convinced that the production's transposition into the 21st century worked. Charles Isherwood, writing in the *New York Times*, found much to praise in the production, but concluded that "Mr Ostermeier's cool and considered "Hedda Gabler" comes a little too close to proving the truth of that platitude used as a prim remonstrance to children whining to be entertained: that bored people are boring people." (2006). Bassett does not believe that genius Lövborg will not have made a backup or printed off a hardcopy of his masterpiece (2008), and Stasio argues that the men in Hedda's life, "deprived of the 19th-century social privileges that would have blinded them to Hedda's subtle wiles, (…) just seem uncommonly stupid" (2006).

Despite those few concerns, for Ostermeier's production of *Hedda Gabler*, the transposition into the 21st century works, overall, because it tells a consistent, cogent, and interesting story, in which the individual elements add up. The changes needed to accommodate the plot within a 21st century context make sense and bring the characters, their words and actions, close to the contemporary German audience—more, so, perhaps, than to the American audience, if the voice of American critic Isherwood is to be taken as representative: his assessment of the production and its characters as cool and distanced misses the point that the monotonous delivery of lines, misunderstood as cool, was indeed characteristic of much of German speaking at the time.

The same principles of story-telling can apply in opera. However, opera plots are often much more removed from real life than plots of theatre plays, at least up until the *verismo* period with operas by Mascagni (1863-1945), Leoncavallo (1857-1919), Giordano (1867-1948) and Puccini (1858-1924). Even in *verismo* opera, no matter how close to real life the plot may have been intended to be, there is still the element of music that creates an additional level of distance between real life and opera. Contemporary directors, especially those who see themselves in the tradition of director's theatre, may feel inclined to update the context of the opera, in some cases allegedly to make it more accessible to a contemporary audience, or to bring new dimensions to a long-established component of the operatic canon. A few examples of this approach over the last few years, with special emphasis on Wagner's operas, will serve as the basis for an assessment of the extent to which the element of cogent story-telling works to make opera productions successful.

An example of a critically well received new telling of a story in opera is Stefan Herheim's March 2010 production of Wagner's *Tannhäuser* at the Norwegian National Opera and Ballet in Oslo. Here is a plot summary, adapted from a text provided by the Metropolitan Opera (New York) website:

> **ACT I.** Medieval Germany. In the Venusberg, the minstrel Tannhäuser praises Venus, the goddess of beauty, who for more than a year has bestowed her love upon him. Tannhäuser wants to leave, but she curses his hopes of salvation when he longs for the simple pleasures and pains of earthly life. In response he calls on the Virgin Mary, and the Venusberg vanishes.
>
> Tannhäuser returns to earth near the Wartburg and meets the Landgrave Hermann and his knights, who recognize their long-lost comrade and invite him to the castle. One of them, Wolfram von Eschenbach, reminds Tannhäuser that in the past his singing won the love of Elisabeth, the landgrave's beautiful niece. On hearing her name, Tannhäuser embraces and joins his companions.
>
> **ACT II.** In the Hall of Song in the Wartburg, Elisabeth hails the place where she first heard Tannhäuser's voice. Wolfram reunites the happy pair. As guests arrive, the landgrave promises Elisabeth's hand to the winner of a contest of love songs. Wolfram delivers an idealized tribute to Elisabeth, whom he too has loved. Tannhäuser, his soul still possessed by Venus, counters with a frenzied hymn to the pleasures of worldly love. Everyone is shocked, but Elisabeth protects Tannhäuser from harm, securing her uncle's pardon for her beloved on the condition that he make a pilgrimage to Rome to seek absolution.
>
> **ACT III.** Several months later, Wolfram discovers Elisabeth at evening prayer before a shrine in the Wartburg valley. She searches among approaching pilgrims for Tannhäuser, but in vain. Broken, she prays to the Virgin to receive her soul in heaven. Wolfram, alone, asks the evening star to guide her on her way. Tannhäuser now staggers in wearily to relate that despite his abject penitence, the Pope decreed he could as soon be forgiven as the papal staff could break into flower. The desperate man calls to Venus, but she vanishes when Tannhäuser is reminded again by Wolfram of Elisabeth, whose funeral procession

now winds down the valley. Tannhäuser collapses, dying, by her bier.
A chorus of pilgrims enters, recounting a miracle: the Pope's staff,
which they bear forward, has blossomed.

Herheim transposed the opera's medieval plot to the 21st century. The set consists initially of an empty stage surrounded by mirror panels. For the overture, images of the outside environment of Oslo's opera house are projected on to those panels. The members of the chorus play men who work in the city, with suits, coats and briefcases. Tannhäuser, a member of the Salvation Army, appears in Salvation Army uniform, and seeks to communicate with the city professionals, but nobody stops to listen to him. So he gets fed up with that environment and seeks out Venus and her pleasures. In an instant, the mirror panels turn, and reveal, at multiple levels from the floor to the ceiling, scenes from opera productions across the canon. Venus appears in a contemporary evening dress in an opera box in the same style as the Oslo opera house where the audience are watching the opera, and invites Tannhäuser to join her there. The sensual pleasures Venus has to offer are thus to be understood as the pleasures of opera. Some of the panels revert to their mirror nature, and now without projections on to them, they reflect the real audience on the night of the performance. The visual effect of this scene is stunning, and it is not surprising that more than 100 stage hands were needed to achieve the effect.

The grand hall in the Wartburg used by the minstrels for the singing contests becomes a Salvation Army headquarters, and the long musical introduction to act two, before Elisabeth starts her aria, is spent by some warden of the Salvation Army clearing the hall of the homeless people who have spent the night there, prior to them receiving free breakfast. Thus there are very impressive sets and scene changes, and those facilitate a cogent re-interpretation of settings within the chosen Salvation Army context. However, the success of the transposition of the medieval context of the original plot to the 21st century comes at the expense of a reduction from Wartburg to the Salvation Army, and the resulting depletion of a potentially spiritual context.

The December 2010 production of *Tannhäuser* at Covent Garden, London, by Tim Albery, seems to have taken some inspiration from Herheim's concept of having Venus seduce Tannhäuser with opera rather than sex. The Venus mountain here is a miniature version of the Royal Opera Covent Garden stage, but without the spectacle, reduced to the much lower technical capacity of that venue compared with the brand-new building of the Norwegian National Opera and Ballet in Oslo. The Wartburg is a further opera house, in ruins in the wake of a war, with the Landgraf and his people in guerrilla uniforms and armed. As Michael White points out:

> When someone remarks to Elisabeth that she hasn't been in this hall for a while, you feel like replying: well, of course she hasn't. It's been under attack and reduced to rubble, there's no roof, why should she? (2010)

In Richard Jones's 2009 production of Wagner's *Lohengrin*, there was no scenic spectacle to distract from the tenuousness of the directorial ideas for transposing this opera's medieval plot into the 21st century. At the centre of that production was the concept that both Elsa and Lohengrin represent, and want to build, a new order. The image used to get that concept across to the audience was to have Elsa design her ideal petty bourgeois, core-family-unit detached home (Gohlke 2009) (during the overture), which she then proceeds to build, white brick by white brick, while the accusations of fratricide are thrown into her face. When her saviour does not materialise on the first call by the Herald, the villagers and soldiers proceed to build a stake from the building materials and bricks, lead Elsa to it and douse it in petrol, ready to burn her in immediate execution of the death penalty. Lohengrin appears, defeats Telramund, and immediately takes up a trowel and joins Elsa in building the house.

A few times a curtain very close to the front of the stage is lowered, and every time it is raised again, the building of the house has progressed considerably, with a finished house with beautiful wooden floors and walls completed by the end of act two, ready for Lohengrin and Else to move in. When Elsa asks the forbidden question, and before Lohengrin reveals his identity, he carries the heavy wooden cradle from the first floor nursery into the ground floor bedroom, throws it on to the bed and sets fire to the bed. The petty bourgeois dream has come to an end. Gohlke comments that the entire subplot involving the clash between pagan views held by Ortrud and the Christian ethos represented by Elsa and in particular Lohengrin, takes place in a vacuum, and that audiences not familiar with the plot will wonder what Ortrud is always so hysterically concerned about

(Gohlke 2009). In this production there is an overall concept, and the concept is applied to the main characters, but it is not very convincing in that context and does not apply at all to the subplot. At least there was more consistency here than in Stefan Herheim's 2009 production of *Lohengrin* for the Berlin Staatsoper unter den Linden, which arbitrarily juxtaposed so many ideas and visual elaborations that critics across the world did not identify any clear overall concept or even storyline (Apthorp 2009; Brug 2009).

Story-telling in theatre and opera can take place through characters and the scenography. In Ostermeier's production of *Hedda Gabler*, scenography and characterisation worked hand in hand: the scenography created an outwardly cold, sterile, "yuppy" living environment dominated by glass and steel, the cynical ideal of 21st century living. In Herheim's *Tannhäuser* the Salvation Army context reduced the spiritual dimension of the original medieval setting, but the idea was thought through fully and across all levels of the plot; the accompanying spectacular scenography compensated for the lack of grandeur in characterisation and context. Jones's *Lohengrin* had a limited and limiting concept, and there was no scenography to compensate, neither was there in Albery's *Tannhäuser* or Herheim's *Lohengrin*. Hans Neuenfels's production of *Lohengrin* at the Bayreuth Festival in 2010 adds a further variety of the interplay of characterisation, concept and scenography: the scenography suggests that the action is taking place as some kind of scientific experiment, with scientists in green laboratory clothes occasionally adjusting the settings and removing faulty participants (or perhaps better: subjects in the experiment). The inhabitants of Brabant (i.e., the chorus) are rats, the King is weak and quite possibly mentally ill, and Gottfried, returned to the Brabantians by Lohengrin at the end of the opera, is a nightmarish adult baby complete with umbilical cord emerging from an egg. However, any disappointment resulting from any perceived lack of cogency of the director's concept as represented by those scenographic choices is by far outweighed by the very intense characterisation of the relationships, between Lohengrin and Elsa, Elsa and Ortrud, and Ortrud and Telramund.

The critical success of a transposition of a play or opera into the present time depends on the kind of story such a transposed play or opera is able to tell. The more components of the story, plot, characterisation, concept and scenography, work together well, the better, as demonstrated by Ostermeier's production of *Hedda Gabler*. In some cases, as in Herheim's *Tannhäuser*, a lack in conceptual attraction can be compensated by scenographic spectacle. In other cases, as in Neuenfels's *Lohengrin*, characterisation can provide the critical mass to outweigh shortcomings in other aspects of a production. In other cases of opera, finally, if a production does not count among its merits either a consistent concept or spectacular scenography or commanding characterisation, critics may instead focus on the music, the achievements of conductor, orchestra and singers despite the perceived paucity of production values.

In the context of consciousness studies and the *Vedanta* model of consciousness, it is useful to relate *storytelling*, as discussed above, to a further key concept in Western theatre: *narrative*. Theatre tells a story, for various purposes. Hayden White proposes a very challenging definition of *narrative*, which both reflects the intellect-dominated paradigm, and offers ways of changing it: *narrative* is the translation of knowing to telling (1990:1). The term *translation* implies a mediation process: in the case of the translation of a given text from one language to the other, translation takes place in the translator's mind, and mediates between the author's and the reader's or spectator's minds. As far as the mind is concerned, the translation process is primarily associated with an intellectual activity, suggesting, by implication, that narrative also functions on the level of the intellect. This view is supported by the use of the term *knowledge* in White's definition: following the Western paradigm, expressed in most Western education systems, knowledge is an accumulation of facts. *Telling*, finally, is usually understood, in the context of the theatre, as referring to the language of the production. It is the amalgam of the various elements that constitute a performance, such as the written text, directing, acting, set, costume, lighting design, sound design, and performance space and all possible sub-categories of those.

The process of telling is the interface at which the realm of the intellect, dominant in the translation process and in the concept of knowledge, *may* be transcended in favour of subtler levels as described by the *Vedanta* model of consciousness. Those levels of consciousness allow a more holistic experience to take place in the theatre. Higher states of consciousness are characterised by maximum spontaneity of action. There is no gap between intention and action to carry out the intention. This is activity informed by the level of pure consciousness, which comprises the intellect. How much the audience will be able to pick up, as it were, from the narrative emerging from this deep level of consciousness will depend on how far they have trained their own minds to experience higher levels of consciousness. In addition, it is possible to argue that repeated exposure to theatre which operates on the level of higher states of consciousness, will be conducive to the development of higher states of consciousness in the spectators.

The reassessment of the concept of narrative from the perspective of the *Vedanta* model of consciousness implies that narrative is no longer restricted to the intellect. With *knowledge* and *translation* firmly rooted in pure consciousness, *telling* becomes able to make use of the full range of possibilities of the theatre, on the levels of pure consciousness and the expressed dimensions of the mind. In one process, all levels of the spectator's mind are targeted, stimulated, and trained to develop towards higher states of consciousness.

Example four. Consciousness and performance: body against boundaries in Raimund Hoghe's choreography

The fourth example, finally, looks at one specific performance choreographed by Raimund Hoghe, interpreting it as an expression of the interaction of components of pure consciousness. Raimund Hoghe was born some sixty years ago in Wuppertal, Germany. He grew up with his mother, about whom he later wrote a book. At an early age he was diagnosed with severe curvature of the spine and developed a hunchback. He did not grow to be taller than 1.54m. He worked as a journalist with the highbrow German weekly *Die Zeit*, writing sensitive portraits of outsiders (famous dramatists, pop singers, and anonymous people, including an aids sufferer, and a toilet woman). Those portraits were later collected in edited books. From 1980 to 1990 he worked as dramaturg with the late Pina Bausch. Since 1990 he has choreographed his own work, initially with other dancers, from 1994 (at the age of 45) with himself on stage.

His work is carefully documented on his website, http://www.raimundhoghe.com/, in German, English, French and Dutch. It carries his schedule of performances, reviews of his productions, and more academic articles. Reviews and articles discuss the choreographies by necessity always in terms of Hoghe's disability: from the simple "how exciting that this man can achieve all this despite his disability", to more sophisticated approaches, in which Hoghe's own views often provide the frame. Hoghe writes:

> Pier Paolo Pasolini wrote of throwing the body into the fight. These words inspired me to go on stage. Other inspirations are the reality around me, the time in which I live, my memories of history, people, images, feelings and the power and beauty of music and the confrontation with one's own body which, in my case, does not correspond with conventional ideals of beauty. To see bodies on stage that do not comply with the norm is important - not only with regard to history but also with regard to present developments, which are leading humans to the status of design objects. On the question of success: it is important to be able to work and to go your own way - with or without success. I simply do what I have to do.

He is most well known outside of Germany, where a disabled performer not kept safely within the amateur or the disabled companies contexts appears still controversial.

I want to develop a new perspective on Hoghe's work, with reference to his *Boléro Variations*, which relate the impact of his choreography, the impact of the bodies moving on stage, in relation to each other, to props, to the set and to the music, to consciousness studies.

The stage is open, empty, framed by black curtains on three sides. There is unobtrusive recorded music in the background. The show is due to start at 8.30pm. At about 8.20, spectators can just about perceive a small figure at the very back of the stage, a little stage left from the middle, who remains immobile until the auditorium lights are dimmed at 8.30 and the stage lights come on in the centre of the stage. A wide range of recorded variations of the Boléro fills the next 150 minutes (there is one 20-minute interval in between). Five conventional dancers (four male and one female) move on stage in relation to those variations, in all possible constellations among each other, and—in relation to the small figure first seen in the shadow at the back of the stage. He is the choreographer, Raimund Hoghe. His presence frames each aspect of the production: sometimes he solemnly walks literally the perimeters of the stage, at other times, he engages in more direct interaction with the other dancers (all or some of them), but remains still the centre of attention, the focal point of the stage compositions. Even when he is stationary, no matter whether in the shade or in the light, his presence remains. Not only does he participate in the performance: at the same time he serves as a witness to it, an involved outsider, and insider on the fringe.

Hoghe's presence on stage is a choreographic depiction of a higher state of consciousness as conceptualised in *Vedanta* philosophy. A higher state of consciousness is characterised by the screen being aware of the projections and observing, witnessing those projections without direct involvement. This is Hoghe's role in *Boléro Variations*: whether interacting with the other dancers directly, or whether stationary in relation to them, or walking the perimeter: he observes, he witnesses, and he is both involved and not involved. All he does on stage (even when he does nothing) comes across as fully alert, emerging from a high level of concentration, ascetic, serious, and playful at the same time, not merely when he rushed around squirting white powder, or water, from a vaporizer into the air or on himself. The reason that Hoghe is the centre of attention during the performance is expressly not his disability. He does take off his shirt, enabling a full view of the hunchback, and in one episode a dancer places plaster cast sheets in water and then on his hunched shoulder, creating a cast that he then places on his knee. That foregrounds the disability, but not *as* disability. The gentle, poetic nature of this encounter of one disabled and one not-disabled performer on stage, and the precision with which the subtly choreographed movements are carried out, suggests the beauty of life in general, in principle, of, or by means of, or, at worst, despite of diversity.

The playful aspect, which the dancers share with Hoghe, is a further characteristic of pure consciousness, according to *Vedanta*. The entire creation emerges from pure consciousness, and that process of emergence is captured as a play, a divine performance, *Veda Lila*, the play of *Veda*, knowledge. It is the interaction of the knower (*rishi*), the known (*chhandas*) and the process of knowing (*devata*), with each other and with wholeness, *samhita*. It may be worthwhile studying Hoghe's work further to look at the choreography more closely and establish whether Hoghe in fact takes on one or more of those roles of *samhita*, *rishi*, *devata* and *chhandas* across the performance.

Chapter Two

Consciousness and Ethics

This chapter takes the discussion from dramatic and performance writing to the work of the actor and director with a reassessment of ethical implications of theatre, acting and directing. The past few years have seen a surge of interest in the ethical dimension of the theatre. Ethics features as a topic in the Palgrave *theatre &* series. A two-fold question is at the centre of Ridout's argument here: "some theatre appears to dramatize ethical questions", while at the same time it is possible to think about ways in which "the practice of theatre (...) might produce distinctive ways of thinking about ethics" (2009: 6). In general terms, Ridout defines ethics to be about being "good and staying good by acting well" (11). He presents his argument in chronological order, from ancient Greece via modern to postmodern approaches. In the Greek context, ethics is based on the realisation of individual potential, in the modern context on the realisation of individual potential, and in the postmodern context on an orientation towards the "other", following Levinas. In the Greek context, Ridout discusses Plato's commonly assumed position that there is something unethical about theatre itself and concludes that Plato is in fact not the anti-theatrical thinker but instead demands more of the theatre than dramatic illusionism, distancing the spectators from the events represented on stage and thus allowing them to think productively about theatre in relation to ethics (24).

Ridout considers the development from Greece to the modern period as one that foregrounds ethics as a means to find a middle way between "do as you are told" and "do as you please". In the context of theatre, he discusses Lessing's role for a national theatre: citizens of a unified German nation attend in order to renew their "emotional and ethical commitment to the idea and reality of that nation" (40). The drawback of this position, however, is its lack of inclusivity: for example, people who do not go to the theatre are, by implication, somehow defective.

Ridout efficiently places the development of the relationship of ethics and theatre from the modern to the postmodern paradigm in the context of a shift in emphasis of post-World War Two philosophy in general. Under the postmodern paradigm, the relationship between theatre and ethics has become increasingly an issue of process and form rather than content. It is characterized by an "openness to the future and the unpredictable rather than a closure around a specific ethical position" (49). With particular emphasis on Levinas, Ridout points out that this openness demonstrates "some suspicion towards the purely aesthetic, and a marked preference for work which can be demonstrated to be effective" (56). Efficacy is not measured in terms of direct political or social impact, but in terms of the "production of ethical relationships and situations". However, ethics does not completely displace either politics or aesthetics: "Aesthetic experience becomes the condition of possibility for a particular kind of ethical relationship. The ethical relationship becomes in its turn the ground upon which political action might be attempted." (66)

Apart from Ridout's survey in book format, there are a growing number of articles in journals, in particular *Performance Ethos*, launched in 2010. Individual productions are at the centre of some of the essays in *Performing Ethos*, discussing their ethical implications in terms of different cultural contexts (Lai 2010, Chen 2010), and specifically in the context of pain (Hazou 2010), and the relationship between the political and the ethical (Tomlin 2010). Stokes discussed the ethical implications of circus acts between the middle of the 19th and the 20th centuries involving wild animals (2004), while Peterson (2007) discusses current practice from a performance studies perspective. Much emphasis in the discussion of ethical issues of theatre focuses on applied theatre contexts where theatre is used in other environments, in many cases for purposes broadly speaking of therapy, such as theatre in prisons or in mental institutions, or of development, when theatre makers go to troubled areas of various kinds to help a section of the local population through their theatre work. An example of the latter is *pandies theatre* in India, which has been working for six years with survivors and victims' families affected by the mass murder of fifty-three children in a slum in India by a rich man and his servant in 2006 (Kumar 2012). Thompson

(2003), Edmiston (2000), Fisher (2005), and Shaughnessy (2005) are further examples. In the remainder of this chapter I consider ethical implications of theatre production and reception from a consciousness studies perspective.

Production

Actors are trained professionally and intend to earn a living from their job, or they are amateurs, acting in the spare time that their full-or part-time jobs allow them. Most amateur actors do not have professional training. Actor training in the UK takes place in drama schools, in Germany in special arts universities, and in the USA university drama departments also offer vocational training. Allegedly, at least implicitly, the philosophy of some actor training programmes, and of some actor trainers, is that on entering the training, trainees have to be "broken" so that they can then be built up again from scratch in line with the ideas and ideals of the respective programme or trainer. Can any act of intentional destruction of what aspiring actors bring with them when they enter professional actor training be beneficial, ultimately? Does the alleged end result (an actor trained according to any one school or ideal) justify the means ("breaking" the actor)? Do those involved in doing the "breaking" have the knowledge needed to ensure that the process of breaking does not leave patients for mental health services for the rest of their lives, rather than leading to well-trained actors? Is any infliction of suffering (assuming "breaking" entails suffering at least temporarily) on another human being justified or even justifiable? Some of these issues have been discussed by Seton (2010).

Even if training does not include "breaking" in order to build up from scratch, it is important to consider, in an ethical context, what kinds of procedures actors are subjected to as part of their training, and what level of qualification, expertise and experience the trainers have in implementing those procedures. An intensive approach based on the American *method*, for example, may involve asking actors to go deeply into all kinds of experiences of their past for them to be able to conjure up the related emotions at will in performance to correspond with a character's emotion that needs to be presented at any given time as suggested in the play or the production. In view of the predominance of negative, undesirable events depicted in drama, and the corresponding necessity for actors to present concomitant negative, undesirable emotions, they are more likely, in their training, to have to engage with, and dig up from the depths of the subconscious, experiences that their psyche would normally repress. If done well, it may work wonders. However, if it goes wrong, the actor trainee can be harmed for life. For trained psychiatrists and psychoanalysts, dealing with a client or patient's psyche is hard work, where every move must be decided and carried out very carefully. Actor trainers are rarely trained psychiatrists or psychoanalysts. This lack of expertise is a potential risk for the trainee actors, and must be considered in ethical terms.

Another example in the context of actor training is a growing interest in applying approaches from non-Western medicine, psychology or spirituality to the training of actors. The indigenous traditions of these approaches in their original cultural contexts imply that the teacher of such techniques will have had literally a life-long training and practice before being allowed to apply their skills in training others. How does that relate to, in extreme cases, a weekend workshop in any such approach, which may then be applied without any control, and with the patchy understanding that a weekend's training provides, in comparison with a lifetime. The dangers must be considerable.

Once trained, the actor enters a very competitive world, where a large percentage of actors will be unemployed at any one time, and few will make it to stardom. The ethical dimension in this context is defined by the limits actors will set for themselves as to what they will be prepared to do to get work and to stay in work. Will they sleep with the director, star, casting director, producer? Are they prepared to appear on stage in any play they are being offered, even if that involves nudity, faked or real intercourse with fellow actors and / or real, random members of the audience? Which degree of explicit violence (including of a sexual nature) are they prepared to be subjected to (real or acted) on stage, or are they prepared to engage in as fictional perpetrators (possibly inflicting real pain on their colleagues, even if unintentionally, by accident)? What about defecating or urinating on stage, real or faked, smearing themselves with real or stage blood, or any other bodily fluid, for that matter, and killing live animals, for real, on stage? It should be noted that there is ample evidence for all of those things having been part of theatre productions on stages across the world.

Actors also have a responsibility towards their fellow-actors in any production they are working on, again with ethical implications, which are at the same time, at this level at least, implications of appropriate professional conduct. Actors need to come to the rehearsals as scheduled and in an appropriately fit state of mind and body, and to the theatre for the performances on time, and in a state of mind and body that allows them to perform as rehearsed. While on stage they must be expected, in conventional theatre where a dramatic text is presented on stage, to deliver their lines precisely as rehearsed, without changes or *ad hoc* improvisation.

In this context, Conquergood's article "Performing as a Moral Act" is relevant; he described four moral pitfalls that performers should avoid. The sin of the sceptic's cop-out is the actor's refusal to participate; the custodian's rip-off implies that the actor engages only superficially; the enthusiast's infatuation implies that the actor celebrates similarities and erases differences, and in the case of the sin of the curator's exhibitionism, the actor puts difference on display to make it appear exotic. These sins, according to Conquergood, constitute a "moral morass and ethical minefield of performative plunder, superficial silliness, curiosity seeking, and nihilism" (1985: 9). In opposition to those sins that the actor should avoid, Conquergood sets

> struggles to bring together different voices, world views, valuesystems, and beliefs so that they can have a conversation with one another. It is a kind of performance that resists conclusions, it is intensely committed to keeping the dialogue between performer and text open and ongoing (1985: 9)

A fascinating ethical issue for actors was discussed by Mary Luckhurst: actors who have to play real people, she argues, find themselves "subjected to specific aspects of ethical stress that they do not suffer from when playing fictional characters" (2010).

Most, if not all issues that affect the actor are closely related to the director: what do they expect their actors to do in productions they direct, in relation to what actors are prepared to be subjected to, both in their private lives by way of career management, and in professional contexts in the rehearsal room and on stage? How do directors react if actors do not agree to do what they may demand from them, privately and professionally? On a level that is perhaps less controversial, but nevertheless highly relevant to the actor's professional and personal well-being: what methods do directors apply in rehearsal? Some allegedly follow the same philosophy of training institutions, of breaking and then rebuilding their actors. Others thrive on tension, which they claim is conducive the flow of creativity (actors hardly tend to agree with them). Some directors have the entire production in their mind's eye and the rehearsals consist of getting the actors to fulfil that vision independent of their own ideas or interpretations of the characters they have to play. Some have no idea at all, either at the beginning, or, so it would seem, towards the end of the rehearsal period, and consequently they ask their actors to try it this way, then that way: they keep changing instructions and requests until the last minute before curtain up on the opening night, with regard to many aspects of acting including blocking, gesture, facial expression and intonation of the lines. How can any actor be expected to thrive under such circumstances? In some companies so much time is spent on rehearsals that no time is left for actors to learn their lines, resulting in the prompt reading all the lines of the play aloud because they just cannot afford to wait for someone to need a line. The amount of nerves this costs both actors and prompt is likely to be considerable, and the artistic value of a production performed in such conditions must necessarily suffer.

The design element of a production combines the directorial concept with ideas contributed, and put into practice, by the designer(s). Ethical implications of this production element focus on the demands the design may make on actors. For a 2003 Newcastle on Tyne-based *Northern Stage* production of an adaptation of Orwell's *Animal Farm*, the floor of the stage was covered in fresh peat; much of the performance consisted of the actors splashing about with lots of water, so that by the end of the performance the stage was a field of mud, and the actors, most of them naked apart from underwear, covered in it. A 1992 production of Shakespeare's *Midsummer Night's Dream*, directed by Robert Lepage at the National Theatre in London, chose a shallow pool of water at the middle of the stage, surrounded by mud flats, which again had all actors in mud throughout the performance (and protective clothes were issued to the spectators seated in the first three rows closest to the stage).

Reception
What impressions, stimuli should theatre subject not only its makers, but also its audiences to? Are there limits, and (this applies to the production side just as well): who decides? Much depends on the audience expectations. Is it fair to expose an unsuspecting spectator to impressions that are intended to be unsettling, disturbing, and / or at least mentally painful? A venue may be known for its avant-garde work, for taking risks, and a spectator choosing to attend a performance at such a venue should not be surprised that some of the work encountered at that venue will be unsettling. If spectators have good reason to expect something disturbing from a specific production, they have the choice to attend or to stay away. If they choose to attend, and find themselves disturbed as a result, they may dislike this experience of being disturbed and decide to change their mind about the kind of performance, or they may acknowledge that they like this kind of experience and seek further exposure to it. Some extreme performance artists are well known for what they do by way of performance, and again nobody choosing to attend would be expected to feel offended. For example, HIV positive Franko B. cuts himself backstage and bleeds on a white set onstage. That's what this artist is known for, and that's what audiences who choose to buy a ticket for his performance will and should expect.

To startle an audience, to shock spectators, seems to be a favourite aim of more recent theatre practice, and the more audiences are exposed to images or concepts that used to be shocking in the past, the higher their threshold rises and consequently the more difficult it becomes to shock them. Theatre needs to develop and invent ever more sophisticated devices to shock an audience. Is it not much easier to shock, to create a scandal, than to create beauty, a deeply moving experience for the spectator in the theatre? Is creating a shock not just a question of how much of their imagination some people are prepared to reveal—how much daring they have to be identified in public with "that"?

Peer pressure may have an impact on spectators and their responses to shock elements in theatre. Will they want to admit openly to have felt affected, disturbed, by what they saw, for fear of being downgraded in their peers' eyes as weak, as softies? Will they want to appear as "cool"? Against a psychology background, are they *sensitisers*, who react very sensitively to shocking stimuli, or are they *rationalisers*, who seem to be able to cope very well with shocking stimuli, apparently unaffected by them? Finally: are rationalisers really not at all affected, even without noticing, by the shocking stimuli?

If not peer pressure, then a spectator's self-image may well affect the ways they respond to theatre shocks. It could take some courage to admit to being adversely affected, and to deal with this insight meaningfully, in other ways than merely thinking worse of oneself, as a weakling. The problem is that in all those questions raised above, nobody provides the answers for us. Each theatre maker, each spectator, will have to find their own answers to these questions, for themselves, on their own, unobserved and in private, and to a lesser or larger extent in public, among friends and family, among peers and beyond. They will need to learn to face criticism if they object to instances of shock in the theatre, or if they define their limits. One such counter-argument is the question whether they themselves have been present at an event they talk about critically—implying that if they have not, they have no right to be critical in relation to it. This argument must be making the day for Holocaust deniers, because if taken to its logical conclusion, this argument implies that once all Holocaust survivors have died, there is no proof for it left. Another comment those critical of certain practices in theatre they may encounter is along the lines that such topics have to be explored in the theatre (often, if you probe further, nothing further emerges), or that we don't like censorship. Indeed the questions raised in this chapter also relate to questions of regulation and censorship or at least self-censorship. Is it necessary to establish further (self-) regulatory bodies for actor training, and where they exist, what do they look at and what are their powers?

I want to conclude the sections on production and reception with three further selected examples of shock value in the theatre, as case studies which address a range of the abstract questions raised so far. In a German production of Verdi's *Macbeth*, the curtain on Macbeth's nightmare scene opened on a stage-high human vagina, realistically recreated, with a number of actors, both male and female, who had as their common characteristic that they were dwarves, crawling out of the vagina and milling around Macbeth on the stage in front of the vagina.

The scene is a theatre in Zagreb in 2000, post-civil war. The audience is comprised of delegates of a theatre critics' conference held in the city at that time, and a remarkably uniform audience of local female adolescents. The play is an "in-yer-face" contemporary play by a dramatist from one of the component parts of the former Yugoslavia. One scene is the very graphically presented, very brutal rape of a young female by a male. The female adolescents in the audience loudly and almost hysterically cheer the rapist. The critics learn later that the actor playing the rapist is a pop idol, and the cheering girls in the audience were cheering their pop idol, and would have cheered him doing anything, it just happened to be rape. The other actors are aware of the problems with this, but have no option of objecting since the pop star assures an audience and they need a job.

A colleague directs a routine student production. A piece of 70 minutes duration, devised by the company. It is set in complete darkness, apart from a fluorescent strip above the exit for health and safety reasons. The production is promenade, the spectators walk around and so do the performers. The first ten or fifteen minutes consist of the performers taking turns in reciting medieval reports of people sighting angels. Slowly the production's emphasis shifts to the presentation of excerpts from a book about the police interviews and subsequent trial in relation to one of the most notorious criminal cases in Britain in the 1990s, that of Fred and Rosemary West, who raped and killed 12 young women, most of them in their home, afterwards dismembering them and burying them under the floorboards of their home. While graphic details of the rapes, murders and dismemberments were recounted by the performers, they moved among the audience and touched spectators. I vividly recall how my neck was stroked while another performer told us how difficult the Wests found it to sever one of their victim's head from the spine as the bone of the young victim (their own daughter) was not at all brittle yet. At the end of that performance I felt physically sick, and had nightmares for several nights afterwards. Not an experience I like to remember, not one I would ever want to be subjected to again.

Up to this point of this chapter I have raised a number of questions, and presented some scenarios for case studies in relation to ethical issues that come up in the context of theatre. Some of the questions include

- Are those who object to some expressions of theatre simply narrow-minded, or conservative to the extent of rejecting innovation?
- Is it all just a matter of taste, and therefore relative, subjective, personal, and therefore ultimately not relevant for or interesting to public / critical / academic debates?
- Are there, should there be limits beyond which theatre should not go—regarding the extent to which the dramatist or director may demand behaviour from the actors that in many contexts other than theatre would be considered highly problematic, morally suspect, possibly with legal implications?
- Could there be any circumstance in which such activity, both gross and subtle is acceptable?
- Is its unacceptability subject to debate?
- What are the criteria a serious critical discussion needs to establish and then adhere to?
- To what extent can the canon of ethical writing provide the context?

The consciousness studies perspective

Everyone has to find their own answers. I want to argue my own position in the contexts of consciousness studies and the *Vedanta* model of consciousness I introduced earlier. This model suggests that development of consciousness towards higher states of consciousness is the purpose of human life, culminating with attainment of enlightenment, unity consciousness or *moksha*. *Moksha* is a state of human perfection, without disease, without problems, conflict or suffering of any kind experienced by the person who has attained that level of consciousness. Such higher states of consciousness are characterized by waking or dreaming or sleeping being experienced simultaneously with pure consciousness, and in terms of, as expressions of, pure consciousness.

I propose, for the remainder of this argument, and as its basis, to accept, as axiomatic, that the purpose of human life is the development of consciousness towards the attainment of *moksha*. On that basis it stands to reason that anything conducive to the development of consciousness should be favoured, while anything not conducive should be considered with caution; anything clearly detrimental to the development of consciousness should be avoided.

While the individual's response to theatre is certainly subjective and personal, consciousness studies allow us to develop generalisations and abstractions to reach beyond the purely personal and subjective. Every person on earth, independent of their background, age, sex, cultural, political, social contexts, is at some stage or other of their journey towards *moksha*, and while each person's profile of that journey is different, the end point is the same, *moksha*. This does not mean that all people will become more and more the same as they proceed on their paths towards *moksha*. On the contrary, the attainment of *moksha* implies that the individual has achieved their own, very personal profile of characteristics and abilities to the fullest extent possible, their full potential, and that is highly different from person to person.

Different people will need different stimuli to help them in their progress towards *moksha*. Those stimuli could be as varied as measures that provide a direct, and intentional impact towards the development of consciousness, such as an active engagement with spiritual traditions and practice of techniques taught in those traditions, such as yoga, or less direct or intentional stimuli that nevertheless provide the individual with incentives towards the development of consciousness (possibly less directly, and possibly not realized by the individual as such): encounters with other people, conversations, and impressions or ideas they pick up from the media. All these stimuli, direct such as yoga, or indirect guidance from impressions in daily life, can have their impacts on their own or in any kind of possible combination.

Theatre can serve as a means towards the development of consciousness on both the direct and the indirect levels. Indirectly, it can provide, as if coincidentally, ideas and impressions that may have an impact on the development of a person's consciousness. Perhaps people are attracted to the kind of theatre they like because it is what they need in terms of development of consciousness. If they happen to like violence on stage, they may need it to come to terms with some dark elements in their own lives or minds. If one were to assume that encountering a fictional dark side in theatre helps some people deal with their own dark side, then censoring the expression, the performance of that dark side in the theatre is problematic. The implication of this argument is a free-for-all, because such theatre might benefit somebody.

However, the argument is weak. We have to ask the question of what happens to those who might not benefit from the expression or the performance of the dark side in the theatre, but who suffer as a result and whose development of consciousness is hindered, blocked, slowed down, and most certainly not supported in its development towards *moksha*. Does the possibility that some people's encounter, in the theatre, with the dark side is of benefit to them in their development of consciousness mean that such theatre should be made at the risk of harming others? If there were no alternative, this question might merit further discussion. However, there is an alternative.

Theatre can be created with the specific intention of supporting the cast, crew and audience's development of consciousness towards *moksha*. That, after all, is the sole and explicit purpose of theatre according to the Indian treatise on drama and theatre, the *Natyashastra*. Much has been written already on the theory of how this may work, and practical explorations of that theory are following suit rapidly.

In view of the potential of direct positive intervention of theatre in the development of higher states of consciousness towards *moksha*, it can be considered not necessary for theatre to engage with the dark side to help some people deal with their own dark side as one means of supporting their development of consciousness. Thus the risk of harming others in their development of consciousness need not be taken. Where such a risk exists, is where, from the consciousness studies perspective developed here, the limits are beyond which theatre should not go, with regard to what playwrights demand of productions of their plays, to the demands directors may want to make on their actors, the extent to which actors are prepared to comply with demands from plays and directors, and what the dramatist and production team want to subject their audiences to.

Chapter Three

Consciousness and the concept of *Guru* in South Asian spiritual and artistic traditions: contemporary relevance and future potential.

The term and the concept of *Guru*

Chapter Three widens the perspective to non-Western theatre and performance contexts in its reassessment of the role of the teacher, or *guru*, for the actor. Much of the evidence in this chapter is based on subjective and anecdotal evidence, demonstrating the importance of this approach to my argument.

The term *guru* is today used in a confusingly wide range of contexts. Entering *guru* into the internet search engine *Google* yields around 434 million hits—there is a *guru* for everything these days: *guru.com* is the world's largest online marketplace for freelance talent, *code-guru.com* is a site for computer programming, and *guru.net* provides its user with instant facts from over one hundred reliable reference works. The *Times Higher Education Supplement* called Professor Steven Schwartz, then vice-chancellor of Brunel University, UK, the government's *fair access guru*, and referred to the job of "guest lecturer" as a "curious cross between tour guide and resident *guru*". Sky News called the marketing manager of the University of Kingston, UK, a *clearing guru*. The leaders of what academics and journalists alike have come to call *New Religious Movements* are referred to as *gurus*, and accounts here vary from critical assessments, anti-cult warnings and escapee reports.

Gurus in this wider context can be persons or software packages, offering, charging for, and allegedly providing knowledge, information and help. In one sense or another, they are teachers. In some cases, reference to such a living or computer teacher as *guru* has a negative connotation, implying at least the potential of charlatanism.

Some experts thrive on the debunking of charlatans, such as Robert Wiseman, Professor of Psychology at the University of Hertfordshire in the UK. The negative connotation might also imply, to varying degrees, an element of ridicule, an accusation that the so-called *guru* is self-appointed, questioning or even denying any acknowledged authority that could have conferred *guru* status to a person credited with that title by others, or who credit themselves. Is it surprising that most *gurus* today are men?

Such profusion and confusion of uses and implications of the concept of *guru* necessitates a reassessment in the context of consciousness studies as relating to ways of communicating knowledge characteristic of the relationship between *guru* and student. The term originates in South Asian spiritual and artistic traditions, where the *guru* is the teacher who imparts to the disciple knowledge (in theory and practice) relating to a specific spiritual tradition or form of art, but extending beyond this to aspects of daily life.

History of *Guru* in the South Asian spiritual traditions

Historically, in *Vedic* times the texts refer to the *acharya*, teacher, and the *brahmacharin*, disciple. Later, the term used for the disciple is shishya. The *shishya* lives in the *acharya's ashram* (a kind of monastery), starting as early as aged five, and staying for up to twenty-four years. The *brahmacharins* serve their *acharya*, and receive knowledge from them. According to Broo, the main purpose of the master-disciple relationship in *Vedic* times was the transmission of knowledge to maintain the *Vedic* canon. Different families were experts in different *Vedic* texts, knowledge of whose recitation was imparted to the disciple (Broo 2003: 73). In *Upanishadic* times (800-400 BCE), the focus of the *guru*'s teaching was the knowledge surrounding the concepts and experiences of *Atman* and *Brahman*, individual and universal self, and ways of understanding and realising that both are one. It was probably more difficult to find a *guru* than in *Vedic* times because the *guru* was expected to have gained *moksha*, enlightenment, and it is difficult for those on the path to that goal to assess a potential *guru*'s level of self-realisation. The *guru* in this era also has more authority (Broo 2003: 74-5). Shankara, in the 9th century CE, moved the *guru* – disciple relationship away from the family context of the *ashram* into monasteries he founded, *mathas*, where the focus was on the *jagadguru*, the *guru* of the world (Broo

2003: 75). The *bhakti* movement represents the fourth era of the master-disciple relationship. *Bhakti* has been defined as the favourable service of a god, such as Krishna, unencumbered by knowledge and work, etc., and free from the desire for anything else (Broo 2003: 33). The principle informing this approach is to draw down mercy from one's own personal god. In the epic period, 500 BCE-400 CE, the *guru* was adored like god, while in the *puranic* and medieval times (400-1500 CE) he was identified with the personal deity (Broo 2003: 33). In the tantric era, finally, *guru* deification reached its climax. The pedagogical relationship of the *guru* and the *shishya* is referred to as the *guru shishya parampara*.

Types of gurus

Thus the concept of *guru* has changed across time. In addition, different philosophical traditions offer different typologies of *gurus*. Regarding whom they teach, the *kula guru* is the guide for the family, the *rajaguru* is the *guru* for the kingdom, and the *jagadguru* is the *guru* of the world. Regarding what they teach, the *vidyaguru* is the *guru* for a particular discipline, the *dharma guru* teaches religion, and the *satguru* is the spiritual *guru*. The *shravana guru* teaches knowledge, and the *siksha guru* instructs in more detailed knowledge of worship and spiritual life; he gives the *vesa* or *sannyasa* initiation. The *diksha guru* gives an initiation through a mantra. At times, the *shravana guru* also serves as *shiksha guru*, but there is no overlap of the functions of *diksha guru* and either *shravana* or *shiksha guru*. In relation to those three kinds of *guru*, the *guru* who provides the first initiation is also referred to as *nama guru*, while the *guru* who gives the second initiation is the *mantra guru*. The *dhaman* or *tirtha guru* introduces his disciple to a holy place and is his guide there, and the *adi guru* is the original *guru* starting a tradition of other *gurus* who follow his teachings (Broo 2003: 96).

Qualities of a satguru

For the purposes of this chapter, from this complex typology I take *satguru*, on the side of *gurus* of the spiritual traditions, as the major term subsuming *shravana*, *shiksha*, *diksha*, *nama*, *dhaman*, and *tirtha gurus*. Most relevant to the performing arts is the *vidyaguru*. The qualities of a spiritual, *satguru*, have been described widely both in *Vedic* scriptures and by later commentators and contemporary academics. The *guru* should be deeply learned in the scriptures, and he should have realised *moksha*, be enlightened. While these are the primary qualities, many secondary ones are also listed—they are secondary because they follow, as it were, rather automatically from the primary ones, or are prerequisites for them. *Gurus* should be of pure descent, clean, devoted to conduct suitable to them, situated in their *ashramas*, without anger, faithful and non-envious, nicely speaking, of nice appearance, pure, beautifully clothed, pleased by the happiness of all beings, thoughtful, humble-minded, non-violent, reflective, affectionate to their disciples, equal when confronted with praise or criticism, devoted to sacrifices and mantras, experts in logic and debate, pure in heart, and a receptacle of mercy (Broo 2003: 110-11). Anne Marshall suggests that *gurus* should not be judged by the number of books they have written, no matter how learned they are, by their oratory, their reputation, or the size of their following. Her list of a *guru's* ideal qualities, compiled after spending a long time in India "*guru*- hunting", is similar: *gurus* must be competent teachers, healthy in mind and body, clean in their habits, and of pleasing appearance. They should not accept gifts and never ask for money. They should have the power of increasing the wisdom, health and happiness of others. They should be selfless and guided solely by wisdom, love and compassion for others (1963: 196). Copley suggests that many established *gurus* share certain features of their lives: they were isolated in childhood, moved by early bereavement, and often indifferent to family ties; often they undertook particular kinds of journeys, or a creative illness prepared a spiritual revelation (2000: 5-6). The *guru* empowers the disciple. Can the same be said, overall, for contemporary Western teachers in relation to their pupils or students?

The *guru*, finally, has charisma, because, Copley argues, he has immense self-confidence in his new revelation (2000: 6). Max Weber defines charisma as

> a certain quality of individual personality by virtue of which he is set apart from ordinary man and treated as endowed with supernatural, superhuman, or at least specifically exceptional powers or qualities (1964: 358)

Weber distinguishes several types of charismatic people. The magician is active purely on a personal level, on his own. The prophet operates on the fringes of society. The sacred legislator codifies or reconstitutes a law, the teacher of ethics gathers disciples and counsels them, and the priest wields institutional charisma. The mystagogue, finally, performs magical actions to bring salvation.

The roles and functions of a guru

Since conventionally the disciple would live in the *guru*'s family—the *guru* was considered more important than the child's parents—the *guru* assumed the role of parent to his disciples. He combined that role with that of teacher. The *guru* preserved the tradition begun by the *adi guru*, and at times renewed a tradition. He is considered mediator between God and his disciples, often regarded as a manifestation of divinity himself, reflected in the title His Holiness or His Divinity bestowed on *gurus*. For the disciple, the *guru* is guide in their spiritual development. The scriptures mandate that a *guru* is needed for such development, and thus the *guru* provides the seeker-disciple with eligibility for such spiritual development in the first place. As the *guru* leads the disciple to enlightenment, he is a kind of saviour (Broo 2003: 83-95).

How to find a guru

Just as there are many different kinds of people, there are many different kinds of *satgurus*. There is not one *guru* that will appeal to everyone, or to whom everyone will be attracted in such a way as to want to have them as their *guru*. From a cross-section of published reports of how people found their *guru*, it is possible to infer that in most cases it was a very personal, highly subjective process and decision, which certainly poses methodological problems in a paradigm of gaining knowledge, and describing outcomes of knowledge in an objective manner that expressly excludes subjectivity. Some people have gone from *guru* to *guru*, seeking their *darshan*, audience, and just knew, without any doubt, but not precisely why, when they had found *their guru*. The concepts of *karma* and *dharma* provide explanations from the perspective of Indian philosophy (see page 128).

Qualities of a disciple

Having a *guru* was considered a matter of pride, as a symbol of security, love, and a sign of great wealth. Someone who did not have a *guru* was regarded as an orphan (not those without parents), and there is even a word in Sanskrit for a person without a *guru*: *anatha*. It was by no means a sign of weakness to seek, and to have a *guru*, as it might be considered in the West. Some scriptures suggest that the disciple should be from a good family, should be fortunate, humble, and intelligent. On the other hand, scriptures suggest that everyone should be able to benefit from the grace of a *guru*, so there seems to be some contradiction here (Broo 2003: 121). There is agreement, however, on the need for the disciple's sincerity, surrender and faith. When it comes to assessing why some people these days become followers of potentially or definitely dubious so-called *gurus*, such as followers of David Koresh in Waco, Texas, Copley argues that they are weak personalities who like to submit their decisions to authority because it implies abrogating responsibility, doubt and anxiety (6). Sri Sri Ravi Shankar points out that the disciple, or devotee, gains most if they come without expectations: "A devotee is not there even for wisdom. He simply is in love. He has fallen in deep love with the master, with the infinity, with God. He doesn't care whether he gets enlightened or not" (1990). He also comments on the service the disciple is expected to perform for the master—in the form of housework when he lived in the master's *ashram*, or in the form of various voluntary work in contemporary spiritual movements led by a *guru*, such as Sri Sri Ravi Shankar's *Art of Living*: "Being a servant is not being a slave, but being a servant is living the dignity of the Master, dissolving into the Master" (1990).

How the guru teaches
The *guru* teaches verbally and non-verbally, in public and private, through setting a personal example and though initiations into *Vedic* practices. In many cases, the *guru* will tell stories, new ones or those from the repertory. They may change traditional stories to adapt them to the specific needs of the people listening. Being with the *guru* is like being with one's higher self. Sri Sri Ravi Shankar argues that "the *guru* makes the abstract more real and what you thought as solid appears to be more unreal. Sensitivity and subtlety dawn. Perception of love, not as an emotion, but as the substratum of existence becomes evident" (1990)

Critique of gurus

As in any field of life, be it private or public, each major *guru*, at least these days, seems to have his or her detractors. They are professional sceptics or lay people, who criticise the *guru*, either from accurate or misunderstood personal experience, or by generalising from reported material without backup from their own experience. In every sphere of life, be it academia, industry, the arts, or indeed the scene of spiritual development movements, no matter whether Eastern or Western, there are unfortunately much competition, jealousy or envy around, which give rise to such a climate of critique. Methodologically, it is important to assess the background of the person voicing criticism of any one *guru* together with the allegations.

The unshakable nature of the *guru*'s authority, and the need for the *guru* to adhere to the principles of what it means to be a proper *guru*, become clear in a traditional story from India, here narrated from childhood memory by a Bharata Natyam dancer—she first heard the story from her grandmother, and it thus forms part of an oral tradition. Below is the full narration literally transcribed—the fluency of the narration is testimony to the depth to which this story is ingrained in the speaker's consciousness.

> Once upon a time there was a war between Gods and demons. The number of warriors fighting in the demon army mysteriously stayed the same, while the number of warriors fighting in the army of the Gods kept depleting. The Gods wondered why this was happening, and they found that the demons had a special *guru*, Shukracharya, who had the ability to bring back the dead, to infuse life back into them, and that was a shastra, a technique, which had to be mastered over the years. The Gods, worried, called a meeting and decided to send a young boy, Kacha, the son of their *guru*, to the demon camp, to the demon *guru*, so that he may learn the shastra, the art of reviving the dead, from him. When he arrived, the demons were of course upset and told Shukracharya that he should not teach a person from the enemy camp. Shukracharya responded that as a *guru* it was his duty to teach his *shishya*, and that he could not differentiate his *shishya*s on the basis of where they came from, including coming from the enemy camp: "He has come to me wholeheartedly as a student to learn something, and I am a sincere *guru*, therefore I need to teach him". Shukracharya took Kacha into his ashram, and as the years passed by, Kacha became Shukracharya's favourite, and the demon boys hated Kacha because he was such a sincere student and fulfilled all his duties and required activities. Shukracharya had a daughter, Devyani, who developed a great liking for Kacha. One day

Shukracharya sent the boys from the village to the jungle to get some wood. The demon boys conspired against Kacha to kill him; they killed him, then returned to their ashram. As the sun was setting, Shukracharya's daughter, Devyani, started getting worried, and asked her father why all other boys had returned but not Kacha. Shukracharya went into meditation and realised with horror what the demon boys had done—they had killed Kacha. Shukracharya then used the shastra and Kacha came back to life. The next day in class with the *guru* the demon boys were completely shocked to see Kacha alive. They schemed again, and after killing Kacha they burnt his body and mixed the ashes into a drink for their Shukracharya. In the evening Devyani could not find Kacha and told her father that the boys might have been up to come mischief again. Shukracharya meditated again, tried his best but could not locate the body of Kacha. With increased effort at meditation and, looking inside himself, he realised with horror what the boys had done. He used the shastra and Kacha came to life within Shukracharya's own body. He told Kacha: "Now the time has come for me to teach you the technique". Kacha was very happy that after so many years of waiting and service he would now learn the technique that would be so helpful to so many. Once he had learnt the technique, Shukracharya said to him: "You will now tear open my stomach from the inside, come out, and then you will use the shastra to get me back to life. That will be my *guru dakshina* and a test for you". This is how it happened. Thereafter Kacha thanked Shukracharya for all the teaching and bade farewell to return to the Gods. Devyani was upset, having hoped to get married to Kacha, and turned to her father for help. Shukracharya responded: "He has been a good student to me, he has learnt his art well, he has given me the *guru dakshina*, and he has passed his test. As a father it pains me to see you so sad when he leaves. As a *guru*, I am very proud of him." Kacha returned to the Gods and applied his shastra to them. (Interviewee One 2012)

The Guru in the Performing Arts
Personal and institutional contexts, past and present
Many of the characteristics of the spiritual *guru* apply to some extent to the *guru* in the performing arts across South Asia and the South Asian diaspora. Traditionally, the disciple learnt from the *guru* in the *guru*'s home, performing service. Not only technique was transmitted in this way, but the artistic context as well, comprising "philosophy, music, sculpture, and mythology" (Venkataraman 1994: 81). Hardly any students of the performing arts in South Asia or the South Asian diaspora nowadays live with their *gurus* in the way it used to be. In India today, there are private *gurus*, where the *guru shishya parampara* may remain most intact. There are dance schools intent on

transmitting technique, and dance is also more and more taught through universities, which become "institutionalised opportunities for local *gurus* as poorly paid visiting faculty" (Banerjee 2010: 39). Jones argues that the close personal relationship characteristic of the *guru shishya parampara* is

> incompatible with the essentially impersonal nature of the expanded institutionalized school. There has been a tendency also toward segregation of beginning, intermediate, and advanced students, whereas formerly, in the traditional method of training, beginning students learned much from observing and from understudying the roles of more advanced students in daily rehearsal in the kalari. At the same time, there has been a trend towards progressive shortening of the training period. (1987: 41)

At university level, there were initially problems when the students were expected to

> extend their interaction with the faculty outside the classroom and to their homes, more so in residential universities. They were expected to do sundry household chores as the disciples used to do in the gurukul or ashram. In return, students were treated like family members and are rewarded with help in completing assignments and dissertations, in evaluation and in the doctoral viva voce examination by appointing known examiners and promoting publications through networks. (Chanana 2007, quoted in Banerjee 2010: 37).

Conventionally, such service is supposed to indicate the student's sincerity and depth of the desire to learn (Owens 1987: 180). The precise nature of this causal relationship between service and leaning has not been explored further. Despite attempts to curb such practice, through student evaluation and more regulations, problems persist:

> I had to devote all my time in completing multifarious personal work for my teacher, like, talking to the reporters, drafting letters, computer jobs despite my busy schedule. I had to pay an extra sum of money for each semester demanded by my *guru* apart from the fees paid to the university. Valuable gifts are often demanded and the denial of affording these expenses would have affected my grades. Who would like to bargain with the final grade in this competitive world? (Personal communication, 2008) (Banerjee 2010: 38)

Banerjee describes her attempts to integrate dance training within a liberal arts curriculum, concluding as follows:

> Instead of supporting an unquestioned transplantation and application of the *guru-shishya* model in miniature form to somehow fit into the paradigm of contemporary liberal arts education within a degree programme, I propose that the dynamics of the dance curriculum should be seen as a translation of the entire process of content development, learning, responding, creating, perceiving and finally evaluating. The 'liberal education dance curriculum' as proposed has embodied technical parameters, socio-cultural dimensions and interdisciplinary areas. (2010: 45)

In the UK, the training in South Asian dance forms has come under the aegis of the ISTD (Imperial Society of Teachers of Dancing). The syllabi emphasise that fundamentals need to be trained through repetition, but apart from that, "a certain amount of independence is engrained in the learning process, established through a holistic understanding of the steps, thus offering opportunities to move away from a traditional dependence on the *guru*" (Prickett 2004: 10).

Subjectively, there is a difference, difficult to pinpoint precisely, between performers who had some kind of deeper bond with their *guru*—representatives of the older generation, usually trained in South Asia, where they at least went to their *guru*'s home, or the *guru* came to their home, on a daily basis, and usually members of the younger generation, especially in the diaspora, who attend classes in a place like the Bhavan Centre, or the Akademi at The Place, both in London, UK, on a once-a-week basis. There was, for example, a marked difference in the way Bharata Natyam dancer Veena Ramphal came across to her audience at her first public performance (*Arangetram*) following training at the Bharatiya Vidya Bhavan in London, and the performance she gave at the same venue a year later, after she had studied with renowned *guru* Padma Subrahmaniam in India for one year thanks to a scholarship. When the older generation is gone, we might not even have "proof" any more of the difference.

Characteristics of guru and shishya
There are similarities between the characteristics contemporary students of the performing arts in India and the Indian diaspora associate with the *guru* and the *shishya* and the conventional

expectations in relation to spiritual *gurus*. Here is one contemporary view:

> *Gurus* should be wise, knowledgeable, inspiring, motivating, someone I can look up to and to whom I want to give back without any expectation on the *guru*'s side. There may be staunch views that all teachers are *gurus* and in that role are due the same level of respect, are to be considered as always right and should never be argued with. However, my open upbringing leads me to consider *gurus* in terms of Carl Rodgers as facilitators of education, who are not necessarily always right. (Interviewee One 2012)

The *guru* has to realise his or her own importance in the education of the *shishya*, and both need to share sincerity and passion (Interviewee One 2012). The *guru* should be convinced of the potential and qualities of the *shishya*: the *guru* should thus not accept everyone as *shishya*. This is relevant for example in the martial arts, where the *guru* needs to be convinced at the outset that the *shishya* will not misuse the imparted techniques (Interviewee Two 2012).

There may be occasions where the quality of the *guru* in terms of this ideal, especially generosity, becomes apparent when they perform with a student of theirs who is better than they are. This is an ideal scenario; there are indications, based on conversations with artists and on relevant publications, that there is today emphasis among *gurus* on fame, money, preferential treatment of family members, and forms of rivalry. However, in a very close-knit community, nobody can afford to address these issues openly; many *gurus* strive to set a good example through their own work and the ways they operate as *gurus* and *shishyas*. For example, Interviewee One seeks to be sincere and to give her students a better experience than she had herself at every stage of their training, and to treat especially children learners as adults, addressing them, for example, with "Ladies, I am disappointed in you, you have not given your best" (2012). This makes them think and is more conducive to inciting improvement than yelling at them or using a stick to hit their feet when errors persist or the student lacks concentration (an experience of Interviewee One's own training, which she, however, attributes to the *guru*'s dedication to perfection and which she accepted fully from her *guru*).

Forms of respect and gratitude

Where possible, the *guru* should inspire and deserve, and on that basis receive, the *shishya's* full respect. Such respect is demonstrated, for example, by the *shishya* touching the *guru*'s feet at the onset of training. This is a gesture that is otherwise reserved as a sign of respect shown by younger people to older people in the Indian cultural context. An older *shishya* touching the feet of a younger *guru* will not represent an indication of respect for the younger person, but for the concept of *guru* manifested in the person who happens to be younger.

Some sources suggest that teachers should not make payment a condition of accepting students, but the *guru dakshina* was an accepted principle: a gift for the teacher to please him or her, not as payment. The assumption here was that anything the teacher taught was so sacred that it could not be paid for by all the wealth of the world. *Dakshina* was considered particularly appropriate at the end of the training. Ancient law according to Manu suggests, for example, that when the student is about to return home (after completing his studies):"he may offer his *guru* some wealth: a gift of a field, gold, a cow, or a horse, or even shoes or an umbrella, or a seat, corn, vegetables or clothes (either singly or together) may engender pleasure in the teacher" (Antze 1991: 32). Students today speak of their esteem and respect for their *gurus*, independent of the administrative arrangements for their instruction. In the case of Interviewee One, the *shishya*'s mother, a good friend of the *guru*, arranged the necessary fee; for some *gurus*, Interviewee One pointed out, the fee forms the basis of their livelihood: as a main means of income. Other *gurus* do not need the money for their livelihood, their interest is in teaching to perpetuate the art form that is considered priceless to the extent that nobody could pay for it adequately anyway. Interviewee Two also gave money as *guru dakshina*, but in addition attended and helped out at all her *guru*'s performances. For Interviewee One, the *shishya*'s appropriate gratitude to the teacher is not limited to, or at an end with, the payment. She sends birthday greetings and every time she starts a new project, or has a performance, she seeks her *guru*'s blessings. The *guru* may respond only with a brief "good luck", but that means a lot to her *shishya*. This particular performer is taking the art form that her *guru* inculcated in her to places beyond India, and her continuing the art form elsewhere might be the biggest *guru* dakshina.

In Interviewee One's own choreographic and dance work, the way she executes her steps, and the way she designs her steps are influenced by her thoughts as to what the *gurus* would say if they saw her perform. They would be encouraging, and would not comment on her creative thought processes, but on the way she executes the resulting dance. In particular, the minute she notices she comes off beat she stops.

Learning through imitation
In the performing arts, the *shishya* learns through imitation. According to Odissi *guru* Sanjukta Panigrahi,

> you just follow him [the *guru*] like a parrot, you imitate what he does. You do not understand the meaning of the dance ... you merely repeat the same positions exactly you do them every time. You follow as if you were blind. We do not ask our teacher how much tension here? How much this should bend? We must follow. (Banerjee 2010: 37)

Critics of the *guru-shishya* tradition consider the lack of questioning in that tradition problematic, suggesting that students are spoon-fed easy solutions, which present a barrier to critical thinking and thus pathways to problem-solving. (Banerjee 2010: 38).

Interviewee Two is adamant that learning works best if it is not accompanied by thinking. Once the body has learnt, thinking can follow. Interviewee One pointed out that today, without the *shishya* living with the *guru*, and in the context of more institutionalised forms of teaching and learning as a result, the critical dimension might be more important than before. When the *guru* had the opportunity to talk about one specific topic, accompanied by demonstrations, for three days in a row, without interruption by other aspects and demands of life outside of the teaching context, taking notes or thinking at length about the topic under discussion were not needed. Learning in distinct, compartmentalised steps is necessary within a more fragmented learning environment which is the norm today, but rigidity should be avoided. A major factor of the change is how people relate to time: fewer people have, or want to spend the time it does take to learn in the established ways.

Guru inside and outside
Sri Sri Ravi Shankar argues that, in the spiritual context, "*guru* is an element, a quality inside you: it is not limited to a body or a form" (1990), and Neki suggests that the *guru* is "*purusha* (person) embodied physically and mentally", and "*nadabindukalatit* (beyond sound, space or time) i.e., devoid of all dimensions, absolute, all-knowing and powerful" (Neki 1973, 1976 quoted in Raina 2002: 179). Antze's Odissi *guru* spoke of his belief that

> the *guru*, or perhaps the concept of *guru* exists within oneself, that one holds the image and power of the *guru* in one's mind/heart. In the initial stages of the relationship, the teacher is responsible for giving birth to the artistic being of the student and for nurturing the pupil's skills by taking the role of second parent. Subsequently, the *guru* and his tradition are assimilated by and become contained within the disciple" (Barba and Savarese 1991: 31).

As Interviewee One put it, the *guru* has to instigate, inculcate certain traditions, but it is up to the *shishya* to realise that tradition: "You can take the horse to the pond, but you cannot force it to drink".

In terms of spirituality, certain traditions of knowledge suggest that the lives of human beings follow a Divine Plan, or, in Indian terms, *dharma*. It may be part of that plan for someone to become and serve as a *guru*, or to need, seek, find and follow a *guru*, in both cases either in the context of spiritual development, or in the context of the performing arts. There is also a more recent tendency, according to geobiologist Hans Binder, suggesting that people need to become more and more independent of guidance from outside in the form of *gurus*, and learn to rely more and more on their own intuition to unearth within themselves the contents hitherto taught, or at least triggered, by a *guru* (2012).

Outlook
The ways of teaching, the ways of imparting knowledge and practice, and the ways of enabling spiritual experience and development are fundamentally different in the one to one context of *guru* and *shishya*, and any other learning or teaching context. The one-to-one scenario is essential in allowing transfer of deep spiritual contents and experience, and it requires a high level of development of consciousness towards higher states of consciousness for someone to

meet all the criteria that a good *guru* needs to fulfil: a high level of spirituality in the *guru* is the prerequisite for the learning process in the uninitiated *sishya* to have any chance of success. Given the spiritual dimension of the performing arts in the South Asian context in which the concept of *guru* originated, it is important to understand the role and nature of *guru* in that spiritual context. In times when learning meant that a teacher who had knowledge gave that knowledge to a student, the *guru shishya parampara* was the ideal way of teaching and learning.

We observe a shift in the nature of learning away from knowledge being handed on from teacher to student, no matter whether in a one-to-one environment or in an institutionalised context, as if knowledge were an object. Today, increasingly, knowledge is experienced as something inherent in every human being, and the process of teaching consists in the teacher engaging in activities that awaken in the student the knowledge that has been within them all along. This shift of experience and understanding was captured well in Interviewee One's comment that "You can take the horse to the pond, but you cannot force it to drink". Further explanation of this mode of teaching and learning that comes to the fore at this point in time is possible again within the context of the *Vedanta* model of consciousness, and specifically its take on communication.

Grammarian Bhartrihari, whose writings critics date around 400-500 CE, describes several levels of language, *vaikhari*, *madhyama*, *pashyanti*, and *para*. *Vaikhari* "is the most external and differentiated level", on which speech is uttered by the speaker and heard by the hearer (Coward 1980: 128). Its temporal sequence is fully developed. *Madhyama* represents, in broad terms, the thinking level of the mind.

> It is the idea or series of words as conceived by the mind after hearing or before speaking out. It may be thought of as inward speech. All parts of speech that are linguistically relevant to the sentence are present here in a latent form. (129)

The finest relative level is that of *pashyanti*. At this level "there is no distinction between the word and the meaning and there is no temporal sequence" (131). Beyond the very subtly manifest level of *pashyanti*, Bhartrihari locates the fully unmanifest level of language, *para* (131). The level of language described by *para* corresponds to the level of pure consciousness in the *Vedanta* model of consciousness introduced earlier in this book.

Bhartrihari associates the *pashyanti* level of language with the concept of *sphota*. It represents meaning as a whole, existing in the mind of the speaker as a unity. "When he utters it, he produces a sequence of different sounds so that it appears to have differentiation" (73). The process of differentiation into sounds proceeds from the *sphota* on the *pashyanti* level of language via *madhyama* or inward thought to expressed speech on the *vaikhari* level. For the listener, the process is reversed. Although he first hears a series of sounds, he ultimately perceives the utterance as a unity—"the same *sphota* with which the speaker began" (73). The *sphota* or meaning-whole thus has two sides to it: the word-sound (*dhvani*) and the word-meaning (*artha*) (12). Sound and meaning are two aspects residing within the unitary *sphota*, which, according to Bhartrihari, is eternal and inherent in consciousness (12). Meaning is thus not conveyed "from the speaker to the hearer, rather, the spoken words serve only as a stimulus to reveal or uncover the meaning which was already present in the mind of the hearer" (12).

Today's *Zeitgeist*, as I have demonstrated in the material in Chapter One about the reasons why there have been so many biographical plays about famous artists over the past thirty-five years, is characterised by increasing knowledge about, and experience, of, pure consciousness and related higher states of consciousness. It is in line with this observation that understanding and experience of the gaining of knowledge shifts in accordance with this development. The shift is one away from the conventional assumption that knowledge is given from one person to the other, or others, or that knowledge is acquired by a person by collecting it from elsewhere (teacher, internet or books). The direction of the shift is towards understanding and experiencing the gaining of knowledge in terms of remembering what has been, and always is, inherent in pure consciousness already.

Chapter Four

Consciousness, warm-up, cool-down and the actor as observer

This chapter tightens the focus further on the actor: warm-up and in particular cool-down have been considered as important for the actor's artistic achievement and personal well-being only relatively recently—the *Vedanta* model of consciousness provides an explanatory framework for their importance and on that basis I discuss a range of practical approaches to enhancing especially cool-down. According to Richard Schechner, the typical experience of acting in the theatre comprises seven more or less distinct elements: "training, workshops, rehearsals, warm-ups, performance, cool-down and aftermath" (1985: 16). From among these seven elements, the chapter focuses on warm-up and cool-down, with special emphasis on the latter, in the context of the *Vedanta* model of consciousness.

Warm-up

Many of the activities involved in warm-up for the theatre actor are physical, allowing the actor's body to be in a state of readiness for the physical aspects of performance, including the use of the voice. Research on warm-up for actors, dancers and sports people points out that there is a useful differentiation between specific warm-up (which involves the performer rehearsing the skills to be used in performance), and general warm-up (which involves activities not related directly to the neuromuscular activity of the forthcoming performance). Among the physiological changes effected by warm-up are increased blood flow and muscle temperature (McHenry et al. 2009: 572). This results in

> faster muscle contraction and relaxation, greater economy of movement because of lowered viscous resistance within active

> muscles, improved oxygen delivery and use by muscles, facilitated
> nerve transmission and muscle metabolism, and increased blood flow
> through active tissues. (McArdle et al. 2001: 575-6)

Research into warm-up, specifically of the actor's voice, suggests, as recently as 2009, that while many actors emphasise the need for vocal warm-up, and it is being taught as part of actor training, "little is known about the effects of vocal warm-up on voice production" (McHenry et al. 2009: 572). Some research suggests that warm-up of the voice leads to a "decreasing viscosity in the vocalis muscle as the result of increased temperature", but this does not impact on the "phonation threshold pressure (PTP) (...), the minimum pressure required to initiate vocal fold vibration" (McHenry et al. 2009: 572, referring to Elliott, 1995). Research by Amir et al. (2005) suggests "that a more holistic warm-up, incorporating relaxation, postural adjustments, and breathing, as well as vocalizing, other researchers found a clear acoustic benefit to warm-up" (McHenry et al. 2009: 573). There may be differences in the ways vocal warm up of any kind affects men and women, or different ranges of the singing voice, e.g., mezzo sopranos and sopranos; the impact of other areas of the body other than the vocal cords on the voice is also subject to research, with often mutually exclusive findings. Van Lierde et al. provide a useful table summarising recent research results on the impact of vocal warm-up exercises (2009: 116-17).

In the context of dance, warm-up and cool-down (not further defined) were found to be associated with a "decrease of incidence of ankle injury" in a study based on self-reports from 159 Irish dancers (McGuiness et al. 2006: 35). In the context of warm-up for sports, a 2006 study concludes that research evidence to date suggests that warm-up before a sports event reduces the risk of injury (Fradkin et al. 2006), a finding supported by a review of relevant literature published in 2007 (Woods et al. 2007). Mandengue et al. concluded that it "is possible to use predictive mathematical models for determining the effects of active WU on subsequent performance" (2009: 9). The findings of this study, conducted in the context of sports, may be transferable to dance and theatre acting.

There is thus, to sum up, some research and associated insight, into physical warm-up. There is much less research and academic writing with regard to possibility, need, or problematic issues regarding emotional warm-up. In the Western context, the largest number of approaches to actor training focus on the actor's emotions, and deal at length with the ways an actor can achieve believable emotions in their portrayal of a character. Most of these approaches, however, focus on the development of a context over the duration of the rehearsal process that will enable the actor to build the character's emotional existence. It is left to the individual actor to find ways of shifting from their daily emotions to those required in the performance, as part of the warm-up, over and above its physical component. The following long quote gives an anecdotal example of how actor and academic David Ian Rabey would warm-up for a particularly intense emotion at the beginning of performances of Howard Barker's *Uncle Vanya*:

> The anger and frustration of the Vanya performer has to set the pace of the first eight pages of the play, up until Serebryakov's initiative of announcing his selling the estate. Up to that point, all other characters are nominally reactive or non-reactive to Vanya's fumings and sardonic outbursts, and the situation is static rather than progressive; so is Vanya, notwithstanding his energy. To drum up enough energy to power me through this sequence - and over a contrasting period of ten minutes physical inactivity whilst the audience first entered the theatre, where I was already sitting motionless - I played myself two tracks on a personal stereo and built up a level of physical momentum in rhythmic and emotional response. First, in the dressing room, I would play Richard Thompson's song 'Can't Win' (the live version from the CD compilation *Watching the Dark*), to invoke and entertain as many as possible of my own feelings of various forms of constriction by others, and my own consequent rage at being forced or expected to be complicit in these constrictions, most of which are manifested in the forms of social determinism which the neo-Chekhovian theatre enshrines. Thompson's performance breaks into a guitar solo which suggests bottled rage, strangulatory concentration and repetitive blows, which I manifested physically against my inanimate surroundings. Then, moving to the darkened corridor at the side of the auditorium, I expanded this into a pacing war-dance to the accompaniment of the Thompson song 'Shoot Out the Lights' (live version from the same CD) - a defiant reaction to the previous frustration, built on an identification of myself with the darkness surrounding me - unreachable, watchful for similarity, purposeful, contagious, grimly pleased with my own capacity for irrevocable destruction (William Burroughs's invocation of 'The Spirit of the Black Hole' in *The Western Lands*, 1988, also combines a number of these qualities). It was helpful that I then entered the darkened theatre space (accompanied only by the performer playing Astrov) and could close my eyes, only to open them when the audience were all present

and visible in the room which I had first occupied. This bred a confidence best summarised by a character in Alan Moore and Dave Gibbons's graphic novel *Watchmen*: 'I'm not locked up with them, they're locked up with me' (Moore & Gibbons, 1988), a confidence in my own energy to which only the other characters - rather than the theatre space itself - could provide impediments. This distinction may sound a minor abstraction, but I found it significant: Vanya should not hate or despair of the theatre in which he is placed, rather he must sense and love its potential energy for disclosure. It is the (self-)restrictive reflexes of the other characters which offend his sense of potential and imagination. Thus I associated with, represented and signified a conscious and purposeful <u>in</u>definition - a spirit of the black hole shooting out the lights of determinism and rationalism: prior and primal inhabitant of a space into which characters and audiences brought their attempted <u>definitions</u>, which I would seek to puncture by exposing their (self-)limitations. (Cornforth and Rabey 1999: 39)

Cool-down

Schechner notes that "little work has been done on the cool-down, at least in the Euro-American tradition" (1985: 125). A 2010 study of singers confirms that trend: of 117 participants in a study of "type, duration and frequency of vocal warm-up" and cool down "regimens in the singing community using a survey",

> only 26 participants [22%] reported that they use a vocal cool-down after singing. Most who indicated that they use a vocal cool-down after singing were females, aged 41 and older, with more than 10 years of singing experience. (Gish et al. 2010: 3)

This study does not explain what activities precisely the cool-down entailed.

As with warm-up, research into cool-down has focused on the physical aspects of performance in theatre, singing, dance and sports. Malliou et al. were able to demonstrate not only the importance of cool-down in reducing injury rate in aerobics dance instructors compared with those instructors who did not cool down, but also of the duration of the cool down exercise: "82% of the instructors who followed cool down up to 5 min, 45% of those who followed cool down up to 10 min and 22.5% of those who followed cool down up to 15 min reported injuries in class" (2007: 32).

In the context of theatre acting, there is consensus that actors may be affected emotionally by the roles they play" (Geer 1993: 151).

Burgoyne found two major types of potentially emotionally distressing affect, which she termed *boundary blurring*.

> In the first type, the actor's personal life may take over in performance, leading to the actor's loss of control onstage...conversely, the actor's character may take over offstage, with the actor carrying over character personality traits into daily life (1991: 161).

Bloch conceptualises the same emotional affect of performance as emotional hangover (1987: 10), while Seton coined the phrase "postdramatic stress" (2006).

Among existing cool-down procedures, Kurtz describes the following:

- Clearly marking the beginning and end of rehearsal / performance;
- Cell-phone (the rehearsal or performance is a period during which the use of cell-phones is not permitted, and performers place their cell-phones in a designated bag at the beginning and retrieve them from there at the end of the rehearsal / performance);
- Transitioning from character to actor (reverse of warm-up); this can be achieved by imagining that the character represents a mask or veil which the actor puts on at the beginning of the rehearsal or performance, and takes off at the end of it; writing a journal right after performance may serve the same purpose, as may discussing the performance with other members of the company;
- Stepping out (part of Susanna Bloch's Alba Emoting: using specific breathing patterns both to get into an emotion, and to abandon that emotion.
- Chaulet represents a subtle energy approach to cool-down: playing a character involves accessing subtle energies relating to the character, which can overshadow the actor's own energies. For the actor, cool-down involves to both consciously separate from the character's energy, and to cleanse their own energy centres (chakras) after performance. (2011)

Cool-down and the Indian approach to consciousness

Over the last decade, developments of thinking within the field of consciousness studies include the position of *embodied consciousness*, understood to mean either that consciousness is not only related to the brain but that other parts of the body are involved in consciousness as well, or, in a more moderate form, that "embodied mental capacities are ones that depend on *mental representations or processes* that relate to the body" (Prinz 2008: 419).

From the perspective of the *Vedanta* model of consciousness, warm-up allows the unity of consciousness and body to shift from the daily mode of functioning to the extra-daily mode of performance. Techniques involved in warm-up may be using the body or the mind, or both, to achieve this result. Given the considerable difference between performative state and daily state of embodied consciousness, it is essential for actors to have at their disposal clearly developed and identified means of returning to the daily mode, to avoid emotional hangover, blurring of boundaries or postdramatic stress.

Consciousness not only relates to, not only leads to, but *is* matter; human bodies are condensed, compressed, compacted, concentrated pure consciousness, and enable the experience of pure consciousness in daily life. Just as *Rig Veda* and *Vedic* literature are an expression of pure consciousness within the realm of the Absolute, human physiology and all other objects within and beyond the range of human perception are manifestations of pure consciousness. Recent research has indicated that *Rig Veda* and *Vedic* literature have their distinctive parallels in human physiology. Such correspondence has been derived in two ways:

> The first is by showing the *functional* correspondence between the quality of a specific area of the *Vedic* Literature and an area of the physiology, and the second is a *structural* analysis of the number of components of the corresponding areas of physiology and the *Vedic* Literature. (Dillbeck and Dillbeck 1997: 15)

Earlier in this chapter I argued that the actor's ability to deal with the emotions they are expected to play is at the centre of the need for effective cool-down, to avoid emotional hangover, postdramatic stress or the adverse effects of boundary blurring. It is here that the *Vedanta* perspective on embodied consciousness, as presented above, is useful in developing further understanding of cool-down. On that basis our ability to develop effective approaches to cool-down can be enhanced.

In neuroscientific studies of emotions, representatives of a basic emotions perspective are looking for specific brain areas in charge of emotions (and have not really found them), while "dimensional theorists insist that the neuronal underpinnings of emotion generalise across emotions" (Shiota and Kalat 2011: 133). The areas of the brain that have been discussed as related to emotions include the limbic system (processing of expressions or experience with regard to emotional contents), the amygdala (especially related to the emotion of fear) and the two parts of the Nucleus Caudatus (if injured, emotional disturbances are among the symptoms).

Nader associates the limbic system with its forty components with the divisions and books of *Kalpa* (1995: 82). This is a body of Vedic texts that deals with ritual. It forms one of six bodies of texts referred to as *Vedanga*, translated as limbs of the *Veda*. The others are *Shiksha* (phonetics), *Vyakarana* (grammar), *Nirukta* (etymology), *Chhandas* (metre) and *Jyotish* (astronomy and astrology).

The limbic system is located in the right and left limbic cortical areas. Nader associates these with a specific aspect of a further *Vedanga*, namely *Jyotish* (astrology). Two of the twelve houses (*bhavas*) in *Jyotish* are related to the limbic cortical areas: the fourth house, *bandhu* to the right limbic area, and the tenth house, *karma* to the left limbic area. Each *bhava* is in turn linked with specific parts of the body: *bandhu* with heart, lungs, chest and indirectly, nose; *karma* is associated with the knees. The astrological function of the *bhavas* are: for *bhandu*, maternal happiness, confidence, belief, comforts, conveyances, mother and home land; for *karma* they are activity, occupation, status, honour, position, respect, profession, vocation, name and fame, father's social status, public life and government (1995: 108-109).

The amygdala, associated with fear on the basis of neuroscientific research, is also related to *Jyotish*: the specific influence from the planets that can be characterised best as "courage, decision, general" (Nader 1995: 96), is associated by way of personification with the deity Mangala, related to the planet of Mars. One of the characteristics of Mangala, or Mars, is fear, which is the link between Mangala, Mars and the amygdala.

Nader associates the lunar nodes in *Jyotish*, *Rahu* and *Ketu*, with the head and tail of the *Nucleus Caudatus*. The emotional afflictions of people with injuries to the *Nucleus Caudatus* correspond to the afflictions described in *Jyotish* when *Rahu* and *Ketu* are out of balance. Nader further associates Mars with the DNA component of cytosine, while *Rahu* corresponds to the enzyme that cuts and removes DNA components (DNAase), and *Ketu* corresponds to the enzymes that rebuild and synthesise DNA (DNA polymerase) (1995: 116).

To sum up the argument of this chapter so far: more research has gone into warm-up than cool-down. The majority of research into both has focused on the body, which is to be expected for fields such as dance, singing and sports. In the context of theatre acting, more research is needed to address emotional warm-up and in particular emotional cool-down, to allow the actor to avoid blurring of boundaries, emotional hangover or postdramatic stress. In the context of approaches to embodied consciousness, *Vedanta* philosophy suggests that the body is consciousness. Nader's research proposes that there is a direct correspondence between texts of *Veda* and *Vedic* literature (as abstract expressions of consciousness) and the human physiology and anatomy (as concrete expressions of consciousness). I selected three such correspondences for description, demonstrating how the location of emotional activity in the brain relates to texts of *Vedic* literature: the limbic system and *Kalpa*, the amygdala and Mangala (Mars) in *Jyotish*, and head and tail of the *Nucleus Caudatus* with *Rahu* and *Ketu*, also in *Jyotish*.

For the actor, the implication of this enhanced understanding of the body as consciousness, and of the correspondence of *Vedic* literature and human physiology and anatomy is this: what cool-down seeks to achieve is to restore balance to the actor's emotions where such balance has been disturbed by the actor taking on, expressing and living the emotions on an "other", of the character. If the body is consciousness, then any emotional imbalance must have a corresponding physical imbalance. Both need to be addressed to restore balance. We have seen that all of the *Vedic* literature (including *Kalpa* and *Jyotish* discussed above), emerge from, and are commentaries on, the knowledge contained in *Rig Veda*. The sounds of *Rig Veda*, and the gaps between those sounds, as pure consciousness, thus represent the source of all *Vedic* literature and human life. The accurate sequence of those sounds represents balance.

Any imbalance is defined, in this context, as the lack of an accurate sequence of sounds. The accurate sequence of sounds, and with it the balance of consciousness at all levels of its expression, including human emotion in mind and body, can be restored for humans, by listening to the accurate sound sequence in *Rig Veda*, or by engaging in such a recital themselves.

For actors whose emotional balance is disturbed due to the activities of their profession, i.e., taking on the emotions of a character in rehearsal or performance, listening to a recital of *Rig Veda*, or engaging in such recital themselves, will restore balance from the most subtle, and therefore most efficient, level of pure consciousness. This can be hypothesised to be a new and efficient approach to cool-down for actors, and empirical measures can be developed to test the hypothesis in practice.

Cool-down and the actor as observer
A further approach to cool-down, which the actor can apply together with *Vedic* recitation as suggested above, or independent of it, follows equally from the model of consciousness proposed by *Vedanta*. One of the experiential characteristics of higher states of consciousness is that the experience of the contents of the waking state is separate from and independent of the experience of pure consciousness. Thus the pure consciousness, or true Self, is independent of the sensory perceptions, thoughts and actions of the ego, or small self. In such a higher state of consciousness, the actor will be able to bring her full attention to any task at hand, including the creation of the character, will not need to build up an excess of adrenalin to achieve a transition between daily life and performance mode, and will, as a result, not need to bridge a very wide gulf to get back to daily life after the performance. Meditation can prove a tool to achieve this state of consciousness; alternatively, the following workshop, consisting of four distinct phases, can serve the same purpose specifically in the theatre context.

Phase One: past, present and future
The purpose of the first phase is to enable participants to experience the difference between past, present and future, and the general tendency to be engaged with past and future at the expense of an awareness of the present. For the duration of the phase, the workshop

leader does not only run the activities as described below, but engages in certain actions that are apparently not related to the workshop, and which the participants will not notice because during this phase their attention is drawn to the past and the future, to the exclusion of the present. The exercise draws on the phenomenon of inattentional blindness discussed in psychology.

For the first exercise in this phase, the workshop leader (WL) asks participants to spend five minutes writing down in as much detail as possible what they did at a time five hours before the start of the workshop. The WL allows as much time as needed for this, and any further similar task. Once all participants have finished writing down their memories, the WL asks them to share what they have written down with a partner of their choice (for larger groups) or with the group as a whole (for smaller groups). If the WL selects the "sharing with a partner" approach, for uneven group numbers, one group should consist of three participants. Once the sharing has come to a close, the WL asks, if appropriate, for all participants to reconvene in one group, and asks all participants whether they expected that they would be asked to share with others their answer to the question of what they did five hours ago, and whether what they wrote down as their answer was in any way influenced by that expectation. Furthermore, the WL suggests that some participants may not have expected the request to share their response to the initial question. Did they read to the other(s) precisely what they had written down, or was what they said aloud different from what they had written down? In the discussion of this question the WL ensures that the participants become aware of the extent to which our action is influenced by what we believe other people might think of us.

In the next exercise of this phase of the workshop, the WL asks the participants to write down what they expect to be doing two hours after the end of the workshop. When the participants have completed this task, the WL asks them to share what they have written down with one or two partners of their choice, or with the group. At the end of the sharing, the WL asks again, as for the first exercise in this phase of the workshop, whether the expectation of sharing what they had written influenced their writing and / or what they eventually said to their partner or the group.

At the end of this phase of the workshop, the WL summarises that we tend to spend much time thinking about the past or planning the future, and those activities are governed, to some extent, by how we feel others might think about us. The WL also alerts the participants to his / her activities not related to the workshop, establishing how many participants noticed those and how many did not. Depending on the WL's assessment of the level of trust within the group, participants can reveal this anonymously if they choose, by commenting on a sheet of paper that the WL collects.

Phase Two: alertness and observation
While a tendency of being preoccupied with past and future was at the centre of the exercises in phase one, the present is central to phase two. The WL asks the participants to spend the next ten minutes observing themselves and their environment. They may talk to each other, about anything they like, they may look out of the window, they may walk around the venue in which the workshop space is located, on their own or with others. During those ten minutes the WL should stay in his / her seat, giving the participants the opportunity to be as unobserved from "authority" as they need. After ten minutes, the WL ensures all participants come back to the workshop venue and then asks them to share with the group as a whole whether it was easy or difficult to get into / be in observing mode? Were they able to maintain the observing mode throughout the ten minutes or did they slip back into non-observing mode. If that was the case, what made them aware that they had slipped? What was it like to be in an observing mode—how did it feel? It is important that in this discussion the WL does not give the impression that any kind of response suggests correct or incorrect behaviour of the participants. The aim is for participants to hear the full range of possible experiences in relation to observation, which might become theirs in due course.

In the second exercise of the second phase, the WL asks participants to share with the group a striking moment they remember from a performance of a play or screening of a film, and how they responded to that moment. The WL should ensure it is clear to the participants that the request is to share a strong moment in a fictional context, not a participant's real-life experience, even if such an experience may have felt like a scene in a play of film. In the discussion, the WL also ensures that the participants realise, as part of this process, that the material that strikes them tends to be very "dramatic" in an everyday sense: intense, fraught with emotions, and that the responses to that moment include a certain distance, or at least that there is the potential of distance as the material on stage or screen is not directly "them".

On completion of this exercise, the WL launches the third exercise of this second phase of the workshop with the request for participants to consider, for a few minutes, each on their own, an emotionally dense moment of their lives. The WL assures the participants that they will not be asked later to share their memories; indeed, they will be asked explicitly not to share them. After a few minutes the WL asks the participants whether they can perceive that moment as if they were a spectator in a theatre seeing this moment on stage in an excellent production, or as a moment in a good film?

Overall, the purpose of the second phase of the workshop is to enable participants to experience the present, and closely related to that: to develop the ability of observation; and thus of experiencing dense or tense moments in their lives, past, present and future, from the distance of the observer of a scene in a play or in a film.

While phases one and two of this workshop cover preliminaries, and have value to life beyond the specific context of cool-down for actors in the theatre, the third phase develops the insights gained in phases one and two further and applies them to the context of theatre.

Phase Three
Actors engage in whatever warm-up routine they have developed for themselves, then rehearse, directed ideally not by the WL but by a director so far not involved with the workshop, a scene from a play selected by the WL for its suitably high level of emotional intensity for all actors involved. This scenario can be changed to suit singers or musicians. If there is a mixed workshop, audition pieces can form the material the participants work on, for themselves. The key is a high level of emotional intensity in the material to be presented.

Following on from phases one and two (above), this approach should lead implicitly to some observation behaviour already during the rehearsal. The discussion after the end of phase three can confirm this or not.

After the rehearsal, which should take one hour, ideally there should be a performance to a real audience. Alternatively, phases one and two can happen before a real performance, followed by

Phase Four

After the performance the WL instructs actors to observe what is happening within them, emotions, feelings, and thoughts, physical sensations, to serve as cool-down.

Thus phases one and two are to prepare the ground, and phase three leads the workshop into a theatre-specific context, while phase four is the activity that performers can apply on their own after each performance independent of workshop context or workshop leader.

PART TWO: OPERA AND CONSCIOUSNESS

Chapter Five

Opera and Spirituality

In Part Two I introduce my thinking about the relationship between opera and consciousness. Chapter Five provides a general survey of this relationship, framed in terms of spirituality as one specific dimension of consciousness.

Introduction

The creation and impact of opera rely on four closely interwoven components: the libretto, the *mise en scène*, the music, and the singing. Those four combine to create the opera's contents, which cannot be found in any one of the four in isolation. For example, plots in many operas have been described as unrealistic, unlikely, overly dramatic or melodramatic, and very unbelievable. Nevertheless, people who like to attend the opera have a propensity of enjoying opera while ignoring those aspects that would most certainly ruin the prospects of success for a theatre play. The strength of the positive attitude of those who enjoy this art form is expressed aptly in the term used for people who attend opera regularly: they are identified as "opera lovers," which contrasts with the less emphatic terms of identification, "theatre-goers," or "concert-goers." Often opera lovers, theatre goers and concert-goers will also self-identify in those terms, while opera lovers are likely to be less happy to be identified with the less emphatic and less emotionally charged "goer", and theatre and concert goers might tend to be more uncomfortable to be tagged as theatre- or concert-lovers, because the association of "lover" with a predominance of emotion might go against their preference of being associated with the more neutral "goer" as indicative of a predominance of more intellectual-critical faculties, without the risk of being overcome by emotion and losing control.

Research into opera audiences has taken up this predominance of emotion in opera lovers' responses to opera, in particular, and music in general (including opera). For the field of music psychology, there has been increased interest in strong emotions in relation to music, physically manifested as, for example, chills, shivers down or up the spine, or an increase of the heart rate. Spiritual experiences feature among the range of strong emotions thus identified. It is on those that I want to focus in this chapter. Not only opera audiences report spiritual experiences: opera singers do so as well. Some contextual frameworks have been developed to explain such spiritual experiences, predominantly for audiences, but they are also relevant for singers. While the libretto is in many cases not likely to support the onset and development of spiritual experiences, some opera librettos might be argued to provide such support. In this chapter, I discuss spiritual experiences reported by singers and review the literature on spiritual experiences reported by audience members in relation to opera, proposing, along the way, relevant additions to the clarification of terminology for, and the explanation of, such experiences. Finally I add a section on the importance of *mise en scène* in relation to the potential of a libretto to induce and maintain spiritual experiences in opera.

Characteristics of singers' spiritual experiences

Opera singers' reports of extraordinary, desirable, spiritual experiences in relation to their singing cover several distinct categories. First, there is the experience of uniqueness. Thus, Teresa Berganza (b. 1935) says that "ultimately nothing can compare with the sensational experience when singing well, and we don't always, but during those rare, near-perfect evenings one almost touches heaven" (Matheopoulos 1991: 255). There are attempts to put those extraordinary experiences into context: Berganza explains, by way of comparison, that the "only thing that could compare with the sensation in terms of ecstasy is the actual moment of childbirth or one of those equally rare moments of rapture in love that occur once in a lifetime" (Matheopoulos 1991: 255). Janet Baker (b. 1933), too, provides an explanation for which criteria music must fulfil for her to experience it as at its greatest: "music at its greatest is for me an experience of the fourth dimension, that is, all human experience plus the extra one of *time*, past, present and future" (1982: 126).

The insight of the uniqueness of such spiritual experiences often coincides with the insight of their short-lived nature. Agnes Baltsa (b. 1944), for example, is filled with "fear and melancholy" because those experiences are "so transient. They are over in a flash and after a few minutes they become just memories (...) sometimes I wish we could hold on to them a little longer. I wish our art were less ephemeral" (Matheopoulos 1991: 235).

There is a tendency among singers to contextualise their extraordinary, spiritual experiences in religious terms. Berganza explains:

> We should therefore treat this gift from God [the voice] as sacred. If one thinks about it, there are very few singers in the world. Therefore, having a voice is clearly a gift. A gift to be used only when we feel in a position to give it everything we have and through it heal and put other people in touch with heaven, too. If I do not feel in a position to do this, I don't sing. (Matheopoulos 1991: 255)

This position is mirrored by Baker: "I believe my voice and power of communication through music were given to me by God, to be shared with others" (1982: xii). Tenor Johan Botha (b. 1965) reveals that he felt from a very young age that his voice and his calling were God-given, to make others happy with. A deeply religious person, he talks about his performances in terms of meetings with God, which transform every performance into a prayer (Harmer 2009).

Placido Domingo (b. 1941) takes the religious dimension of singing further when he discusses the way he feels about Wagner's opera *Parsifal*:

> As for the finale of this Act, where Parsifal brings back the spear to the knights, heals Amfortas and is able to unveil the grail and once more bestow its blessing on the knights, it is such a mystical moment that I don't know that I can find words to describe it. I feel as if God is about to come on stage, to bless and lift us all up higher, to a kind of resurrection. I *feel* the presence of God coming down to touch us all for a moment. And at the moment Parsifal bestows this blessing I find myself wishing I could reach out, embrace and bring peace to everyone, the audience and the whole world. It is a profoundly emotional experience (...) I must say that participating in this work— one of the greatest, if not the greatest ever written—in any way is a privilege. It brings you so close to God, to our faiths and beliefs. (Matheopoulos 2000: 215-216)

For sopranos and tenors in particular, the high notes, especially the high C, has particular potential for yielding a thrilling experience for both singer and audiences. Luciano Pavarotti (1935-2007) says:

> When singing high notes, I feel like a show jumper before a two-metres-plus bar (…) Stretched to my limits. Excited and happy, but with a strong undercurrent of fear. The moment I actually hit the note I almost lose consciousness. A physical, animal sensation seizes me. Then after it has been successfully negotiated, I regain control. (Matheopoulos 1989: 123)

An analysis of video and DVD material about achievements of high notes from the opera repertory reveals a range of common characteristics: on the high note itself, singers open not only their mouths wide, but also their eyes, which tend not to blink at least for the duration of the note. After the end of singing the high note, there is a combination of heavy breathing, reflecting both the aftermath of the strain and relief. It may take a while for the singers to close their mouth again, and many also close their eyes. Sometimes they visibly struggle to keep their composure, and on occasion burst into tears (Risi 2010).

Desirable extraordinary experiences extend from one singer to encompass all singers on stage at the time of the experience, and the audience as well. Matheopoulos quotes from, and comments on an interview with Montserrat Caballé (b. 1933):

> "I know this may sound strange to many people, an example of what I mean are those extra-special moments that occur from time to time in every artist's career, moments when you no longer feel you are on a stage making music but in a different dimension, inside, at one with music, and no longer aware of the act of singing or conscious of yourself or your body. The body is a concrete thing made up of physical matter. But when you are in this state of fusion with music, you are totally unaware of it. You feel light, weightless, and afterwards (…) you feel so heavy again". Sometimes during performances Caballé is aware of colleagues or conductors experiencing the same sensation "this sort of trance when all of us feel we are not wholly here, and suddenly it's over in a flash, we look into each other's eyes and know we've just woken up and are no longer in another world but down here, on the stage, making theatre. I don't know why this happens, or how to explain it, but I know that it does and that audiences feel it, too. One of the worst things that can happen at such moments, when you are suspended in a dimension beyond, out of time and space, is applause. (1991: 61)

Anna Tomova Sintov (b. 1941) emphasises the need for opera singers to remember, while they are on stage, that "we are mere instruments in the realisation of a work and that our function is to merge with our colleagues until we are at one with them, the conductor, and through the latter's imagination with the composer" (Matheopoulos 1991: 221). Sherrill Milnes (b. 1935) provides this report of the most extraordinary, spiritual, of performances he participated in (a performance of Verdi's *Otello* at the Vienna State Opera):

> Right from the start we felt a sort of electricity in the air, the feeling that tonight the stars are in the right place—a Sternstunde as it's rightly called in German—and by the end of our Act II Otello-Iago duet the place exploded! It went berserk! At the end, we took our bows, the soli, the tutti, and half an hour of forty to fifty curtain calls after, we were still there. By then we were all getting tired of smiling, the way that you do at wedding receptions, and finally, an hour and a half and 101 curtain calls later, we got away! (Matheopoulos 2000: 178-9)

Barbara Bonney (b. 1956) describes the spiritual magic of a performance of *Der Rosenkavalier* by Richard Strauss during the Vienna State Opera's tour of Japan in 1994:

> (...) it took off in such a magical way that we all felt that this is it. Now we can all be run over by a truck because we have done it. This evening we made this work come alive in the way we feel Strauss wanted. Nothing can ever be like this performance. Even the remaining performances of the run under the same near-ideal conditions were a disappointment after what we had experienced on that fourth evening. (Matheopoulos 1998: 7)

The extraordinary, spiritual experiences reported by opera singers affect them profoundly. Here is a sufficiently long report by Baker to serve as an example.

> I believe my voice and power of communication through music were given to me by God, to be shared with others. This I have tried to do, but it has been with a sense of duty rather than of joy. Recently, through the help of close friends (...) I myself have come to understand and participate in the joy of performing. This is something new to me, and in the sense that I have been relieved, both of the responsibility for the end result and of the terrible fear, which has dogged me all my life, it is a miracle. I have reached a point where I feel myself to be an empty vessel. There must always be a personality

involved in any human action, but I now stand out there, silent within, and allow the music to speak through me. It used to worry me greatly that there are always people in an audience who are unmoved, unreached by what I do; I have always wanted *everyone* to understand my own particular message. Now, I realise that this is simply not my concern. All I have to do is prepare myself musically, physically and psychologically for a performance, and then stand aside to allow the music to speak for itself. It is interesting to notice from audience reactions in a hall, from people's words to me afterwards, and from letters received through the post, that the reaction I now produce is much more violent than before. Those "for me" are more so, those "against" likewise. I see this as an extremely positive situation. (1982: xii)

Explanatory frameworks

Conceptual frameworks for making sense of such spiritual experiences have been developed in the context of Transpersonal Psychology and consciousness studies. In Transpersonal Psychology, Abraham Maslow developed the concept of peak experiences, which represent rare and transforming moments in peoples' lives. The qualities of the extraordinary spiritual experiences discussed above are precisely those characteristic of peak experiences: uniqueness (Berganza), the short-lived nature of the experience (Baltsa), the religious connotations (Berganza, Baker, Botha, Domingo), the experience of unity (Caballé, Tomova Sintov, Milnes, Bonney), and the profound impact on the singer (Baker). In the context of consciousness studies, the experiences make sense within the framework of the model of consciousness proposed by Indian *Vedanta* philosophy in terms of higher states of consciousness: as the frequency of the experience of higher states of consciousness increases, so does the clarity of the experience, and its depth. To a person initially unfamiliar with experiences of higher states of consciousness, they will come across as unique. Initially, at least, they are short-lived. Their very nature is such that many people experiencing them may be able to do so best in religious terms, as there is currently not much of an alternative. The experience of unity is typical of higher states of consciousness within the *Vedanta* model, as the highest level of experience is characterised by the very unity of the experiencer with everything and everyone in the world (Meyer-Dinkgräfe 2005).

Research into strong emotional responses of opera audiences

Compared with little research into peak experiences or altered, higher states of consciousness as reported by opera singers, more research has been undertaken to explore and explain similar, spiritual experiences of audiences. The following passages will summarize this research, much of which is in the context of the general impact of music, including opera but not exclusive to it. In 1980, Panzarella published a study based on his PhD dissertation, in which he proposed a phenomenology of aesthetic experiences in the music and visual arts areas on the basis of Maslow's concept of peak experiences. The results are based on 103 responses from among 2,000 subjects initially invited to participate in the study. They were asked to report on "intense joyous experiences" of listening to music or looking at visual art (Panzarella 1980: 71). In addition, they provided information about age, gender, educational background and other items, and completed questionnaires to establish personality traits that could be correlated with the responses to the peak experience question. The ability of music, including opera, to lead to joyous experiences in their listeners has never been in doubt, but Panzarella's study was one of the first to put such insights into a conceptual framework.

In later years, Csikzentmihalyi's concept of *flow* was added to the characteristics of peak experiences. It is a "state of consciousness where people become totally immersed in an activity, and enjoy it immensely" (Bakker 2005: 26). Bakker studied flow in the context of theories of emotional crossover or emotional contagion—how and why "positive and negative emotions can crossover from one person to another" (29)—and found that the peak experience of flow does indeed cross over from teachers to students. It is likely (a hypothesis, in empirical terms) that the occurrence of flow (or other peak experiences) in opera spectators crosses over to other spectators, and that similar crossovers take place among opera singers and between singers and spectators in both directions. Crossover can thus be related to the experience of unity as described by opera singers, as one possible way in which such unity can emerge.

Most recently, peak experiences or higher states of consciousness in music, including opera, have been discussed in terms of *strong experiences with music* (SEM). This research has been pioneered by Alf Gabrielsson of Uppsala University. Subjects were asked to describe "the strongest, most intense experiences of music that you have ever had. Please describe your experiences and reactions in as much detail as possible" (2010: 551). Supplementary questions were whether this experience occurred only on the first time of listening to the music, or as well on subsequent occasions of listening; how the respondent felt "before and after the experience", "what the experience had meant in a long-term perspective" (551), the cause of the experience, and whether such experiences were encountered in situations that had nothing to do with music. In total, 953 people participated in the project, 250 of those provided more than one report, so that the analysis is based on 1354 reports (552). The analysis takes the shape of a descriptive system for SEM (SEM-DS), with seven basic categories, each with a different number of sub-categories. The basic categories are: general characteristics, physical reactions and behaviours, perception, cognition, feelings/emotion, existential and transcendental aspects and personal and social aspects.

The experience categories of the singers discussed above fit into the SEM-DS. Uniqueness features among the general characteristics, as does the fact that the SEM are hard to describe. The experience of unity comes under the cognition category, within the sub-category "changed experience of situation, body-mind, time-space, part-whole" (557), religious experience is a sub-category of the basic category of "existential and transcendental aspects," which also includes spirituality. The impact SEM have on the singers is represented in the "new insights, possibilities, needs" sub-category of the basic category "personal and social aspects."

While Gabrielsson points out that the number of psychological studies into what he calls SEM is very small, and calls for more work to be done in this important but neglected field (2010: 571), it is useful to highlight some of the other findings and debates. One relates to the study of thrill (also referred to as chill or frisson), defined by Goldstein as "subtle nervous tremor caused by intense emotion or excitement (as pleasure, fear etc.), producing as slight shudder or tingling through the body (1980: 126). He found that thrills are typically described as tingling sensations starting, and spreading out from the neck. A strong thrill spreads to the scalp or via the spine to arms and legs. Some thrills are accompanied by visible goose bumps on the arms, or by weeping, sighing or the feeling of a lump in the throat. Panksepp provides an explanation for the relatively small number of studies into this phenomenon: "Such as enquiry has, no doubt, been neglected because of the subjective nature of the phenomenon and perhaps also from the suspicion that chills will turn out to be quite idiosyncratic and variable from individual to individual" (1995: 173). He noted the importance of familiarity with the piece of music triggering the chill (his preferred term), and sought to identify aspects of the music itself that may serve as triggers, finding that sad or melancholic music is more likely to lead to chill effects than cheerful music. The relation between expectation (closely related to the aspect of familiarity) and thrills was further analysed by Huron and Margulis (2010) with reference to what they call "frisson". They summarise Panksepp's explanation for frisson as follows:

> the emotional power of the frisson lies in the receptiveness and receptivity of the auditory system to infant distress calls. Since the principal caregivers in most species are mothers, females would be expected to be more attentive to separation distress calls, and so would be expected to be more reactive to music-induced frisson (2010: 597-8)

A disadvantage of Panksepp's theory is that it does not account for frisson not induced by music. Huron developed his *contrastive valence* theory to address this issue. He argues that frisson arises when an "initial negative response is superseded by a neutral or positive appraisal" (2010: 599). In the context of opera, this would mean that we perceive the frisson-inducing element, probably most typically a tenor's or soprano's high C, initially, for milliseconds, as potentially threatening. However, almost immediately we recognise them as aspects of music, not threatening, and the physiological responses that has been initiated over the first few milliseconds after perceiving the sound, are now perceived as something pleasant rather than unpleasant. Such an effect is likely to happen repeatedly because the initially evoked defensive reaction is resistant to habituation. Huron also argues that "large violations of expectation" can lead not only to chills, thrills or frisson, but also to laughter and awe (2010: 600). Awe, in turn, can be related to spirituality, in so far as awe is a frequent reaction to a spiritual experience, and becomes part of it.

Research suggests that the stronger the emotional arousal described by the subjects in studies, the stronger the physiological arousal (Rickard 2004). However, the causal link between music and emotion is controversial. Thus Konečni et al. sought to establish whether there is a causal link between music and emotion, and came to doubt the existence of such a link—a finding in opposition to that of Lundquist et al. (2009). It is beyond doubt that music has a strong impact on the listener; the centre of the debate is on how to conceptualize that experience. According to Konečni et al., listening to sad music may not induce sadness, but may, instead, lead, in the listener, to imagine sadness. In response to this finding, Konečni developed a theory of *aesthetic trinity*, "involving the responses of thrills/chills, being moved, and aesthetic awe" (2008: 305). Being moved, in this conceptualisation of the impact of music on the listener, is the predominant response. Aesthetic awe encompasses being moved, is much less frequent, and is considered "the ultimate human aesthetic state: a response to the sublime stimulus that—among other attributes—includes colossal size" (2008: 305). This is the essence of spiritual experience.

In summary: there has not been much empirical research into the relation of music, including opera, and emotions. What research there has been seems to agree that emotions reported in relation to music go along with specific physiological patterns, and there seems to be a causal relation between the intensity of reported emotional arousal and corresponding intensity of physiological arousal. The causal link between the nature of the music and the nature of the emotion is in doubt, as it may be possible, for example, that the allegedly aroused emotion may in fact be the imagined experience of an emotion rather than the emotion itself. A considerable proportion of the responses reported as allegedly triggered, or at least related to music, are such that they go beyond conventional categories of emotions: they are spiritual in nature. While some researchers try to keep them under a widened concept of emotions, such as the SEM-DS, others try to move away from reference to emotions in favour of concepts such as "being moved" for the "normal" range of responses to music, and "aesthetic awe" to capture peak experiences. Thus, while there is consensus that there are experiences in relation to music (and that includes opera) that go beyond the norm, that are extraordinary, strong, exceptional, rare, and spiritual, there is no consensus as to what to call them and how to explain them.

Expanding the explanatory framework

It is necessary, based on the findings summarised above, to seek to further enhance ways of understanding the nature and the causes of extraordinary (desirable, enjoyable, blissful, etc.), spiritual experiences while performing in, or receiving opera—the latter can take the forms of attending a performance of opera in an opera house or concert hall, or listening to opera at home on CD, or watching a DVD at home, or attending a live broadcast in the cinema. In this section of the chapter I want to explore conceptually a range of possibilities to enhance our understanding of the nature of extraordinary experiences in opera performance and reception. A methodological note will help to contextualise my approach in this endeavour. What follows is in many ways an extended contemplation of the issues raised above, freely tying in interdisciplinary approaches and my own experience as an opera-goer. The end result offers an enhancement of our understanding of spirituality and opera, but is as much a beckoning toward further exploration as a final conclusion.

Vedic linguistics

In this section I want to explore how we can understand better opera's spiritual dimension for singers and spectators/listeners alike from a holistic perspective, taking all aspects of opera together: singing, music, *mise en scène*, and plot. In Chapter Three (page 129f) I introduced the Vedic model of language, with its four distinct levels language, spoken (*vaikhari*), thought, (*madhyama*), finest relative (*pashyanti*) and absolute, on the level of pure consciousness (*para*). Malekin and Yarrow describe *para* and *pashyanti* as follows:

> *Pashyanti* is pre-verbal, marked by unity of subject and object, non-discursive, immediate, devoid of any sense of spacetime, a holistic cognition. *Para* is prior even to *pashyanti*, a first stirring towards speech, a sense of "something to be said", and arises out of unconditioned mind (non-contingent consciousness). (2000)

Communication, according to this model of language, does not work according to the currently accepted sender-receiver scheme, with the receiver obliged to decode the sent code. Rather, when the hearer hears a spoken word, he or she remembers the contents of the word, which has existed already on the level of the hearer's pure consciousness.

I propose to extend this model for spoken language to the language of opera as a whole. The acts of creation of the component parts of opera, on their own and together (music, singing, libretto, *mise en scène*), arise in specific relation to the level of pure consciousness: more or less of pure consciousness is integrated into the creation, depending on the degree the composer, singer, librettist or director and scenographer is able to create from a higher state of consciousness. The more an opera has been created from its composer and librettist's higher states of consciousness—that is from the *para* and *pashyanti* levels of consciousness—the more the production team will be able to experience the same higher levels of consciousness that are inherent in the opera when working on a production and when presenting performances of the production. The more of the spiritual levels inherent in an opera the production team are able to translate into the production, the more the spectators will be able to perceive them, leading in turn to their own spiritual experiences.

Perception of the spiritual potential of opera and production, for production team and spectators, does not depend merely on cognitive recognition of codes, but, as for spoken language, the language of opera triggers in those encountering that language (production team, singers, musicians, conductor, and spectators or listeners) a memory of the contents contained in the language which already existed, and exists beyond any dimension of time, on the level of *para* or pure consciousness. What conventional linguistics refers to in terms of understanding is limited to intellectual, cognitive meaning. In comparison, contents on the level of *para* or pure consciousness is all-encompassing, holistic, thus including not only the meaning that literary criticism of the libretto might elucidate, not only an understanding of the music that is the subject of musicology, and not only the sensual dimension of the *mise en scène*. Rather, contents on the level of *para* or pure consciousness includes the entire field of non-conceptual and non-sensual, or even better, trans-conceptual and trans-sensual impact of opera relating to feelings, emotions, intuition, and pure consciousness itself.

Sex, eros and femininity
With reference to a combination of Lacanian psychoanalysis and neuroscience, Zuccarini argues that the nature of the pleasure experienced by the listener/audience in response to opera is erotic

(2008), and that the peak of that experience is an operatic orgasm or *jouissance*, triggered by the voice that in such moments separates from contents and becomes pure sound. This argument conflates eros and sexuality, while more attention to the nuances of those concepts yields better results for the enquiry into the nature of strong emotions and experiences of spirituality triggered by opera. Eros in the Platonic sense is the ultimately unfulfilled and unrealisable yearning for ideal beauty. In this context, sexuality is of a lower order than eros: it can be fulfilled and realised in the physical encounter with another person's body. The strong emotions and spiritual experiences potentially generated by opera fall within the realm of eros, since all components of opera conventionally strive to combine to create beauty on a grand scale: the impressive environment of the opera house, the size of the stage, the splendour of the set and costume design, and the nature of the music and the singing. Such beauty of form and content together has the power, in Platonic terms, of reminding the soul of, and thus guiding it towards, the ideal of beauty, whose attainment is the ultimate aim of life overall. In terms of *Vedanta*, the elements of opera on their own and even more so taken together are perceived as beautiful, and create the experience of beauty; that experience serves as a vehicle for consciousness not only to perceive individual and collective beauty, but to transcend those perceptions so as to allow the experience of pure consciousness.

The principle of beauty in relation to opera, together with a major appeal of opera to the emotions rather than intellect, both as far as music and plot are concerned, lead to a further aspect of understanding the spiritual dimension of opera more comprehensively: opera as a predominantly feminine art form. According to St. Germain, one of the Ascended Masters in theosophy and other esoteric traditions, the purpose for souls to be incarnated as humans on the planet earth is for them to be able to develop the feminine side of their nature, irrespective of whether they are born as man or woman (2004). Opera thus helps humans develop their feminine side in a way that assists their spiritual development. Below, I return to this point and tie it into the overall discussion.

Mise en scène
Opera is sometimes presented in concert format, with only orchestra and singers (often using the score). While still impressive, it is not the

"real thing": it lacks the production aspect comprising set, costume, light and sound design, and the singers performing their parts in an arrangement' on stage developed by the director. In most operas, the orchestral score and the music for the singers have been written to support the plot, and vice versa. Music, singing and plot thus form a unity, carrying the range of emotions characteristic of any given opera, and aiming to convey those emotions to the audience. This insight might suggest that a production is most likely to achieve the aim of deepest impact on the audience if it manages to tell the opera's story at the opera's own level. Take, for example, a production of Wagner's romantic opera *Lohengrin*. Here is a plot summary, provided by the Metropolitan Opera (New York) website:

> ACT I. Antwerp, c. 900s. On the banks of the Scheldt, a Herald announces King Heinrich, who asks Count Telramund to explain why the Duchy of Brabant is torn by strife and disorder. Telramund accuses his ward, Elsa, of having murdered her brother, Gottfried, heir to Brabant's Christian dynasty. (Gottfried was actually enchanted by the evil Ortrud, whom Telramund has wed.) When Elsa is called to defend herself, she relates a dream of a knight in shining armor who will save her. The herald calls for the defender, but only when Elsa prays does the knight appear, magically drawn in a boat by a swan. He betroths himself to her on condition that she never ask his name or origin. Defeating Telramund in combat, the newcomer establishes the innocence of his bride.
>
> Act II. Before dawn in the castle courtyard, Ortrud and the lamenting Telramund swear vengeance. When Elsa appears serenely in a window, Ortrud attempts to sow distrust in the girl's mind, preying on her curiosity, but Elsa innocently offers the scheming Ortrud friendship. Inside, while the victorious knight is proclaimed guardian of Brabant, the banned Telramund furtively enlists four noblemen to side with him against his newfound rival. At the cathedral entrance, Ortrud and Telramund attempt to stop the wedding — she by suggesting that the unknown knight is in fact an impostor, he by accusing Elsa's bridegroom of sorcery. Though troubled by doubt, Elsa reiterates her faith in the knight before they enter the church, accompanied by King Heinrich.
>
> ACT III. Alone in the bridal chamber, Elsa and her husband express their love until anxiety and uncertainty at last compel the bride to ask the groom who he is and whence he has come. Before he can reply, Telramund and his henchmen burst in. With a cry, Elsa hands the knight his sword, with which he kills Telramund. Ordering the nobles to bear the body to the king, he sadly tells Elsa he will meet her later to answer her questions.

Escorting Elsa and the bier to the Scheldt, the knight tells the king he cannot now lead the army against the Hungarian invaders. He explains that his home is the temple of the Holy Grail at distant Monsalvat, to which he must return; Parsifal is his father, and Lohengrin is his name. He bids farewell and turns to his magic swan. Now Ortrud rushes in, jubilant over Elsa's betrayal of the man who could have broken the spell that transformed her brother into a swan. But Lohengrin's prayers bring forth Gottfried in place of his vanished swan, and after naming the boy ruler of Brabant, Lohengrin disappears, led by the dove of the Grail. Ortrud perishes, and Elsa, calling for her lost husband, falls lifeless to the ground. (2010)

If the *mise en scène* created around this plot chooses to take Wagner's aspirational intent seriously, its visual, intellectual, symbolic and kinaesthetic aspects will work together to create spiritual experiences, including their physical expressions such as frisson. My argument here supports the view expressed earlier regarding the disadvantage of Panksepp's theory of frisson: it is not only music that has the strong potential of evoking this experience.

In evoking the religious and spiritual contexts so evident in the plot, which are, furthermore, reflected in the music and should serve as a blueprint for the *mise en scène*, Wagner clearly sought to create a religious feeling in those involved with the opera as performers and as spectators. Assuming that a religious feeling in performer or spectator represents an expression of a higher state of consciousness, Wagner thus sought, at least implicitly, to raise the state of consciousness of performers and spectators. Domingo's account of his response to *Parsifal*, discussed above (page 147), confirms the potential also inherent in *Lohengrin*. The plot of *Lohengrin*, as succinctly summarised above, provides an imaginative production team with an abundance of rich opportunities for varied and diverse interpretation within its own terms, as a medieval fairy tale (as in the 1977 Elijah Moshinsky production at the Royal Opera Covent Garden) or a timeless piece of depth psychology (as in the 2006 Baden Baden Festspielhaus production by Nikolaus Lehnhoff).

In other words, there is ultimately no need for radical interpretations that deconstruct the plot, the meaning carried by the plot, or seek to update the contents to make it, allegedly, more meaningful to a contemporary audience, or to younger audience members. Such justifications either sell a director's ideas under a false pretext, or do serious injustice to the abilities and sensibilities of today's opera audience, no matter what age. It is the very potential of the plot and *mise en scène* for inducing religious and spiritual experiences that makes it so clear to spectators and critics that a production is not cooperating with Wagner's aspirational intent. I have described productions where the potential of the plot was not fulfilled: Jones's 2009 Bavarian State Opera production of *Lohengrin*, and Herheim's 2009 production of the same opera for the Berlin Staatsoper unter den Linden (see page 98).

Conclusion: opera and spirituality

In conclusion, I now seek to bring together the individual strands discussed in this chapter to present a picture of opera and spirituality that encompasses the full range from the universe to the individual. On a universal level, in the Divine Plan of the God and Goddess, Saint Germain tells us, planet earth has the purpose of allowing souls to develop their feminine side by way of incarnating as a human being on earth. One of the ways created by humans themselves to facilitate this development of the feminine aspects of every human being's nature is opera with its emphasis on the feminine elements of emotion and beauty. It is part of the Divine Plan that different humans will best respond to different means of developing the feminine side of their nature, therefore it is the case that opera does not appeal to everyone, nor is it necessary.

Opera is a whole, which is more than the sum of its parts—plot, libretto, score, music, singing and *mise en scène*. As a whole it, and its constituent parts, affect the participant (orchestra, conductor, singers, and spectators) in every single performance in a potentially holistic, spiritual way. All opera has that potential. In principle, the extent to which that potential is tapped and put into action and practice depends on the extent to which the component parts are carried out in spiritual terms. The range of that extent is quite wide, as the number of supporters and detractors of any one singer, conductor, or opera, among opera-lovers, will confirm. Depending on what any one opera lover needs, in terms of spiritual development and according to what the Divine Plan has determined for them individually, they will like the interpretation of the score by von Karajan or by Solti, will prefer the tenor voice of Ben Heppner or Klaus Florian Vogt, and the production by Nikolaus Lehnhoff or Stefan Herheim.

A holistic understanding of how opera creates its spiritual impact is possible with reference to the *Vedic* model of language: combined together, all aspects of any particular performance of opera may stir, in the pure consciousness of the musician, conductor, singer and spectator, an intuitive glimpse of the eternal ideal of beauty that the genre potentially offers—an experience which is available at a level of consciousness independent of time.

From the holistic level we proceed to the individual level. Those two levels exist in mutual interdependence, not at all in opposition to each other. On the individual level, the spiritual experiences of the singers, as well as research into the impact of music, including that of opera, on an audience, are relevant. I discussed both earlier in the chapter, within their respective explanatory frameworks of music psychology, transpersonal psychology and consciousness studies. The *mise en scène*, finally, has its own role to perform among the constituent parts of opera that can make the experience of opera spiritual. Future research can explore any level of the argument presented in this chapter further, in theoretical and empirical contexts and terms.

Chapter Six

Spiritual Aspects of Operatic Singing:
Klaus Florian Vogt

"Time is different during opera. You live before and after. During the performance itself time stands still."
"Wenn nicht jetzt, wann denn dann? / If not now, when then?"
(Klaus Florian Vogt)

Introduction
The singing of German tenor Klaus Florian Vogt (b. 1970) initially puzzled, and continues to fascinate those who hear his voice on stage and through transmissions and recordings. In this chapter I provide a brief biography of Vogt, followed by an account, based on interviews with Vogt (including my own) on how he relates to his major roles, his voice, his acting and experiences with director's theatre, his way of preparing for a role in rehearsals and on a day of performance, how he relates his experience of singing to that of flying a plane, political views on the need for opera in the regions, the differences between singing in a fully staged opera and an aria recital, how he experiences singing, and the impact on it of orchestra and conductor, magic moments and anecdotes of unexpected events in performance. These two sections provide sufficient information to allow the readers to form their own image of Vogt. In the third section, I address the reception of Vogt's voice and singing in the media, and provide a context of spirituality to account further for the exceptional nature of Vogt's voice and singing; here I also relate information provided in the first two sections to the development and expression of spirituality.

Biography
Klaus Florian Vogt was born in 1970 in Heide, Schleswig Holstein, Germany. He has five siblings. His father had embarked on studies of music before changing courses to study medicine instead. He became a GP, but maintained his keen interest in music, leading all of his six children to appreciate music and play instruments, in a way that allowed them to discover the enjoyment of learning to play music. Vogt got his instrument, the horn, on his 10th birthday: his father had always wanted to found a wind quintet, but had difficulties finding a suitable hornist (Bscher 2009). Vogt enjoyed playing the horn so much that in due course he studied it in Hannover and Hamburg. Then he auditioned for the Philharmonisches Staatsorchester Hamburg, which, in addition to symphony concerts, plays for all the opera and ballet performances at the Staatsoper in Hamburg. He was accepted, and after a customary probationary year, he received the official letter from the cultural authorities informing him that his position with the orchestra, as deputy principal horn, was now for life (Bscher 2009).

At that time, he was not at all interested in singing; he had joined youth orchestras, rather than youth choirs (Vogt 2010 b). He was introduced to the world of singing through his girlfriend, later wife, Silvia Krüger, but initially that ability to see behind the curtain alienated rather than attracted him. Vogt was suspicious of the world of singers, especially the distance between stage and orchestra pit which he considered psychologically or mentally quite vast (Vogt 2010b). He took flying lessons with the first money he earned in the orchestra.

For a family celebration, Vogt and his wife rehearsed the *Cat Duet* by Rossini (with the male part written for a baritone), and those present suggested that the sound of Vogt's voice was good enough to merit having it checked by a professional singing teacher. The teacher told him that he was a tenor, not a baritone, and that he had considerable potential. His wife maintains that initially she took his singing more seriously than he himself, reminding him of the need to practise (Bscher 2009). On the side of his full time post in the orchestra, Vogt took up studying singing at the Hochschule für Musik in Lübeck, an hour's drive from Hamburg. He did not tell his colleagues in the orchestra anything about his studies (Vogt 2010b), but one day a decision had to be taken.

In 1997 he made the decision to abandon his career with the Staatsorchester in Hamburg, on the condition that he might return to his post within one year—a deal agreed by the entire orchestra (Bscher 2009). The decision was a difficult one. On the one hand he has a secure position, for life, and he loved his profession, having worked hard throughout his studies to get there. On the other hand, having reached the position he had, there was not much further he could progress, and the prospect of serving in the orchestra for another 30 odd years was frustrating. Looking for alternatives was one decision; finding the alternative and actually resigning from his post was a different matter altogether (Vogt 2010b). He took up a one year contract with the Landestheater Schleswig Holstein in Flensburg, singing operetta and light opera, including Tamino in Mozart's *The Magic Flute*. This move involved a loss in income (from around 8000 DM at the orchestra to 3000 DM at the theatre [4000 Euro to 1500 Euro] per month), and a fundamental risk (Bscher 2009). It also felt sad, Vogt reports, to leave behind such a major period of his life (Vogt 2010b), and one which he had worked hard for to achieve and thoroughly enjoyed (Vogt 2011b).

From the next season, 1998/99, he was a full time company member of the Staatsoper in Dresden. Since 2003 he has been freelance, making his debuts at major opera houses across the world: the Metropolitan Opera in New York (Lohengrin, 2006), La Scala, Milan, as Lohengrin in 2007, the Vienna State Opera (2007), Bavarian State Opera, Munich (2007), and sang Parsifal in Hamburg (2004), where he was welcomed back warmly by his former colleagues in the orchestra. In 2007 he stepped in at short notice in Katharina Wagner's production of *Die Meistersinger*, at Bayreuth, after the originally cast Robert Dean Smith withdrew due to disagreements with the production concept. Vogt repeated this role there in 2008, 2009 and 2010, followed by Lohengrin in 2011 and 2012.

He lives with his family, wife and four sons, in the north of Germany, very close to the North Sea, where he likes to take long walks with his family and their dogs (Bscher 2009). His sons are developing an interest in the arts, the piano, film and acting (Vogt 2011c).

Vogt on Vogt

The voice

Vogt maintains that while there was, by necessity, a certain natural gift for singing, his professional career started with a few high notes, and the rest was sheer determination and hard work. He seeks to develop an appropriate technique that allows him to sing fully with his voice (Vogt 2010b). He still works with a singing teacher, Irmgard Boas, which helped him not to get a hoarse voice within minutes without knowing why, and which now allows him to sustain long parts such as Lohengrin or Stolzing (Vogt 2010b, Bscher 2009).

When it comes to the challenges of singing Wagner, i.e., long parts over many hours, Vogt is able to differentiate, most probably an important condition for success. Whereas in *Lohengrin*, the majority of singing happens in the third act, in *Meistersinger*, Walther sings across all three acts, with much singing already in act one I, culminating in the rejected song. While act two is relatively brief for Walther, the kind of singing required here is quite dramatic; for the third act he has to return to the very lyrical mode of singing required for the development of the prize song, and the song itself then develops into dramatic singing at its end (Vogt 2010b). In addition to the individual requirements that vary from role to role, the framework of the opera house adds to the challenge. In Bayreuth, for example, Vogt has to take into account the need to maintain alertness and readiness to perform across very lengthy intervals in between Acts (Vogt 2008).

Whereas many singers in the Heldentenor line may have started as baritones, Vogt trained as a tenor from the start, and his first parts, at the Landestheater Flensburg, were in the light lyrical line, followed by some operetta. Vogt believes that operetta has been underrated: operetta, too, has big arias, accompanied by a large orchestra, and the tessitura is similar to that of many of the Helden-roles (Vogt 2008). For Vogt, operetta parts prepared his voice for Heldentenor parts, and he used them as tests to assess where his voice was going (Vogt 2008). He refers to predecessors who combine singing Wagner and operetta (Rene Kollo comes to mind, a singer whom Vogt expressly mentions as a colleague who impresses him considerably [Vogt 2010b]). Against this background it is important to note that Vogt expressly seeks to maintain the lyrical qualities that are always part of so-called Helden-roles. For him, singing Wagner is not the same as roaring, yelling, or speaking, but demands beautiful singing (Vogt 2010a). Ultimately, for example, Lohengrin is not that far distant from Tamino in Mozart's *Zauberflöte*: Tamino, too, has dramatic passages, such as the scene with the speaker in act two (Vogt 2010b).

A massive orchestra sound can tempt a singer to do all he can to persist in relation to it. Vogt does not consider this an appropriate attitude. It results in considerable wear and tear of energy, with some notes at the end of a performance sounding not as beautiful as they should. If he encounters conductors intent on a volume that he considers inappropriate for his voice he just won't cooperate—he won't set his volume against that of the orchestra, because in that contest he is bound to fail (Vogt 2008). In his experience, if he offers a more differentiated approach, or a piano (often in places where it is noted in Wagner's score), orchestras and conductors tend to accept this, possibly not having asked for it in the first place because they did not expect a tenor to be able to offer a more lyrical approach to a given passage (Vogt 2010b). Vogt emphasises that "lyrical" does not mean, as some myth has it, to sing with only half the voice. Singing with a strong voice but with distinct arches is also "lyrical" in his view. The size of the orchestra is not at all a disadvantage: if sixteen violins play piano, the impact is much more beautiful than if that same sound is created by eight violins (Vogt 2008). This is the essence of this music, its magic, which is ruined by volume.

Based on the success he had with lyrical parts, Vogt tested his ability for more dramatic parts initially with opera in which the more dramatic tenor part does not cause so much of a stir as in Wagner operas (a new tenor in a major Wagner role, almost in any Wagner role, come to think of it, will cause a stir. A new tenor in a tenor role in an opera that is relatively unknown is much less likely to cause a stir). For example, Vogt sang a part in *Es War Einmal* by Alexander von Zemlinsky, and *Schwanda der Dudelsackpfeifer* by Jaromir Weinberger. Those parts, and others like them, allowed him to explore whether he was able to sing in a sustained composition, with the need to maintain one's readiness all the time, and to preserve an appropriate level of freshness of voice even by the end of the opera—all in contrast to operas that rely on individual arias. Vogt observed how the voice worked in such roles, what it did, how he felt at the end of a performance in such a part, or on the day after that (Vogt 2010a). In parallel, he further mastered his singing technique. In due course he sang his first Lohengrin (Erfurt, 2002), which he considers a further stage in this learning process, which is ongoing.

He is aware that his body needs sufficient time to regenerate, comparable to a sportsman who cannot engage in competition after competition without breaks. His ideal is 40-50 performances a year, affordable at an evening salary that is more than his monthly salary with the orchestra. He does find it difficult, however, to reject interesting offers over and above this self-set limit (Bscher 2009). Vogt is aware of the high expectations that any performance brings with it. He tries to keep the pressure of such expectations at bay, just as much as the warnings about the failures of major singers in specific roles or passages of roles (Bscher 2009).

He is also aware that his voice changes, and that in particular the middle range of the voice is improving, adjusting to the needs. As a result, the range of possibility of what he can achieve with his voice in the lower and higher registers also improves, because the middle register represents the link between the other two. As long as he was searching around in the middle register, as was the case for Vogt certainly earlier on in his career, the more difficult singing was, especially in the lower register, but also in the higher one. The middle register is developing further, establishes itself, and becomes more comfortable. As a result, the lower and higher registers are also becoming more comfortable (Vogt 2011a).

The way Vogt experiences his voice is initially and mainly through a process of sensing (Erfühlungsprozess), which takes place not limited to the throat as the seat of the vocal cords, but throughout the body. The entire body contributes to a complete sound. Vogt is aware, consequently, that it is very difficult to sing if he is even only a little ill. Then the body does not really want to support the singing. He senses difficulties, or inadequacies of his voice in this way, and then, or thus, also hears them. On many occasions, it feels worse for him than it sounds to others. If such a feeling comes up, Vogt takes note and addresses the issues in his daily practice. He realises what the feeling should be like, and seeks to re-create that feeling on every occasion of singing. As the voice develops, there will always be irritations and the need to reassess and adjust: the process of the development of the voice is a long and arduous one (Vogt 2011a).

For Vogt, playing the horn has links to singing—starting with the idea that wind instrumentalists seek to make their instruments "sing". In addition, breathing is important in playing wind instruments; thus the body is used to make music, and the player gets used to concepts and related practices related to breath, such as support and phrasing. The main difference is that what the singer hears himself is different from what the others hear. "You can learn only what a tone must feel like" (Vogt 2010b, 2011a). In particular, the horn allowed Vogt to get used to the aspects of the instrument and of music in general that are unpredictable. Thus, playing the horn and learning to sing professionally complemented each other for a certain time, before they ruled each other out (Vogt 2010b). These days he plays the horn only occasionally, and while he gets used to it quickly, he admits that he does not have the stamina any more required for playing the horn professionally—a very physical activity that requires regular practice and training that his singing career does not allow him time to engage in (Vogt 2010a).

The impact of orchestras and conductors
The relationship between Vogt and the orchestra can depend to a large extent on the conductor, but can just as well depend on the orchestra itself. There are orchestras that make him feel comfortable and integrated right from the start, and he realises that the colleagues listen to him. On the other hand, there are orchestras where the musicians do not listen when he is singing, where they ignore his singing. On those occasions in particular, the role of the conductor to connect the singer and the orchestra is important. Some conductors are more successful than others. Vogt is impressed that on some occasions a shaky start can lead, mediated by a good conductor, to a sound basis on which the singer and the orchestra find each other. Of the many factors that determine the nature of the orchestra in this respect, Vogt emphasises the constellation of the individual musicians that make up the orchestra, and possible traditions within the orchestra. While it is not possible to generalise, a symphony orchestra might be more geared towards bringing out its own brilliance, and may therefore find it difficult to stand back behind a singer; an opera orchestra might be more likely to be used to listen to and accommodate the singer. A further difference is the orchestra that accompanies a singer on the concert platform as opposed to the orchestra pit in the opera house, because in the pit the musicians hardly hear the singers at all and the

role of the conductor becomes even more essential in mediating between them (Vogt 2011a).

The most important qualities that he seeks on a conductor are empathy with the singer, and the ability to lead, and openness, in addition to a sufficient level of respect for the singer but also for the work. He likes conductors most who are not primarily concerned about themselves but about the work, and who create their music from their guts to the same extent that he does (Vogt 2011a).

Preparing for a role – rehearsals and the day of performance
During the course of rehearsals, Vogt creates a kind of path through the role from beginning to end, which combines singing, acting, text, and interaction with the other characters. He can walk along that path mentally in preparing for a performance, and in performance he notes that the other people on stage will react differently on each occasion, which he then engages with, leading to changes on the path. To be able to achieve this to the best possible effect, he needs a healthy degree of stage fright (Vogt 2011c).

On days of performance, Vogt tries to avoid travelling, arriving at least the day before, unless he has to step in at short notice. He gets enough, but not too much, sleep, and has as normal a day as possible, with a tendency to take it easy rather than an emphasis on exercise, and to do other things to distract himself, rather than focus all day on the evening ahead. He treats his voice with care—not trying to avoid speaking at all costs, but on many occasions when he is on his own, this is not a problem, but not all that intentional. He has a good lunch, at least three hours before even an early start performance—to be able to get over the natural tiredness that follows a meal by the time he has to perform. His lunch is followed by a rest. Then he walks through the path of the role mentally, makes his way to the performance venue for the makeup session, and then the performance begins. If a performance lasts for five to six hours, then he will not have had anything to eat for up to eight hours after lunch, and this aspect has implications for the foods Vogt chooses to eat on days of performances (Vogt 2011c).

Major roles
The key role in his career to date has been Wagner's Lohengrin in the opera of the same name. It is Vogt's favourite part, he can identify

personally with many things the hero does in the course of the opera. He likes the qualities of love, trust, honesty, noble-mindedness (Vogt 2010b). Even after eleven years of having sung the part regularly, Vogt still discovers new dimensions of it, especially in the Grail narration. For example, Vogt thinks that he was probably not able to start it as softly in earlier years as he is able to now. He experiments with this, for example, exploring how soft it can go and remain good, and when it starts getting not so good any more (Vogt 2011c). Another example is the range of the voice: how far he can expand to the dramatic dimension without hurting himself, and without losing the ability to return to the lyrical dimension (Vogt 2011b). Every evening, the music (particularly with reference to Wagner's *Lohengrin*) is so strong that it is irresistible.

Interviews with Vogt demonstrate the depth of understanding he develops for the characters he portrays. Thus he considers Walther von Stolzing in Wagner's *Meistersinger* as a multi-layered character: he is naïve, rebellious, in parts insecure, and those facets serve to stir the set and conservative world he enters. He does not come with the intention to stir, to change the conditions, or even to destroy the traditions. However, he represents his mind-set, and thus causes upheaval in the gridlocked society he enters. He realises that he has this impact on this society, and that in turn changes him. In addition, he is in love with Eva and wants to win her for himself, and to achieve this means that he has to comply with the new society to some extent (Vogt 2008).

Acting and "director's theatre"
Acting was part of the training as a singer, but Vogt has also learnt a lot from observing more experienced colleagues, by taking advice from those directors who are capable of explaining how to put ideas into practice, and by listening to suggestions from his wife during the rehearsal period (Vogt 2010b).

In the 1999/2000 and 2000/2001 seasons in Dresden, he was part of the controversial production (by Peter Konwitschny) of Kalman's operetta *Die Czardasfürstin*, and in 2005 he sang Florestan in a controversial production (by Günter Krämer) of Beethoven's *Fidelio*. In both productions, audience protest brought the performances almost to a premature end. Katharina Wagner's controversial Bayreuth production of *Die Meistersinger* (from 2007) also received considerable booing at curtain call. Not only in such circumstances, does Vogt note the mood of an audience. He considers it important to sense the audience's mood at the beginning of a performance, and if the mood is good he considers this immensely helpful for the performance (Vogt 2008). Even if the boos are not directed at himself, he maintains that any booing, no matter for whom, is felt deeply by the entire team working on a production, and all suffer from it (Rausch 2009).

On the basis of such experiences, Vogt, who works predominantly in Europe, might be hesitant about European, in particular German, "director's theatre". His position is sophisticated. On the one hand, he is aware that director's theatre can be taken to unnecessary extremes. On the other hand, he realises and appreciates if directors representing "director's theatre" work at markedly high levels of technical competence and craft. They are able to support the singer in transforming directorial ideas on stage, in contrast to other directors with possibly equally brilliant ideas (Vogt 2008). In 2010 he stepped in at short notice to replace Jonas Kaufmann as Lohengrin in Bayreuth, in the controversial new production by Hans Neuenfels. He considered the production ultimately as conventional: there are new and different ideas, but the character of Lohengrin follows Wagner's views and has not been turned upside down completely (Martens, 2011).

Opera in the regions
Vogt returned to Flensburg in 2010 for an event to help save the theatre in times of financial difficulties resulting from funding cuts. He maintains that it is essential for rural areas such as the one served by the theatre in Flensburg to have access to the wonderful art of opera just as much as people in more urban areas. It is also essential for the new blood of artists to find available to them an appropriate infrastructure, where newcomers can join smaller theatres to get to grips with the system and its requirements, and to build their careers. This infrastructure has been built up over many decades and is the object of envy from many other countries in the world. It would be irresponsible to neglect this infrastructure, because once lost it will be lost forever (Vogt 2010b).

The critics

He cannot pretend that he is not interested in reading reviews, but he is reserved. He considers it disrespectful if he pours all his heart and soul into a five-hour evening and then receives, if he is lucky, one good, and if he is unlucky, one bad adjective. This does not do justice to such an evening. He considers himself his own harshest critic, and he will know if something did not work out as intended (Vogt 2011b).

Critical views

Critical comment on Vogt in individual, single reviews is indeed neither very detailed nor varied, independent of whether it is voiced in blogs or by newspaper critics. However, the range of words the critics have used to describe his voice come together to form an interestingly complex image. Here are a few representative examples. His voice is wondrous (Vogt 2011c), without baritonal base (Clarke 2008), the highest tenor timbre among Heldentenors (Luehrs-Kaiser 2011), like that of a chorister (Sinkovicz 2008) or boy (Krause 2009), achieved through the strangely constant maintenance or admixture of the head register (Sinkovicz 2008), bright, small but sonically very strong (dpa 2010), free-moving and silvery (Krause 2009), androgynous (Brug 2009a), and hard as a laser beam (Spahn 2009). Critics have mentioned his disarming *mezza voce* and beguiling cantilenas, powerful top notes, and exemplary articulation (Clarke 2008). His singing has been described as straight-line (rather than baroque) (Sinkovicz 2010), effortless (dpa 2010a), of finest lyricism (dpa 2010a) and lyrical gracefulness (dpa 2010b), heartfelt and free from lubricating grease (Brug 2009b), ethereal and devoid of body (Brug 2010) and radiant (Lange 2011).

Longer descriptions can be found in blogs, which are not restricted in the space allowed for a review, for example:

> For starters he *sings* Wagner. His performance might have been as surprising and unusual to the audience as when Wolfgang Windgassen first hit the stage with what was then considered a confoundingly light voice. Vogt, at home in everything lyrical in Wagner, hits the high notes with shameless (vertical) ease; his clarion voice (with that aforementioned element of choir-boy) ringing delightfully. Especially for Lohengrin, whose otherworldliness and naïveté set him apart from the other characters, this is particularly suitable. (I imagine Vogt's would be a very fine *Parsifal*, too.) (jfl. 2007)

Some reviews early on in his career, when he was "new", also use more words:

> He has got a bright, very lyrical tone, and starts off as if he were singing old music, can boost his tenor smoothly to the heroic, commands a large volume. He can still gain in colours, he remains too much on one single track, but one that he masters perfectly. (Keim 2006)

Comments following the immense success of his official Bayreuth debut as Lohengrin on 27 July 2011 were longer, with similar descriptions of his singing as weightlessly high, bright, solid, gleaming, effortless, powerful, sweeping, and even, with beautifully-heartfelt piano passages, which nevertheless reach all remote corners of the opera house; critics also commended his clear diction, which allows audiences to hear and understand every word (Zibulski 2011, Döring 2011, Schreiber 2011, Anon. 2011).

The various short descriptions of Vogt's voice and his singing are all accurate on their own, and taken together they provide an attempt at expressing in words the range of experiences of listening to that voice. The extraordinary number of interviews with Vogt over the past few years, serving as the basis of portrait articles, or printed on their own, or broadcast on radio and TV, demonstrates the public fascination with that voice. The questions Vogt is asked to address naturally focus on the exceptions: they relate to his career path—because he was a professional horn player at the highest possible level of employment and job satisfaction before he trained as a singer; they relate to the repertory he sings—because it is not easy to pin down in terms of *Fach* (a concept Vogt explicitly does not consider helpful in his case); finally, interview questions relate to the quality of his voice—because it is fascinating to find out more about how precisely he achieves this sound, and how much is due to natural gift and how much to hard work.

The spiritual context

It is here that reference to spirituality comes in meaningfully to explore Vogt's voice, and the appeal of that voice, further. Spirituality is understood for the purposes of this book as a concept that is in principle not exclusively religious, but may encompass religion. It is used in terms of the development of higher states of consciousness as conceptualised, for example, in the *Vedic* literature of India. In this context, higher states of consciousness, as states of increasing spirituality, are characterised by the coexistence of either the waking state, or the dream state or the sleep state of consciousness with the state that is transcendent to them all, at their basis, pure consciousness (also termed *samadhi* in the *Vedic* literature, or *nirvana* in Buddhism).

Hearing versus seeing

It is striking how many terms used to describe the experience of listening, and to describe the nature of the sounds heard, are taken from descriptions relating to a different sense altogether, especially that of sight, and how few terms are specific to the sense of hearing. The difficulty that critics and listeners have in putting that experience into words is at least twofold. Firstly, we are still living in a world that has been dominated by the sense of sight for as far as we can think back ourselves, or trace experience back through history.

This phenomenon has been explored in depth by Berendt (1987). The result is the dominance of sight-related terminology to describe auditory experience. In some cases terms relating to other senses, still not specific to hearing, are used to describe sounds, such as "velvety". Berendt explores the dominance of the eye as related to the Chinese *yang*, "male, aggressive, dominating, rational, surface-oriented, analysing things", while the sense of hearing corresponds to *yin*, "female, receptive, careful, intuitive and spiritual, depth-oriented, perceiving the whole as one" (1987, 5). According to St. Germain, one of the Ascended Masters in theosophy and other esoteric traditions, the purpose for souls to be incarnated as humans on the planet earth is for them to be able to develop the feminine side of their nature, irrespective of whether they are born as man or woman (2004). This position supports Berendt's argument that humans need to develop from a seeing to a hearing being. Vogt's voice and singing fit this context ideally as they are suffused with feminine qualities, as I explore further in the next section.

Spirituality of voice

Both Vogt's voice and his singing operate in ways that appear new and therefore unfamiliar, challenging critics and lay listeners to engage with them at a level of depth that is not considered necessary for other singers—because their singing is more familiar to listeners' ears. This striking novelty factor is the reason for the considerable number of interviews with Vogt characterised by an emphasis on questions that focus on that very difference to other singers, and on how he achieves his almost unique way of singing. In an attempt to shed further light on Vogt's voice and singing, I refer to *Vedic* knowledge about sound, *nada*, as described in the *Sangita Ratnakara* (*SR*), the second major classical Indian text about music, dance, drama and theatre besides the *Natyashastra*. This analysis links in with the comments on the feminine source of hearing discussed above, in so far as *nada* emerges from Shakti, the feminine principle in the unity of *Shiva – Shakti*.

Nada is the Sanskrit term for *sound*. The syllable *na* stands for *prana*, while *da* stands for *Agni* (*SR* I,3:6) *Prana* is life force, while *Agni* represents fire, or the intelligence of the inner dynamics of all transformations at the basis of any evolution (Hartmann 1992: 94). *SR* considers *nada*, thus defined as the combination of infinite life force (*prana*) and pure intelligence of eternal dynamics of consciousness (*Agni*) as the ultimate source of all existence. *SR* differentiates two kinds of *nada*: unmanifest, and not created physically, for example by plucking a string (*Anahata Nada*), and manifest *nada*, created physically (*Ahata Nada*). As Biswas explains, in Western terms, the note "A", for example, is "a particular rate of vibration", and that vibration has been determined to be 440 Hz, a parameter that can be measured. In the context of the *SR*, the manifest sound, *nada*, is also referred to as *swara*. However, *swara*, as Biswas explains, does not exist without a musician performing the sound, as a Western *note* does: "When sung it [*swara*] is a function of my particular body and breath, and the space and time in which it occurs. It is the vibration of this embodied moment" (2011: 100). A further development of *swara* comes into existence when *swara* is sung perfectly: then *swara* becomes more and more independent of the singer, ceases to be the singer's vibration, becomes pure resonance, and the "notion of me or mine becomes vestigial" (100). In other words, manifest sound, *Ahata Nada*, is traced back to its origin, *Anahata Nada*, and in the process approximates it as far as possible, even if never fully.

Against this background, it is possible to understand Vogt's voice as capable of expressing a very high degree of *Anahata Nada*, which is the primordial quality of sound. As such it represents an expression of femininity (*Nada* as expression of *Shakti*), which is central, according to St Germain, for the development of souls on planet earth. These related contexts thus go some way to explain the special nature of Vogt's voice (its expression of a high level of *Anahata*). The increasingly unanimous critical praise for Vogt's voice is due both to people getting used to it and learning to appreciate it as a result of repeated exposure. On a subtler level, it can be taken to represent one instance of progress, on the global scale, of development of the feminine side of humanity (St Germain).

Spirituality of life
The spiritual dimension of Vogt's voice, which I have discussed in this section so far, is not isolated from Vogt's life and career. I now address some of the characteristics of Vogt's career, voice and singing in the order I presented them in the first two sections of this chapter.

1. All humans are in the process of spiritual development, at different stages according to the Divine Plan (St Germain 2004). For all humans, their individual paths include the necessity to make decisions, major or minor, at many junctions and cross-roads. For Vogt, the major crossroads of his life was the choice he had to make between continuing a safe and well paid career as horn player in a major German orchestra, which represented the goal of his adolescent ambitions and was, to some extent, very fulfilling for him. The choice was to continue in this post until retirement, or to take the risk of jeopardising those qualities of life to start afresh as a singer, with uncertain prospects, given that contracts in opera are never for life, as in the orchestra. His success as a singer suggests that he made the right decision.

2. A further crossroads, not as strongly at the forefront of interviewers' interests as the horn player versus singer one of 1997, came in 2003 when he decided to abandon his full time contract with the Semperoper in Dresden in favour of a freelance career. This decision had further implications, and came with apparent sacrifices, with the need to decide priorities—another characteristic of spiritual development. On the one hand this 2003 decision allowed Vogt to launch his international career, which has taken him, by now, to almost all the opera houses in the world that he would want to sing in (Vogt 2011d). On the other hand, it meant that he would be away from

his family for considerable amounts of time each year. This decision also affected Vogt's wife, Silvia Krüger, who had been a celebrated soprano with a high profile career in opera, operetta and musical, including the German production of the musical *Phantom of the Opera*. She had to give up her career so that she could take care of bringing up their by then three, now four children. In the 2009 TV documentary about Vogt, she recalls this sacrifice with tears in her eyes (Bscher). Vogt and Krüger have recently taken up singing together on special occasions, with duets from operetta. Interviews suggest that this enforced distance from his family makes that family even more precious to him, as he arranges his working life in such a way that allows him to be with his family as much as possible (Vogt 2011d), returning home in between performances and taking his entire family on extended holidays over the summer to Bayreuth (Vogt 2010a).

On the night before the first press performance of *Die Meistersinger* in Bayreuth, in 2007, his wife went into labour. It was Vogt's free day, and he flew back home, was present at his fourth son's birth at around 8.15pm, stayed in hospital with his wife and the other three children until well after midnight, took the children home, got a few hours' sleep, went back to the hospital in the morning and then flew back to Bayreuth early the next day. Stronger winds and low cloud delayed his flight, so that he reached the festival house an hour before the rehearsal began, in the presence of 17 camera teams from across the world (Bscher 2009).

3. The key role in Vogt's repertoire, Lohengrin, is a role with whom Vogt identifies very much; the role is that of a major knight of the holy grail, the son of the grail's ruler, Parsifal. Lohengrin, as created in Wagner's opera, is an ideal embodiment of spiritual development, chosen by the grail due to his purity of mind and spirit. Vogt's primary identification with this character suggests an implicit affinity towards spirituality.

4. Any path of spiritual development, independent of the means or tools employed, such as meditation, or contemplation, or indeed singing, involves hard work—it does not just happen, or come on a silver spoon. This aspect of spirituality fits in with Vogt's insistence that apart from a few high notes, and a natural gift for singing, it was

sheer determination and hard work that allowed Vogt to develop his voice.

5. The body is essential in any spiritual development, or development of consciousness. It serves as the basis for such development, and its medium. It is essential to achieve balance between the spiritual and the physical; Vogt achieves such balance by alternating his artistic work in rehearsals and performance with considerable engagement in sports, such as football, badminton, wind surfing, skiing, snowboarding, horse riding, jogging, and walking his two dogs (Bscher 2009, Vogt 2011d).

6. Vogt's views on flying his plane mirror and expand on his spiritual experience of being fully and only in the present while singing—for him, "Time is different during opera. You live before and after. During the performance itself time stands still" (Bscher 2009). Vogt's experience of flying goes even beyond that peculiar and specific experience of time: he is adamant that as a pilot you have to be ahead of the plane at all times. You have to sense what is coming your way, to be aware what will happen now, and to play through it in your head. Thus you live in the present but have the immediate future at the back of your mind all the time (Bscher 2009).

7. On occasions of aria recitals, as in Hamburg in March 2011 or in Berlin, July 2011, Vogt appears on stage as himself and engages in the conventional exchanges with the conductor, orchestra and audience. In the few seconds between the applause ending, the orchestra beginning to play and the moment he has to start singing, Vogt visibly changes into character. This is indeed what he aims at. For him, presenting opera arias from a concert platform sets the challenge of deciding whether to be himself, demonstrating that he can sing the aria in this way, or whether to seek to enter the character. It is possible to get the appropriate access to and expression of the individual arias only if one is ready and prepared to put oneself into the character's position. Otherwise a certain distance will remain between the work and the artist. In that sense there is always an emotional or mental dimension involved, and Vogt makes the conscious effort of achieving the necessary level of involvement. He finds that he is more or less successful in this—more successful for arias of characters he has

already performed. If he has not, he tries to get an idea of the character through studying the part and the subject matter. For arias from operas that he has performed on stage, he thinks himself into a scenic image to be part of a production (Vogt 2011a).

8. While Vogt acknowledges the difference between very good performances and exceptional performances, he seeks to achieve an exceptional performance for himself on every occasion. Whether it works or not depends on many factors, including outward factors such as the weather. The highest number of magic moments he has encountered were in performances of *Lohengrin*. Others were in relation to the run of performances of *Die Tote Stadt* in Frankfurt, or a concert performance of Dvorak's *Requiem* with Mariss Janssons conducting. What is characteristic of these magic moments is that he feels himself swimming on the same wave as the conductor, the orchestra, the work, and ultimately also the audience (Vogt 2011a). While experiences of spirituality are rare and while people are not accustomed to them, whatever their contexts may be, they will come across, and be described, in terms of magic, of the exceptional. As spirituality develops in human life, it loses some of its novelty factor, its exceptional nature in the sense that it happens only briefly and occasionally. Thus it is experienced more and more clearly and more often and for longer periods of time. This is what Vogt aims for in his own terms.

9. The experience of spirituality is deep, but such depth does not imply dry seriousness. A good part of the experience of the depth of spirituality is a deep level of enjoyment: the experience of pure consciousness, or *samadhi*, is one of pure bliss. It is very evident how much Vogt enjoys singing. He emphasises that rendering his experience as "having fun" ("es macht Spass") can give the impression of a superficial experience. It is far from that: it is a deeply felt emotional joy, which is in part also a deep awe, or reverence that one is allowed to do this work. Even after a good many years as a singer, Vogt still considers his singing as a huge godsend. When he realises that he has been able to transmit that joy to the audience, and that he has enabled the audience to share his experience of joy, the audience's applause is the best reward (Vogt 2011a). In the same context, Vogt is aware of the unpredictable nature of live

performance, and is able to see the funny, comical side of unexpected events. He is thus open to the lighter side of spirituality. Two examples may serve to support this argument. When Vogt was at the beginning of his career as a singer, he was involved in an open air production of the operetta *Gräfin Maritza*. Before one particular performance there had been rain. When he sat down in an armchair he realised that the staff had forgotten to dry that armchair, so that he ended up with a wet bottom. He knew that his baritone colleague had to sit down soon after that as well, so he managed to whisper a warning to him—"too late" came the reply. On another occasion he had to stand in at short notice as Lohengrin in Madrid, and for his first entrance he had to come up from below stage on a lift. The lift broke down about a metre below the surface of the stage. Vogt had to heave his sword, and then himself in full metal armour, up on stage and then sing his role (Vogt 2011a).

It will be interesting to observe how Vogt's voice develops further, and how he will bring new approaches to the singing of further roles in his repertoire. Will critical attempts of describing his singing in words develop the critical vocabulary? Is it possible, if considered desirable, for empirical studies to operationalize some or all of the argument presented in this chapter and put them to the test? Will more voices like Vogt's emerge, or are they already among us?

Chapter Seven

Spirituality and Operatic Conducting

This chapter focuses on operatic conducting, with reference to a range of extraordinary experiences reported by conductors in relation to their art, and special attention to three conductors in three separate case studies: Peter Schneider, Karen Kamensek and Sir Roger Norrington. In chapters Six and Seven, the subjective element of consciousness studies comes to the fore in the use of interviews, with Vogt, Schneider, Kamensek and Norrington; this approach honours the processes of individual minds in the exercise of conscious activity. It also tends to relate myself as researcher/writer/critic directly to the source of the data (that is, the interview or conversation) so that the generation of a study of consciousness comes in the form of a dialogue in which two minds are intermingling. The effect of the subjective approach to consciousness studies is sometimes like panning for gold in a narrative that does not intentionally isolate it because it does not know what it is looking for. In fact what it is searching for is only later discovered when the data is reviewed. The subjective, as I use it in my interviews, captures the technique's true essence, the embodiment of emotion, also the embodiment of wisdom. The interview structure becomes the embodied source of discovery and insight. This structure has been overlooked by scientific study which tends to dismiss it as anecdotal and not replicable. What science fails to recognize in its dismissal of the subjective is that the subjective often becomes the source of scientific insight and contributes the seeds of future scientific exploration. Thus, my emphasis on subjectivity and spirituality in the context of consciousness studies develops, in effect, a new perspective on theatre and opera.

In 2012, BBC Two, the UK's public TV channel with a "culture" remit, broadcast *Maestro at the Opera*, a programme of three one-hour episodes over three weeks. In it, four people well known to a wide TV audience as a presenter of a science programme, a judge in a dance competition, a DJ and a comedy actress, were trained to conduct opera. On the basis of their ability to conduct an aria, four contestants were reduced to three; the next elimination round was based on conducting an entire scene from an opera, leaving two contestants in the frame. They had to work on the full second act of Puccini's *La Bohème*, and the winner had the opportunity of conducting that act a professional performance of the opera at the Royal Opera House Covent Garden. The programme demonstrated vividly the importance of the conductor in the coordination of all aspects that come together in the performance on stage, including the orchestra, the chorus, and the singers. The three professional conductors who trained and advised the contestants, led by Sir Mark Elder, emphasised the need for the conductor's technical proficiency, such as their ability to read music fluently in the score, and to be aware of the appropriate movements for right arm and hand to convey the rhythm and beat to orchestra and singers on stage, and the left arm and hand to convey nuances of feeling as they perceived it in the music and as they wanted to transmit it through the orchestra and the singers to the audience.

The conductor's technical proficiency will serve as the lowest common denominator for the profile of a conductor's abilities. *Maestro at the Opera* provided excellent insight into the amount and extent of hard work that it takes any aspiring conductor to achieve a good level of such technical proficiency. Analysis of interviews with conductors suggests that once conductors have achieved this technical basis, they do not need to place their attention on the technicalities anymore; as a result, a greater percentage of their attention is free to explore and interpret the musical depth of the score in the moment of performance rather than in preparing for the performance; in addition, experienced conductors can afford more attention to the needs of the singers on stage.

Analysis of interviews with conductors also suggests that the "great moments" that make their work so special, have technical proficiency as their precondition. As Herbert von Karajan (1908-1989) put it: "We wait for them, and we prepare for them, but we cannot summon them the way that you can summon a waiter. This ... something just comes, and it's the grace of the moment" (Matheopoulos 1982: xviii). In this chapter I want to discuss the nature of those "great moments" further.

To start with, music itself is a mystery, according to Carlo Maria Giulini (1914-2005): "Take the string chords of a violin. There is no sound until they start to vibrate, and when the sound comes, it is always different and varies according to acoustic conditions". While it is possible to consider music as mathematical in the sense that we know that "two is the double sum of one", it remains a mystery because we do not know what "one" is. Words in a poem are concrete, while the notes of music are not the sound of music itself, which has to be created by the musicians. The role of the musicians and the conductor is to read behind the notes, and to try to understand what the composer wanted to say with those notes (Matheopoulos 1982: 170).

The position of Bernard Haitink (b. 1929) is similar: in music are contained, he argues, all human emotions, as well as "tenderness, power, sense of form and beauty, everything". It is the most "subjective and least tangible" of all arts, and has its own language which reaches beyond human spoken language and becomes mysterious as a result (Matheopoulos 1982: 196). Zubin Mehta (b. 1936) likens the perfection and beauty of music to God (Matheopoulos 1982: 357).

Here, conductors begin to touch on the *strong experiences with music* (SEM), in Gabrielsson's terminology. Not only music itself is mysterious in the experience of conductors, but their art as conductors as well. Riccardo Muti (b.1941) points out that there are certain aspects of a conductor's work that can be "learnt and understood", such as, how to give an upbeat, "how to beat in four, in five, or in seven". However, reference to technique cannot explain

> *why* a certain conductor can obtain a certain kind of sound, a certain kind of forte, a certain kind of piano or pianissimo and *how* he succeeds in holding a hundred and twenty people together—which does not involve merely the technical ability to hold them together but also the inner will to do so— (…) (Matheopoulos 1982: 360)

Sir Georg Solti (1912-1997) picks up on the relation between technique, mystery and the conductor's will, in terms of control, conceiving of the art of conducting as an alchemical mixture of the right amounts of "spiritual, inspirational and interpretational guidance with mental control". If there is too much control, intensity is lost, and with too little control the conductor becomes "too rhapsodic and abandoned" (Matheopoulos 1982: 405).

The work of the conductor reaches into this mysterious realm, in particular, for Haitink, when musicians who are fair rather than good or outstanding as far as their skills are concerned, possess a mysterious magic, a charismatic personality to draw more out of the orchestra than an outstanding musician is ever able to (Matheopoulos 1982: 196).

James Levine (b. 1943) considers the relationship between conductor and orchestra as mysterious when it gets beyond tangible aspects of communication. As with interpersonal relations, at some point "it's in the air, it has vibrations, and there is no way that this element can be controlled. It either happens or it doesn't (...)" (Matheopoulos 1982: 284). Mstislav Rostropovich (1927-2007) considers technique to be perhaps as little as thirty percent responsible for the relationship between conductor and orchestra: "What matters is projection, projection of your personality, and this, of course, is like magic. Because if your musical mind is strong and definite, the orchestra understands perfectly and immediately" (Matheopoulos 1982: 484). Pianist and conductor Vladimir Ashkenazy (b. 1937) finds it difficult to generalise about the "necessary human qualities required for conducting". In principle, two ingredients come together: musical qualities and the ability to communicate—and it is in the latter that Ashkenazy locates the mystery of "why some can and some cannot" (Matheopoulos 1982: 471). These characteristics of the mystery of the art of conducting are the characteristics of spiritual experience and the experience of higher states of consciousness.

Just as singers, conductors report experiences of special moments. Giulini has an ambivalent attitude towards these experiences, and finds them almost something to be afraid of, in terms of a simultaneity of control and freedom (reminiscent of Solti's position):

> If a performance ever comes *near* to being ideal, it's almost dangerous because while performing, the concentration is such that you often don't know who or where you are. You exist in a different dimension.

> If the ideal should happen and these two opposite forces came close to fusion, you would probably lose control. (Matheopoulos 1982: 191)

Levine describes extra-special performances in terms of getting close to the essence of the work, to the "composer's intentions, inspiration, vision and challenge". Such a performance is not free of technical mistakes, but those are weighed up by "such truth" and "such depth of communication and fidelity to the essence of the work" (Matheopoulos 1982: 290). Ashkenazy experiences moments of the same kind of elation characteristic of "extra-special" concerts as soloist or conductor not only in public performance but also while practising the piano at home, and while learning new pieces (Matheopoulos 1982: 481). These characteristics of special moments of conducting are the characteristics of spiritual experience and the experience of higher states of consciousness.

In some cases, conductors remember not necessarily moments of relatively short duration as outstanding events in their careers, but also productions they were involved in, or debuts with particularly renowned orchestras. Thus, Sir Roger Norrington recalls the production of Monteverdi's *Orfeo* at the *Maggio Musicale*, an annual music festival, in Florence, Italy, in 1984. He was given *carte blanche* about the production. He worked on the production with his wife, dancer and choreographer Kay Lawrence. She choreographed, he prepared the music, and they co-directed. They sought to create a historical production, with orchestra musicians in costume, for example, and a whole production that did not require a conductor. Altogether the project took two years to prepare and stands out in Norrington's memories of his long career (2012).

The experiences of the mystery of music and of conducting, and experiences of special moments have an impact on the conductors encountering the experiences: humility (Guilini), energising (Giulini), emotionally draining and problems sleeping after performance (Levine), daily routine (Levine), physical relaxation (Seiji Ozawa (b. 1935), loss of identity (Giulini, Leonard Bernstein (1918-1990).

The Derren Brown experiment with conductor Robin Stapleton and the Orchestra of the City might be relevant in this context: Brown asked Stapleton to think of a famous tune from a piece of classical music, and write it down, and put the sheet of paper with the details face down on his stand. Then Brown tied Stapleton's hands behind his back, and asked the orchestra to play at random and to come up, without Stapleton's input, with the piece he had written down. Indeed, within two or three minutes of random playing, the tune Stapleton had chosen and written down, the Ode to Joy from Beethoven's Ninth Symphony, emerged. It would appear that between conductor and orchestra, information is exchanged in ways that have not been understood fully, if at all, in conventional science. A mode of interaction is at work here that might also account for phenomena such as dogs moving to the door to wait for their masters at the very second those masters, in some cases miles way, make their decision to come home. Sheldrake has sought to develop explanations for this kind of interaction, and I have written about it in terms of a newly discovered form of matter, cold dark, soft matter (2005: 143-4; 2006).

In the remainder of this chapter, I present three case studies of contemporary conductors and their views on conducting, covering both mundane aspects of technique, the repertory and working as a general music director, and aspects considered in terms of magic or mystery in the material presented above.

Case study one: Peter Schneider

Peter Schneider was born on 26 March 1939 in Vienna. His father was a war invalid who enjoyed military marches, while his mother enjoyed listening to, and imitating opera arias, to the extent that on occasion neighbours would come and ask them to turn the radio volume down. He remembers that the house he grew up in was next to the one that was home to the Arbeiterzeitung, and through the nights he could hear the printing press. The house is now a hotel, and the house between the two parts of the hotel is the one Schneider grew up in (2011a).

At some point in his youth he noticed that he liked singing and that he had a beautiful voice. His primary school teacher suggested to his parents that he should become a Wiener Sängerknabe. His mother took him to the entrance examination when he was not quite eight years old. He was successful and underwent preparatory courses for two years in the Hofburg, and at the age of ten, in 1949, he joined the reserve choir: when conductors needed additional singers, they approached the reserve, had suitable singers audition for them and selected those suitable for the occasion. Until 1953 he sang with Furtwängler, Karajan, Böhm, Hollreiser, and Moralt conducting; however, he was not aware of the fame of those conductors. He was introduced to opera as chorister in a production of *Carmen*, where he was impressed by Sena Jurinac as Michaela, and sang in *Turandot* with Maria Cebotari and Maria Reining (2011a).

While Schneider is unable to remember precisely when he decided to become a conductor, he does remember that it was quite early on in his life. His mother took him to see a children's opera with full orchestra and conductor, and he said that he wanted to be a conductor. After his Matura in 1957 he studied composing with Karl Schiske and conducting with Hans Swarowsky at the Akademie für Musik und Darstellende Kunst in Vienna. In 1959 he embarked on his first professional employment, as musical assistant at the Landestheater Salzburg, followed by a post as Kapellmeister in Heidelberg, 1961-1968. During those years he also accompanied song recitals for the Richard Wagner association, and instead of payment received a one-off scholarship to attend the Bayreuth Festival. While in Heidelberg he met his wife, actress Dagmar Soerensen, in the canteen of the theatre. She now teaches at a Munich acting school. They have two daughters who are working as actresses, and are married to an actor and a deputy head of a TV satellite channel respectively. Each has three daughters. His son is married and lives in Toronto (2011a).

From 1968 to 1978 he was First Kapellmeister at the Deutsche Oper am Rhein Düsseldorf/Duisburg, from 1978-1985 he was Generalmusikdirektor in Bremen, while at the same time continuing to conduct most of the considerable Wagner repertoire at the Deutsche Oper am Rhein. In 1981 he received his first invitation to conduct at Bayreuth, where to this day he holds the record of having conducted in the largest number of seasons, twenty in 2012. From 1985-97 he was Generalmusikdirektor in Mannheim. He was meant to be there for five years but left after two years in favour of a freelance career. From 1993 to 1998 he was Chief Conductor at the Bavarian State Opera, followed by a number of years there as First Guest Conductor. He made his debut at the Vienna State Opera in 1984, and at the Met in New York in 1995. He conducts frequently at the Semperoper in Dresden, as well as in Zurich and Hamburg. He has become renowned as conductor of operas by Wagner, Strauss and Mozart.

He likes it when the directors of productions he conducts allow him to discuss the production with them. Thus for the 1990 production of *Lohengrin* in Bayreuth, for the scene of Ortrud and Elsa on the way to the wedding, in act two, he suggested to director Werner Herzog that the chorus, especially the women, need to be doing something rather than remaining stationary. There are passages in the music, he pointed out, that do not make sense if there is no corresponding action on stage. Herzog responded from the perspective of the film director thinking about a close-up when he asked Schneider whether he did not see that the women in the chorus are looking from one side to the other (2011a).

Schneider is popular with orchestras and singers because he is known as a conductor who does not seek to achieve good performances through harsh tempers. In conducting the repertory he considers it essential to prepare fully, and to observe and control his way of conducting, for example developing a very clear beat with his right arm so that the musicians recognise beyond doubt his intentions. As far as the singers are concerned, it is important for Schneider to breathe with the singers. He notes into his score where the singers take breath. For those moments he needs to give the singer sufficient space, even if that is on the scale of fractions of seconds. Singers are aware of that space being available to them or not. Schneider is aware if he pushes the singer too much, or if he has selected a tempo that is difficult for the singer because it is too slow. Due to his own background as a singer, he is able to sense this with singers, but not with dancers. Some of his colleagues who come from a symphony orchestra background tend to be of the opinion that singers must follow their beat just as the musicians. Musicians in turn sometimes have the same opinion, and in such situations Schneider has to explain to them why singers may not be able to do this always and as precisely as the musicians (2011b).

He considers himself as phlegmatic sanguine, who does not like to burst into fits of anger to achieve high performance from his orchestra. Many years of experience of conducting the repertory at the Deutsche Oper am Rhein, Bremen and Mannheim, taught him to achieve a high level of self-discipline. He is not the kind of conductor who buys CDs to study new works quickly, but takes a long time to study and learn new scores (2011a). His way of conducting has been called very transparent, detailed, and of considerable intensity (2011a).

For music of the Vienna classicism, studying the score allows him to hear the music in his head. For more complex scores he helps himself by playing the lines on his piano, or, failing that, with the computer. With the help of these tools he finds out the sequence of harmonies, and is then able to see them in the score, and forms an inner conception which he then tries to put into practice during rehearsals. In the early days of his career he sought to press for his interpretation, while nowadays he takes into account the considerable level of experience that the orchestra musicians have to bring to the performance. For example, in preparing for the performance of the overture of Weber's *Oberon* in July 2011, he discussed the beautiful clarinet solo with the clarinettist, raising the concern that the musician had chosen a tempo for this solo that made the piece take on the nature of an adagio, while the score suggests allegro, although it has been composed very broadly. The clarinettist on that occasion indicated that he did not intend this change of tempo, and asked Schneider to ensure he was not too slow for this solo. (2011b)

At this point in time he considers himself a specialist for Wagner and Strauss. He is more hesitant about Mozart: while Mozart has been central to Schneider's career, he is nowadays offered less conducting engagements for Mozart's operas because of the current preference for conductors who seek to perform Mozart on period instruments. Such an endeavour is less of importance to Schneider: for his interpretation of Mozart, the key is the tempo, and in some of the allegedly authentic performances of Mozart's works, that tempo is not accurately realised. The tempo is more important to Schneider than the issue of whether to use a natural trumpet or a wooden timpani (2011b).

Schneider achieves minute detail within a coherent overall structure. In particular with Wagner, Schneider wants to achieve for the audience the experience of the large arcs that are characteristic of Wagner's music. He has not been able to experience for himself, and thus relay to the audience, the idea or assumption that an entire opera might constitute such an arc, but certainly he does realise the arcs across and within individual acts. Once identified, he seeks not to break those arcs by superficial effects of details, not to exaggerate some traditions to the extent that the wholeness breaks apart. If wholeness has been broken, the music has to begin from the start, and the arc has been lost (2011b).

His attempt to make music with the aim of achieving a synthesis of all its elements is rendered difficult when he works under the conditions of a live performance being recorded for the later creation of a CD. In such a context, analysis needs to dominate, with concerns that lead from instance to instance, the neatness of entry of that instrument, or a musician failing to produce a specific sound that is essential for a given piece. Many of his colleagues, especially those who are much in demand, may not have the time to study a score in depth, a tendency helped by the easy availability of recordings on CD or DVD (2011b).

Schneider enjoys studying the scores in detail even for pieces he has conducted many times in the past, and often he discovers new elements and characteristics. In this process he tends to question and scrutinise traditions, querying how and why those traditions came into existence. He noted that such traditions have the tendency to become more and more extreme. For example, at the beginning of the overture of *Die Fledermaus* by Johann Strauß, traditionally a slight delay is added on the upbeat in bars 228/29. The score edited by Swarowsky specifically annotates this passage: "without delaying the upbeat and without slowing down the tempo, continuing the tempo of *allegro moderato* that is to be beaten two bars before" (...) Schneider notes that a very slight delay adds beauty to the performance, but considers an exaggerated delay as nonsense (2011b).

Another example is the beginning of the overture of Wagner's *Tristan und Isolde*. The score says "langsam und schmachtend" (slow and languishing). The question is what precisely the instruction "slow" refers to. Schneider notes the tendency of conductors to consider the instruction "slow" to refer to their way of conducting, not necessarily to the music. The beginning of the overture has to be beaten in quavers: "slow" is then applied to the beat of the quavers. This causes the entire beginning of the overture to become too slow. Schneider applies the instruction "slow" to the half-bar. The long pause that follows could not be kept in the conventional understanding of "slow", but makes more sense in his reassessment (2011b).

In the case of *Lohengrin*, in the third act bridal march, there is a passage that Schneider always felt should be conducted more slowly than indicated in the score. He did conduct this passage more slowly, and was attacked by some Bayreuth spectators for superimposing his own views on a sacrosanct score. He later found a letter from Franz Liszt to Wagner. Wagner was in exile in Luzern, Liszt was involved in the first production of *Lohengrin* in Weimar. In the letter Liszt writes about the same passage in the bridal march, and about his feeling that

that passage should be conducted more slowly. Wagner's response confirms Liszt and Schneider's intuition: Wagner had merely forgotten to write into the score for this passage "bedeutend langsamer" (considerably more slowly) (2011b).

The overture and the grail narration in *Lohengrin* begin with four split solo violins. The entire string section is in four voices, up to a certain point in the overture where the number of voices is reduced to two. In the transition from four to two voices there is a problem because the second and third voices make a complicated shift. That is how it is seen in the score. Another letter from Wagner suggests that he did not intend this shift in this particular way. The printed allocation is that first violins take the first and second voices, and the second violins take the third and fourth voices. What Wagner really intended was for the voices to be interlaced, with first violins playing first and third voices, and second violins playing second and fourth voices. The passage during which the four voices change into two voices became very straightforward and logical, and much easier to perform in this revised version (in which not a single note is changed) than in the one that is printed in the scores. Schneider was disappointed that such insights into Wagner's composition were not adopted by fellow-conductors. (2011b)

A further example of Schneider's alertness to the music is his observation that overture of Mozart's *Zauberflöte* contains the story prior to the opening of the opera: following the Sarastro chord, Mozart represents Tamino's flight from the snake in the form of a fugue, and the music shows Tamino running in zig-zags. The sliding movement of the snake is also represented by the music. (2011b)

The meaning of the term *fermate* is conventionally taught to be elongation. In truth, *fermate* means stop: the conductor does not go on conducting at this point. It is at the discretion of every conductor when to carry on. This means that a *fermate* sign over a long note, or over a pause sign, can in fact lead to an abbreviation of the note or pause—it is not automatically an elongation. A good example is Wagner's *Götterdämmerung*. In the conversation between Gunter and Siegfried, Siegfried asks "Und wie heißt deine Schwester?" (And what is your sister's name?). This is followed by an entire bar with *fermate*. If that *fermate* is taken as a pause of a bar's length, the singer of Gunter has the problem of how to fill that pause, as if he could not remember his sister's name. Wagner wanted to achieve a caesura, distinct but brief, not a long pause. In Tamino's aria *Dies Bildnis ist bezaubernd schön*, in Mozart's *Die Zauberflöte*, in contrast, there is a bar without notes after *Was würde ich*, which does not have a *fermate*, and needs to be counted fully (2011b). The monumental introductory chorus in the *St Matthew's Passion* is written in 12 quaver beat. The last bar of this chorus is one note, to be counted as 12 quavers, and this has a *fermate*. Here, elongating the note would not be feasible for the singers: the *fermate* allows the conductor to conduct this bar intuitively (2011b). In other situations, especially the ends of overtures of operas, where the score does not show *fermate*, musicians tend to play as if there were one, elongating the notes. (2011b)

At the end of every Bayreuth season, the festival directors ask Schneider whether he would object to any one member of the orchestra being invited back the next season. In the twenty seasons that Schneider has conducted at Bayreuth, he has not had reason to object to any one player. The musicians of the orchestra are the most highly motivated Wagner specialists (Kröner 2011).

The detail of his knowledge of the score and its intricacies becomes particularly evident in his chapter "Climbing Mount Everest: On Conducting *Die Meistersinger*" in a book collecting articles on this opera from 2003.

Different productions do not fundamentally affect his way of conducting, given that he has the score to put into practice. In the times of *Regietheater*, in which the production does not see as its main aim to get out of the opera whatever is possible, but to add something to it—the director's concept—, he is satisfied if whatever appears on stage when the curtain opens fits the music. For example, for one *Ring* he conducted, the curtain for the ride of the Valkyries opened to reveal someone sitting and knitting. There was nothing on scene to reflect the thunderstorm that the music suggests. His conducting cannot add to this, because, as he puts it, he cannot make a knitting music out of a thunderstorm (Kröner 2011).

Some critics attribute "routine" to Schneider's conducting. Fewer critics are able to appreciate the subtlety of his interpretations and their nuances. Those that do are also able to put not only the observations of subtlety and nuance into words, but also comment on the paucity of appreciation:

> All this lead by a man who demonstrates that hype and quality have
> nothing to do with each other. Peter Schneider achieves, almost

unnoticed by the daily newspapers, one highlight after the other. The relatively brief applause did not do justice to the achievement at all. We were lucky, on this occasion, to be able to relish Peter Schneider's gestures and body language from a box on the side of the stage: those hands are music. We were happy to note that Mr Schneider is obviously in such good physical health that he was able to conduct the four-hour opera without problems while standing. This offers hope for the future, because we opera lovers do know what we have got with him. (Jahnas 2011).

Other critics comment favourably that the orchestra (of Zurich Opera) plays with noticeable joy and at a very high level of musical achievement, emphasising further that the musicians play with "silky, repeatedly sensual sound", interspersed by "drama and resounding moments". The transitions from scene to scene are smooth and the tension is maintained. While this may sound like something that goes without saying, experience elsewhere suggests that it is special after all. Schneider is able to achieve this because of his unmistakable sense for tempi, combined with knowledge and experience for the relationship of tempi among each other (Voigt 2011). Voigt emphasises the visible joy of musicians and singers alike in performances conducted by Schneider also in other reviews (2012).

On Schneider's interpretation of *Tristan und Isolde* at the Bayreuth Festival, Willner comments that Scheider can, as no other conductor, bring the score alive, and emphasises, as other critics do, Schneider's "unmistakable sense for the right tempo" and notes that Schneider finds a very colourful and flourishing pulse that transforms listening to the score, supported by the acoustics of the Festspielhaus, into an experience of happiness (2011). Pitz-Grewenig's review mirrors this view:

One has to be as sure of one's work as Peter Schneider in order to be able to translate the score into sound so stringently, on the basis of an understanding that is both poetic and internal. This must surely come close to Wagner's intentions, because it is those two adjectives that he used often when he wanted to describe his music. Peter Schneider was able, too, to integrate the formidable ensemble of singers into this continuum of sound. (2012)

Schneider's achievement of maintaining intensity and balance is praised repeatedly:

What Schneider is able to do above all is to set the music in motion and to maintain its flow. He moulds the sound through dynamics and clever choice of tempi. Both experience and routine have their impact here. The way that Schneider directs the balance of the voices, structures the phrases and achieves highest possible transparency even in tutti-passages, without losing himself in excesses of sound deriving from ego, are great examples of the "old school". (Scheider, 2006a)

The Bayreuth veteran Peter Schneider was conducting at his twentieth Bayreuth Festival and led a performance that was far from routine and that had the vigour of a much younger man; it was full of mystery, transcendently rapturous and magisterial by turns. He was helped by his almost-perfect orchestra who also deserved their appearance on stage at the end to share in that standing ovation for all concerned. (Pritchard 2012)

With regard to Schneider's specialism in opera by Richard Strauss, critics point to similar achievements. Thus, Schneider is able to

elicit the Strauss-sound so typical for Dresden, to form it and to enhance it. With Schneider this never sounds superficial or excessive, but astutely developed, brilliantly illustrating, occasionally lapsing into a kind of conversational tone, in order to launch new soaring flights of sound, secure in achieving the effect and maintaining high levels of transparency of sound. This is not excessive Strauss of superficial emotions, but Strauss that is thought of in terms of theatre and that communicates with the singers. This approach ensures clarity and dramaturgical cogency and foregrounds the score's lively combination of lyrical and comedy elements, which must have been what Strauss and Hofmannsthal had in mind. (Schneider 2006b)

Case study two: Karen Kamensek

Biography

Karen Kamensek was born on 2 January 1970 in Chicago. Her parents had emigrated to the USA from Slovenia. They continued speaking Slovenian at home and kept Slavonian traditions alive. In her home, Kamensek was subjected to Slovenian male choirs and Polka bands, Vienna waltz and many recordings of operetta (Umlauf 2004). Her mother was a musician flutist, and before the family's emigration to the USA, her father had been a dentist. In the USA he did odd jobs for many years because he could not continue working as a dentist there, and in the 1980s he founded a company with friends to do with computers.

Kamensek started learning the piano from the age of four, and the violin from the age of eight. She taught herself playing the flute in between. From age eleven Kamensek knew she wanted to be a conductor. From age twelve, she led orchestra rehearsals on a daily basis at her high school, led a choir and did voice rehearsals. Her school was quite remarkable in fostering musical talent: to date, another ten graduates went into the music industry: Mark Newbanks is the manager of conductor Gustavo Dudamel, Carey Syleiman is chief of press of the Toronto Symphony Orchestra. Kamensek graduated from High School at the age of seventeen because she had started schooling at the age of five and skipped one year.

She then studied piano and conducting at Indiana University in Bloomington. A few years of conducting in the USA followed, without much of a breakthrough, and leading to frustration and a near-decision to give up. However, three years before this point at the career cross-roads, Kamensek had waited at the stage door after Simone Young had conducted a performance of *La Bohème* at the Metropolitan Opera in New York, and told Young: "You need an assistant? I am the assistant!", and gave her a videotape of her work. Now, three years later, and just after Kamensek was ready to give up, she received a postcard from Young asking her whether she wanted to assist her now. She accepted, and Young arranged for her agent to hear Kamensek at work with Young's orchestra. The agent then arranged a trial with the Vienna Volksoper, which turned out so successful that before long Kamensek worked there as a full time Kapellmeister from 2000 to 2002.

Moving on, from 2003 to 2006 she held the post of General Music Director at the Stadttheater Freiburg, and from 2007-2008 she was Chief Conductor at the Slovenian National Theatre in Maribor. From the 2008 to 2011 she was deputy General Music Director at the State Opera in Hamburg (with Simone Young as General Music Director), and took over the post as General Music Director at the State Opera Hannover in summer 2011. She has guest-conducted at the opera houses in Frankfurt, Berlin (Deutsche Oper, Komische Oper), Stuttgart, Bordeaux, Melbourne, Kopenhagen, Houston, New York (City Opera), in addition to conducting concert performances with numerous other orchestras, including Linz, Braunschweig, Brussels, Dortmund, Duisburg, Halle, Klagenfurt, Basel and Kuala Lumpur.

Some time before she took up her current post as GMD in Hannover, Kamensek went to Africa for a few months, placed as a volunteer for work with animal welfare. During those months she came to the insight, essential for her well-being, that she could live, happily even, without her life focused around music. Work with animals might have been an alternative career choice early on and in the turn of the century crisis. The time in Africa was essential also because it made her realise, and finally accept, her leadership qualities: even among her fellow-volunteers, who were mainly much younger people interested in working with animals, she became the leader. The experience in Africa made her feel earthed—simply remembering one of the baby animals she cared for while in Africa makes her feel calm (Mende 2012).

In her current post as general music director of the state opera in Hannover, she is supported by a team of staff. She works with the dramaturges and the Intendant to plan forthcoming seasons of opera and concerts. When she is invited to guest-conduct, she is now prepared to ask for certain pieces that she is asked to conduct to be replaced with others that she is more ready for (Mende 2012).

Gender

So far she does not feel that she had more difficulties of succeeding in her profession because she is a woman. Although she is aware that the number of female conductors is very small (probably below ten world-wide on the internationally known circuit), she is against a quota for women in the field, convinced that the ideal, that the person who plays best, sings best or has the best charisma gets the job, should work (Neumann 2011).

Kamensek believes that in principle women can conduct just as well as men. It is more of a question of work-life balance for women than for men, however: if you are on tour for two thirds of the year, having a family is difficult for a woman. While some women conductors of Simone Young's (b. 1961) generation were able to combine family life with children and their profession, Kamensek has not been able to do this so far. According to Kamensek, a conductor also needs a sense of rhythm which she can demonstrate physically. Additional qualities are a good ear, technique and skill, so that in the end something special is created, rather than a piece just being played through (Irler 2010).

Conducting

Kamensek is convinced that being a conductor involves leadership, which needs to be practiced, because not everyone is a born leader. She knew had this leadership potential—from an early age she organised puppet shows at her home without her mother's knowledge, and in the string quartet which she joined in music school, she was the one to explain the direction to the others although she played only second violin (Irler 2010). She emphasises the need for a professional relationship between her and her musicians, even if she has known them for many years. The reason for this is the institutional power the conductor has, from giving a written warning to terminating a contract (Mende 2012). She assumes, perhaps naively so, that all musicians will give their best, and if they do not, then there is a solid reason for this, which she has to take into account. Her role is to catch those that are below their best, and inspire all to give their best. She does not expect all to be equally good on all days, but would hope that in the course of time the overall achievement improves. She quotes Gandhi: "Be the change that you want to see in the world". Thus she has the same expectation for improvement of herself (Mende 2012).

In 2004, at the age of 33, she described the "Slavonic soul" as young, cheerful and heated, and explains the phenomenon of the Slavonic soul as a kind of melancholy, a yearning for something unfathomable, a certain temperament, an inner pulse (Umlauf). She is still in the process of finding some balance between private and work life. She tended to have feelings of guilt that she did not work, study, or read enough. At the same time she was completely burned out. Then she took stock and asked herself what life was for in the first place. As a result, now she works in a more goal-oriented manner, for example to study more intensively but for a shorter period of time, and has developed the attitude that it is not essential for survival if she can or cannot do something to do with music today.

Kamensek compares conducting with top-level sports, a view confirmed by her physiotherapist who comments that Kamensek has the back of a professional swimmer or tennis player, and recommends to her to do half an hour of special exercises, including Yoga, every day. Physical fitness and appropriate diet are important for her, and she feels the difference if she has not had the time to exercise (Mende 2012).

Kamensek uses different coloured pencils to mark up her scores for phrasings, sections and different instruments (Mende 2012). She has no problems with learning to work with a score, but is not too keen on learning work completely by heart. She could get through without the score, but wonders, in her case why she should create such extra stress for herself in a job that is difficult enough as it is. When she turns a page in the score, one glance at the new page will be enough for her to know that page, to remember it. When she then turns to the next page, the previous one will have left her memory again. It is a question of practice, and works together with the inner ear, allowing her to hear what she sees in the score. On one occasion she was so involved with the music that she did not know, on conducting a specific fermate, whether this was the first or the second, i.e., where precisely in the score she was. She conducted a general upbeat and the music went on and she knew again where she was. Since that event she tries not to get lost in the music. The conductor, she concluded, has to think approximately ten to twenty seconds ahead of the orchestra (Mende 2012).

She is aware of the differences between orchestras, different chemistries. Within an orchestra there are also many possible issues that could cause problems, and the conductor has to be aware of these and must be prepared, and capable, of addressing the issues. It is essential in this context for the conductor not to take everything personally (Mende 2012).

Rehearsals should lead to a performance during which the audience is aware that something is being created in the very moment. Thus she will not give her all at the dress rehearsal. In this way the audience can leave the with insight that going to the theatre offers more than listening to the music on CD. On the other hand she likes the additional thrill of stepping in at short notice to replace an indisposed colleague, without rehearsal, possibly without having worked with the orchestra before (Mende 2012).

She would not like to conduct Puccini's *Madama Butterfly*, knowing that she would be angry throughout the performance as she would be angry at the entire attitude reflected in the opera, which is hostile towards women, against her as a woman. and thus she would not be able to relish the music (Mende 2012).

Interview

The following is a transcript of an interview conducted by phone in June 2012. It develops the profile of this conductor further.

DMD

How does the idea of the music form in your mind? I.e., when you read a score and prepare for a performance, do you hear, in your mind, the music as you see the score, does a sound-scape form in your mind, of what you want the music to sound like?

KK

Music is a lifestyle for me, it has been the basis of every day since I was four years old. Thus the whole language of vocal music and symphonic music has been with me since as long as I can remember. Given that this is a lifestyle choice, things start to happen naturally. You work with people and you work on your own, to get the best results out of certain people, certain instruments, certain types of singers, certain types of personalities. I do not know what specific effect that has on my preparation, but I know what to expect, where I can push and where I cannot, depending on the level of the group that I am working with. When you are in your teens and early twenties when you start working with people you are very nervous, about being prepared, do I know what I am doing, do I really know the music, do I know enough about every instrument to ask for certain results or am I just fishing. But that tends to go away with time and experience.

DMD

How do the individual elements of the sound relate to the overall soundscape?

KK

I work a little bit like a sculptor or a potter, who has a lump of clay, working it or chiselling away at it until he has a shape, and then I work backwards from the whole to the more individual. The other side is that I am an avid jigsaw puzzle doer—having to start with the framework and filling in the details. I like seeing where the missing pieces are and then try to fill those gaps. Thus I work from the bigger to the smaller and not the other way round.

DMD
How do you translate your ideas when you work with the orchestra / the singers?

KK
This depends on the orchestra I am working with. With my own orchestra in Hannover, we have a relationship that was built when I was guest conductor there for the last five years. We benefit greatly from that now. I tell them a little bit about the history of the piece that we are doing if it is an unknown piece, and I try to have some continuity in programming so that we can work specifically on styles over a continuous period of time; for example, at the moment we are doing a lot of French music, which is good for many, many aspects of sound production through all the instrument groups and much different from the Italian or German repertoire as far as the sound is concerned. I do not give them too much historical background. I give them literature tips, tell them which painters were painting at that time, or which part of the world it comes from, to give them a little bit of a flavour. I ask for a certain level of preparedness in terms of their playing so that we do not have to spend time on struggling to stay together as an orchestra. Then, depending on the mood and on the repertoire we are doing that week, and how tired we all are because we are playing every night and have rehearsals every day, I let them play through an entire piece once to feel the ground under our feet, or whether I start working right away. When I come as a guest conductor and the orchestra does not know me and I do not know them, I generally play for longer stretches of time so that they build up a physical trust with me immediately. In general, when orchestras meet a new conductor, they are a little sceptical: can this person drive the car? Once the orchestra realises that someone does have a good stick technique, and a brain to go with it, and a sense of humour and joie de vivre also help, and then the whole body language of the orchestra relaxes. With an orchestra that I guest conduct often but have not seen for a year or so, I usually ask whether they would prefer to play for a while so that we can get to know each other again, or should I get right to work, and let them decide. There is a lot of group psychology involved here; for me it is important to remember the difference between a dictator and a leader. I have my feelers out to what the group is offering me.

DMD
Can you tell how much of the ideal you achieve?

KK
I am a bit of a marathon runner in that I can always go a long distance but not quite get to the goal. That is not always good, but I think that is just the perfectionistic musician, also having to confront my own doubts, my own self-doubts as a person, as a musician, we all have them; some people take those doubts out on a group and others try to work them out within themselves. There is a process I go through, again depending on how many rehearsals we have and what the goal is: is it a repertoire performance, a premiere, a concert; is it a children's concert with one rehearsal, or a full concert with five rehearsals, is it a concert repeat a month later with no rehearsal—then I have to prepare the orchestra for longevity, so that the piece can go into repertoire. I have to take all these into consideration so as never to allow things to get below a certain level. It is like training a horse: do you train the horse to be a sprinter, to run cross-country, or to be a dressage horse? I often laugh after the first rehearsal especially if I work on something new to the repertoire and am still not sure about how I feel about the piece or maybe it was a stretch in repertoire for me where I am saying hmm, maybe I am not ready for this piece right now but it presented itself so I am going to deal with it because I have the technique to do it but maybe I need a little bit more time to do it; after the first rehearsal I see the goal come closer, it does not seem as unreachable. The first goal for me is to survive, to be able to say: we're going to do it. It may not be perfect, but it will get there. Each orchestra, each group, whether it is a chorus, or en ensemble of singers or an orchestra, has its definite strengths and definite weaknesses. I need to take all that into consideration and make the best of it as I can. The minority of musicians will say: that was really good. There is always a tendency to say that it could be better. We never reach perfection but we are taught from a young age to strive for it although we have no idea what it is.

DMD
Can you tell why you have achieved?

KK

Definitely. I am always in discourse with myself because people are always in discourse with me. There is always a lot of feedback going on in all directions. Interestingly enough it most often comes in the form of a compliment when you are in an everyday setting of working with the group. In this way I also provide feedback, to myself and the others: the strings have come so far with this, or finally we are playing all the cords together, there is not always someone trailing behind, or the dynamics are getting better as a group, or things that I do not have to say any more in the first rehearsal, like: can we all play softly when it says "soft" in the score? In working with a group, as in a marriage, these things become part of your every day. Then you can bring more individual nuances out, more character and variety. It is a constant juggling between looking at the big picture and looking at what you have in front of you.

DMD

How do you achieve diversity in unity?

KK

With reference to this particular production of *Walküre*: it is a Wiederaufnahme. In other words I was taking over an existing production that was created a few years ago. For this *Ring* cycle the previous conductor is doing *Siegfried* and *Götterdämmerung*, and I am doing *Das Rheingold* and *Walküre*. Because it had been prepared initially by someone else, I felt I had to find ways to make it mine. On 17 June 2012 was only the second time I had conducted *Walküre*. The first time was one month before that. We had three orchestral rehearsals and two stage orchestra rehearsals, basically a dress rehearsal over an entire day. In the first rehearsal we were definitely swimming because I was of course different than the previous conductor. The orchestra had only done *Walküre* with that conductor, because they did not have several conductors coming through and changing things quickly. I said what kind of things about the sound I wanted to change, without criticizing the previous conductor, but I need to make it mine in a very short amount of time. The first performance went quite well. The second performance was cancelled for a variety of reasons and then it rested for a month. My manager had come to the first performance of the *Walküre* and advised me to bring more individuality out of various groups, out of the texture, as it can be a wash. I told this to the orchestra at the rehearsal for *Rheingold*: try individually to bring out the Leitmotifs a little bit more, listen who you give the theme away to and try to make it a little more seamless. Then I kept demanding that they play softer and softer and softer. That's when it becomes fun: instead of just controlling the volume, that's when you can bring details up, when you trust that they will not just boom up and overpower the stage or overpower the pit. I asked them to honour the dynamics: Wagner is very specific about what he wants. Not everybody makes the diminuendo at the same time. So I might say: over these sixteen measures, please play the dynamics exactly as you have, because it is not one massive diminuendo or one massive crescendo; play exactly what he wrote, and to do at a level suitable to your instrument. If he says crescendo to a mezzo forte, just because the instrument next to you makes a bigger crescendo, chances are that instrument has a crescendo going to fortissimo one bar later. I make them aware of those things. The composers were very scrupulous about those things, they knew what they were doing.

DMD
How do you work with the singers on their own? How far can you go /overlap with coaching, here the vowel is too open, here the intonation is not clean

KK
I work with them on a one to one basis. I come from a long line of voice preparation—during my studies at the University of Indiana, from the age of seventeen I played for all the teachers and I studied voice for two years myself and I am definitely a conductor who intervenes. I have never had a singer tell me to stop. Because I know what I am doing, I studied for a long time. I treat the voice as an instrument and I tell people some truths, that they do not want to hear, in a very careful way, naturally, and depending on the level of the singer, I will change my tone. The beginners are eager for any piece of information that you can give them and that they can take back to their teacher and their other coaches to talk about. When I worked with Klaus Florian [Vogt], I would ask him questions because his voice is so unique, and he comes from a different perspective, being a horn

player: his ability to sing long lines without taking a breath is phenomenal, and during one performance of *Lohengrin* two years ago in Hamburg he ran out of breath in one phrase where he never ran out of breath. I went to him to apologise: oh my God, was I too slow, did I not give you time to breathe, and he said: no, I was negotiating my own vowel, you know, I am not perfect, and I got caught in one place at the wrong time. At that highest level a singer knows when conductors really know about voice. I also play for my singers, I still coach, I play cembalo for my Mozart operas; I come from the violin school and the vocal school, for sure.

DMD
How do you support the singers, in principle, and on any given day? Do you make allowances for differences on the date of performance?

KK
That comes with the territory, a little bit. Generally, if they are nice to me they are telling me they are having a down day, or they are not hearing so well, or they are at the start or the end of a cold, and I know what that means, or I have phlegm, or migraine, or jet-lag; as a huge generalisation, when singers are tired they tend to hang on to their notes even longer at the end of the phrase and they get sloppy. I tell them: OK, do whatever you need to do, take more breath, keep the rhythms crisp and don't hang on to notes at the end of phrases. I'll give you more time, but don't get sloppy. Usually when I am preparing singers they have a pretty good idea of the concept and I can give them a lot of artistic liberty within that concept, even a little more time on a note, but they know what the general goal is. If you have been working with people over six week then it gets much easier. For example, the rehearsal the day before yesterday for *Walküre* was so much easier than the one before because Kelly God [Sieglinde] and Vincent [Wolfsteiner, Siegmund] had not worked with each other before, and we had just started piano rehearsals for *Il Trittico*. Through the orchestra rehearsals and performances of *Il Trittico* came a real trust so that they were so sure that I would always give them time and that I can always catch them if there is a mistake. We had built up trust over six weeks. It is fabulous when that happens, and it happens more and more now that I work with colleagues repeatedly on various occasions.

DMD

When you work on new productions, how do you like working with the director?

KK

It depends on where I am. In my own opera house, unfortunately I do not have as much time to go to the staging rehearsals as I would like, because of the administrative responsibilities, auditions for instrumentalists and singers. Since I came to Europe I have done seventeen premieres, and in four of those the experience was really positive: the director and I met very early and we talked about the concept. On the other occasions I just showed up as scheduled and we got along and the result was really good and sometimes it was not so good.

DMD

How do you find out about singers you have not known before? Do you to see performances elsewhere? Are you approached by agents with demo material? Are you approached by singers themselves with demo material?

KK

In principle all of the above. The least of all at the moment is travelling to hear other singers. When I travel I try to see performances. At the moment I have a team of people who are here to do that. They send me CDs, DVDs, recordings, or youtube clips and say: what do you think. We may then invite them for a working rehearsal or for an audition. I know a lot of people anyway, and our team goes to a lot of competitions. I depend on my creative team. Managers will send me things, a lot of them know me already, so we talk.

Case study three: Sir Roger Norrington
Biography

Roger Norrington was born on 16 March 1934, son of Sir Arthur Norrington (1899-1982), former Vice-Chancellor of Oxford University. He studied the violin from the age of ten and singing from the age of seventeen, and read English Literature at Clare College

Cambridge. After a number of years as an amateur violinist, tenor and conductor, he studied at the Royal College of Music under Sir Adrian Boult. In 1962 he founded the Schütz choir, from 1969 to 1984 he was music director of Kent Opera, in 1978 he founded the London Classical Players, serving as their musical director until 1997. Further major roles include principal conductor of Bournemouth Sinfonietta (1985-89), Camerata Salzburg (1997-2006), Stuttgart Radio Symphony Orchestra (1998-2011). In the 2011/12 season he started his role as principal conductor of the Zurich Chamber Orchestra. He was made an OBE in 1980, CBE in 1990 and Knight Bachelor in 1997. In the early 1990s he was diagnosed with cancer, but has been treated successfully, with over 100 pills per day and a tailor-made diet prescribed by an American specialist.

Norrington's name has been associated first and foremost with endeavours to perform music today as much as possible in the way that we must assume, based on research, it to have been played at the time when it was composed. This means using period instruments, and taking special account of descriptions of the music as found in treatises, diaries and letters of the time. In particular, Norrington insists that vibrato for strings was not the norm until early in the 20th century, and should not be used, strictly speaking, in performances of music composed before that time. His views and practice have earned him both praise and criticism.

Interview

DMD
How does the idea of the music form in your mind? Same for instruments and singers?

RN
At this point in my life, I can say that I know most pieces at least to some extent: some very well, I may even have played in them, or sung in them as a chorister. If, on the other hand, it is a world premiere, you have nothing to go on except the score, and then you have to hear what is in the score. On the basis of this general knowledge, I actually like to hear the music, so I learn it through the ear as much as through the eye. I will thus listen to recordings and will get an idea of it in that way, of how people generally do it, and what it generally sounds like.

Then I look at the score and see whether actually they are doing anything like what it says. Then you correct what you heard or what you learnt about a piece in the past, and put it right, in your mind. When I then come to conduct it, it does not sound anything like the record I heard, unless, of course, it is a terribly good recording: in such cases you listen to a record and you think you would imitate the recording, but I don't. I have learnt that even if I hear a record which I want to imitate, for example Benjamin Britten conducting his own music, so I want to do it like that. However, when it actually came to it, when I hear the subsequent recording of a radio broadcast, or something like that, I am amazed at how different it is. Perhaps slightly worrying in some ways, but it just shows that if you have lots of ideas you probably use them.

The score, or course, is terribly important because it allows you to see what is written down by whoever wrote it, and, if you are well trained, what those marks mean. They do not mean the same to us now than they did then. There are quite a lot of examples for this—in the same way that words change, music writing has changed. When Jane Austen wrote *Sense and Sensibility*, she does not mean "now do be sensible, my dear", she means "sensitivity". She lives in the same time as Mozart, and the way the notes are written down has changed and we need to know about that. So you try and sort out exactly what the writing in the score means, particularly in terms of speed. Here you have to make a big point of not being influenced by what you have heard before, which is quite a hard thing to do. Music works a lot by tradition, tradition of how you do things. That is a real danger. Mahler said: tradition is laziness—"Tradition is Schlamperei". That is very true, but it is also that music is so difficult to perform and therefore it is handy to have a tradition. The danger is that it can work like Chinese whispers: tradition is handed on and it gets more and more bent. Therefore, you really have to be careful to avoid tradition of any kind.

In the end, which is where the ear comes in, very prominently, I do many pieces from memory anyway. Listening is very important: music is about sound, about what you hear, it is not about what you read, it is not a book. Books are, on the whole, not written to be read out aloud, but music is. If you conduct from memory, you start listening to what is coming out from the orchestra or chorus much more than if you were looking at the score at the same time. A certain part of your concentration is used up by looking at the score. Thus, if you are not looking at the score, you focus all your concentration on listening to what is coming towards you. Both the score and listening are important, like riding two horses: one of them is telling you to get it right, in historical terms, and the other is saying: "use your imagination, boy, don't be hamstrung". When you have both at once, it is very exciting.

DMD
Does the public performance add more to the performance of the music than could have been achieved at the rehearsals, due to enhanced attention in the presence of an audience?

RN
That is the case if you are lucky, there might be an extra dimension. If you are unlucky, you may have had a brilliant final rehearsal and something goes wrong in the performance: musicians might get nervous, and not play as well as they did at rehearsal. I think it depends on how carefully prepared you are. If you are over-prepared, it may not have any life to it. If you are under-prepared it will have lots of life but also gaps. The performance is, in a way, another rehearsal.

DMD
Sometimes, performances provide a soundscape that is very undifferentiated, while others develop a diversity in unity, where the conductor develops a general soundscape at early states of a rehearsal to a highly differentiated sound through a process of stopping, emphasising, making requests for changes, clarifying proactively or in response to questions from the musicians, to bring out the differences of strands, of voices, instruments, rhythms…

RN
You have answered the question for me, thank you very much. This is exactly what you do. And it is different with different kinds of music. For Mozart, the notes would be very easy, and we would be talking a lot about detail, about phrasing. In the Tippett *Fantasia concertante on a Theme by Corelli*, the textures are very difficult, and some of the time you are just trying to get it right. It does sound good if it is just

right. You do not have to put a lot of extra magic into it, because it is much more "written" than that. In comparison, you have to put a lot of detailed work into Haydn and Mozart—without that it can sound slightly tedious. Haydn symphonies can sound quite boring if they are not properly phrased. There are thus different ways of rehearsing different pieces.

DMD

How do you work with the singers one to one? How far can you go /overlap with coaching, here the vowel is too open, here the intonation is not clean

RN

Usually I work with good people where one to one work is no longer needed. Exceptions are some stars, with very big or difficult arias, such as "Abscheulicher!" in *Fidelio*. I can certainly do it if they want it. Usually I leave that to assistants. I find it more useful to work with the company, because there the singers can learn from each other, they can hear how I want the style to develop. This approach develops a family feeling, and that's why I like to work with the whole cast. This is particularly effective for unaccompanied recitative, in Händel or Mozart, for example, to make it sound natural. Some singers are good at it, others not so, and they can then listen to the good ones and realise how to do it better.

DMD

When you work on new productions, how do you work with the director?

RN

I have enjoyed working with many directors such as Jonathan Miller of Nicholas Hytner. I am happy for a director to make suggestions about a pause here, or faster tempo there, and I might make suggestions, too, for example asking for a singer to stand in a specific place half a bar later. Such interaction allows for a very fluent production. My ideal production is one where it looks as if the composer had directed it: all flows out of the music.

DMD
From this I gather that you are not much in favour of *Regietheater,*
Regieoper

RN
Or *Eurotrash*, as we call it. I am very happy with *Regietheater* if the
production has anything to do with the opera. That's fine by me. But
the idea that the Regie is going to pull the music apart and deliver a
kind of gesture which has nothing to do with the music is what I do
not like. I would not agree to working in the context of such a
production, or I would walk out. Many productions I see are most
extraordinarily unsuitable to the music.

DMD
How do you support the singers, in principle, and on any given day?
Do you make allowances for differences on the date of performance?

RN
I provide a clear rhythm with the orchestra, and getting them to take a
lot of responsibility for the drive of the music themselves, already in
rehearsal. I do not like the idea that they get into a boat at the
beginning of an aria, sit in it and get delivered at the other end by the
orchestra. They need to be rowing it. The best way I can support that
is by getting them to support themselves, from day one.

The context of spirituality
The activity of conducting, in the contexts of opera and beyond, has
its share of experiences reported by conductors that come under the
heading of *strong emotional experiences with music* as defined and
researched by Gabrielsson, or the heading of *spirituality*. Many
conductors consider at least aspects of music itself is mysterious and
potentially of a spiritual nature; their art of creating the sound of
music with the musicians of the orchestra together with the singers
goes well beyond the craft that can be trained—indeed, greatness, the
spiritual dimension of conducting, enters only once the conductor has
learnt craft and technique to the extent that they come without having
to think about them any more. The conductor's charisma, energy, or
electricity, their chemistry with an orchestra and the singers, are
related to their success in going beyond craft and technique, and to the

questions of *why* and *how* certain conductors can achieve individual differences between the ways they interpret the same scores. In most cases, it is possible to make the case of something special happening, but it is difficult to pinpoint precisely what the differences are, even though their existence is beyond reasonable doubt. As in the case of opera singer Klaus Florian Vogt, the profiles of the three conductors at the centre of the case studies in this chapter reveal a number of similar characteristics of spirituality:

- A range of important decisions where the artists are at crossroads in their lives; in its extreme, in Norrington's case, of physical survival, assuming that survival involves decisions at the highest spiritual level.
- the hard work that is necessary to transform any natural gift into a life-long career and maintain it;
- the importance of the body, of physical fitness.

Conclusion and Outlook

Compared with my 2005 *Theatre and Consciousness: Explanatory Scope and Future Potential*, summarised in the introduction to this book, the material and insights presented in this book have taken the topic from theatre to dance and opera, and have widened the argument to increasingly subjective areas of first-person experience in the context of a dimension of consciousness studies that has been increasingly of interest to researchers over the past eight to nine years: *spirituality*, as a sound, reliable and verifiable category of experience that must be understood beyond its conventional use in the context of religion. Against this background, the insights developed in this book can be summarised as follows:

1. A consciousness studies approach can add to our understanding of history in general and theatre history in particular. Considering theatre history as a series of important events, independent of chronology, it is possible to relate distinctive qualities of theatre in each specific and defined epoch to characteristics of pure consciousness, from where those qualities emerge in the first place.

2. Further, it is possible to relate the specific sequence in which those qualities of pure consciousness emerge, to the specific epochs of theatre history, and thus to begin a discussion of why the sequence of epochs developed as it did.

3. The phenomenon of a particularly large number of plays written and performed in the UK that have a famous artist as main character can be related to the phenomenon, in consciousness studies, of self-referral.

4. Drama and theatre have developed an interest in sets of experiences central to consciousness studies, such as plays with characters that have *synaesthesia*.

5. The critical success of a transposition of a play or opera into the present time depends on the kind of story such a transposed play or opera is able to tell. The more components of the story, plot, characterisation, concept and scenography, work together well, the better, as demonstrated by Ostermeier's production of *Hedda Gabler*. In some cases, as in Herheim's *Tannhäuser*, a lack in conceptual attraction can be compensated by scenographic spectacle. In other cases, as in Neuenfels's *Lohengrin*, characterisation can provide the critical mass to outweigh shortcomings in other aspects of a production. In other cases of opera, finally, if a production does not count among its merits either a consistent concept or spectacular scenography or commanding characterisation, critics may instead focus on the music, the achievements of conductor, orchestra and singers despite the perceived paucity of production values.

6. The analysis of one of Raimund Hoghe's choreographies from a consciousness studies perspective adds a dimension to understanding to his work that is important and not available without this approach.

7. A consideration of ethical implications of theatre (production and reception) from the perspective of consciousness studies allows a series of cogent answers to be developed in relation to a range of important questions that are often left unanswered because they are considered too personal and thus relative.

8. In view of frequent misleading use of the term *guru* in a wide range of current contexts, it is essential to re-assess the meaning of the term in its original context—South Asian spiritual traditions—and in its past and present contexts of South Asian performing arts.

9. The consciousness studies perspective adds meaningfully to the debate about the need for actors not only to warm up to prepare for their performance, but also to cool down to achieve a smooth transition from performance to daily life.

10. A consciousness studies perspective allows us to consider the full range of opera in general, and singing and conducting in particular, from the universe to the individual. On a universal level, planet earth has the purpose of allowing souls to develop their feminine side by

way of incarnating as a human being on earth. One of the ways created by humans themselves to facilitate this development of the feminine aspects of every human being's nature is opera with its emphasis on the feminine elements of emotion and beauty.

Opera and its constituent parts affect the participant (orchestra, conductor, singers, and spectators) in every single performance in a potentially holistic, spiritual way. All opera has that potential. In principle, the extent to which that potential is tapped and put into action and practice depends on the extent to which the component parts are carried out in spiritual terms. A holistic understanding of how opera creates its spiritual impact is possible with reference to the *Vedic* model of language: combined, all aspects of any particular performance of opera may stir, in the pure consciousness of the musician, conductor, singer and spectator, an intuitive glimpse of the eternal ideal of beauty that the genre potentially offers—an experience which is available at a level of consciousness independent of time. From the holistic level we proceed to the individual level. Those two levels exist in mutual interdependence, not at all in opposition to each other. On the individual level, the spiritual experiences of the singers and conductors, as well as research into the impact of music, including that of opera, on an audience, are relevant. The *mise en scène*, finally, has its own role to perform among the constituent parts of opera that can make the experience of opera spiritual.

Of course, this book covers neither all the issues that the 2005 one left over, nor all that has emerged since as possible areas to investigate further, but it has broadened the horizon and further consolidated consciousness studies as a cogent approach to addressing phenomena of production and reception in the performing arts. Future research can explore any level of the argument presented in this book further, in theoretical and empirical contexts and terms.

Bibliography

Adalian, Yvonne. 2000. The Art of Theatre: Magic or Illusion? *Consciousness, Literature and the Arts* 1 (3).

Alexander, Charles N. and Robert W. Boyer. 1989. Seven States of Consciousness: Unfolding the Full Potential of the Cosmic Psyche in Individual Life through Maharishi's *Vedic* Psychology. *Modern Science and Vedic Science* 2 (4): 324-371.

Amir, O., N. Amir and O. Michaeli. 2005. Evaluating the influence of warmup on singing voice quality using acoustic measures. *Laryngoscope* 19: 252-260.

Angelaki, Vasiliki. 2007. Structuring Consciousness through Objects: Fluctuating Roles and Selves in Crimp, Pinter and Ionesco. In *Consciousness, Theatre, Literature and the Arts 2007*, ed. Daniel Meyer-Dinkgräfe, 126-133. Newcastle: Cambridge Scholars Publishing.

Anon. 2011. Sternstunde der Oper: Vom Feinsten: der "Lohengrin" reißt die Besucher der Bayreuther Festspiele zu Beifallsstürmen hin. *Welt Online* July 29, http://www.welt.de/print/welt_kompakt/kultur/article13514088/Sternstunde-der-Oper.html (accessed August 2, 2011).

Antze, Rosemary Jeanes. 1991. Oriental Examples. In *The Secret Art of the Performer: A Dictionary of Theatre Anthropology*, eds. Eugenio Barba and Nicola Savarese, 30-33. London: Routledge.

Apthorp, Shirley. 2009. Lohengrin, Staatsoper Berlin. *Financial Times*, April 9. http://www.ft.com/cms/s/2/7176ed16-2389-11de-996a-00144feabdc0.html#axzz1B0A3Ew6z (accessed December 16, 2011).

Ashperger, Cynthia. 2008. *The Rhythm of Space and the Sound of Time: Michael Chekhov's Acting Technique in the 21st Century*. Amsterdam: Rodopi.

Baker, Janet. 1982. *Full Circle. An Autobiographical Journal*. London: Julia MacRae.

Bakker, Arnold B. 2005. Flow among teachers and their students: The crossover of peak experiences. *Journal of Vocational Behaviour* 66: 26-44.

Balme, Christopher. *Global Theatre Histories*. Online at http://global-theatre-histories.org/about-the-project (accessed April 10, 2011).

Banerjee, Suparna (2010). Designing a dance curriculum for liberal education students: problems and resolutions towards holistic learning. *Research in Dance Education* 11 (1): 35-48.

Banes, Sally and Andre Lepecki. 2006. *The Senses in Performance*. London: Routledge.

Barba, Eugenio, and Nicola Savarese (eds). 1991. *The Secret Art of the Performer. A Dictionary of Theatre Anthropology*. London and New York: Routledge.

Barber, John. 1984. *Daily Telegraph*. 18 January.

Bartlett, Chris and Nick Awde. 2006. *Pete and Dud: Come Again*, London: Methuen. Performed at The Venue, London, 7 March to 3 June, 2006. Reviews in *Theatre Record* 2006: 251-253.

Bassett, Kate. 2008. Hedda Gabler, Barbican, London. *The Independent*, March 2. http://www.independent.co.uk/arts-entertainment/theatre-dance/reviews/hedda-gabler-barbican-londonbr-the-vortex-apollo-shaftesbury-avenue-londonbr-artefacts-bush-london-790146.html (accessed December 15, 2011).

Bennett, Alan. 2009. *The Habit of Art*. London: Faber and Faber. Performed at the
    Lyttleton, Royal National Theatre, London, from 5 November 2009.
Berendt, Joachim-Ernst. 1987. *Nada Brahma: Music and the Landscape of
    Consciousness*. Rochester: Destiny.
Berson, Misha. 1988. Whites Only in Fugard's *The Road to Mecca'*. *San Francisco
    Chronicle Datebook*, 7 February.
Billington, Michael. 2007. The Giant. *The Guardian*, November 9.
    http://www.guardian.co.uk/stage/2007/nov/09/theatre2?INTCMP=SRCH
    (accessed August 23, 2010)
———. The Line. 2009. *The Guardian*, November 24.
    http://www.guardian.co.uk/stage/2009/nov/24/the-line-
    review?INTCMP=SRCH (accessed August 23, 2010).
Binder, Hans. 2012. Personal communication, Email.
Bird, R.J. 2005. Shakespeare as Mathematician: The Use of Iteration and Recursion in
    Much Ado About Nothing. *Consciousness, Literature and the Arts* 6 (1).
Biswas, Ansuman. 2011. The music of what happens: mind, meditation and music as
    movement. In *music and consciousness: philosophical, psychological and
    cultural perspectives*, eds. David Clarke and Eric Clarke, 95-110. Oxford:
    Oxford University Press.
Blair, Rhonda. 2007. *The Actor, Image and Action: Acting and Cognitive
    Neuroscience*. London: Routledge.
Bloch, Susana, Pedro Orthous and Guy Santibañez. 1987. Effector Patterns of Basic
    Emotions: A Psychophysiological Method for Training Actors. *Journal of
    Social and Biological Structures* Jan.: 1-19.
Bockler, Jessica. 2006. The Actor's Self: A Transpersonal Exploration of the Actor-
    Character Relationship. In *Consciousness, Theatre, Literature and the Arts*,
    ed. Daniel Meyer-Dinkgräfe, 60-69. Newcastle: Cambridge Scholars
    Publishing.
Böckem, Jörg. 2010. Im Hier und Jetzt zu sein, wie ein spielendes Kind. *Zeit Online*,
    November 3. http://www.zeit.de/2010/44/Traum-Katharina-
    Schuettler/komplettansicht?print=true (accessed December 15, 2011).
Bonshek, Anna. 2004. *Reverie II*: A Video Installation: Revelation, Consciousness
    and Peace. *Consciousness, Literature and the Arts* 5 (1).
Bown, Abi. 2002. *Hey There Boy with the Bebop*. In *The Drama Book. EMC KS3
    English Series*, eds. Michael Simons and Lucy Webster, 27-60. English and
    Media Centre.
Boyko-Head, Christine. 2002. Mirroring the Split Subject: Jean Genet's *The Balcony*.
    Consciousness, Literature and the Arts 3 (2).
Brahms, Caryl. and Sherrin, Ned. 1979. *Beecham*. Not published. British Library
    Playscript 899.
Brask, Per. 2003. The Reflective Actor. *Consciousness, Literature and the Arts* 4 (2).
———. 2006. Acting and Archetypes: A point of departure. *Consciousness,
    Literature and the Arts* 7 (2).
Bray, Peter. 2009. "But I have that within that passes show": Hamlet's Soliloquies as
    an Expression of Shakespeare's Loss and Transformation. *Consciousness,
    Literature and the Arts* 10 (1).
Broo, Mans. 2003. *As Good as God: The Guru in Gaudiya Vaisnavism*. Abo Akademi
    University Press.

Brown, Ben. 2006. *Larkin with Women*, London: Faber and Faber. Performed 1999 at the Stephen Joseph Theatre, Scarborough, and revived in 2006 at the Orange Tree, London.

Brug, Manuel. 2009a. Herheim und Barenboim scheitern an Lohengrin. *Die Welt*, April 6. http://www.welt.de/kultur/article3509974/Herheim-und-Barenboim-scheitern-an-Lohengrin.html (accessed August 2, 2011).

———. 2009b. Zarah Leander als Operettenstar. *Die Welt*, August 18, http://www.welt.de/die-welt/kultur/article4343306/Zarah-Leander-als-Operettenstar.html (accessed August 2, 2011).

———. 2010. Wagner leuchtet. *Die Welt*, July 7, http://www.welt.de/die-welt/article4072663/Wagner-leuchtet.html (accessed August 2, 2011).

Bscher, Astrid. 2009. *Der Meistersinger – Klaus Florian Vogt*. DVD. Directed by Astrid Bscher. Köln: WDR.

Burge, Anton. 2008. *Whatever happened to the cotton dress girl?* Not published. Performed at the New End Theatre, London, 17 June to 20 July. Reviews in *Theatre Record* 2008: 729f.

Burgess, Chris. 2005. *Sophie Tucker's One Night Stand*. Not published. Performed at the New End Theatre, London, 8 December 2005 to 14 January, 2006. Reviews in *Theatre Record* 2005: 1618.

———. 2008. *Lunch with Marlene*. Not published. Performed at the New End Theatre, London, 28 March to 27 April, 2008. Reviews at *Theatre Record* 2008: 361.

Burroughs, W. S. 1988. *The Western Lands*. London: Picador.

Chanana, Karuna. 2007. Situating the academic profession in Indian tradition, modernisation and globalisation: Implications for research and knowledge. UNESCO. Available at: http://portal.unesco.org/education/en/files/54063/11870007425Karuna_Chanana.pdf/Karuna_Chanana.pdf (accessed October 28, 2012).

Chen, Yilin. 2010. Gender and homosexuality in Takarazuka theatre: *Twelfth Night* and *Epiphany*. *Performing Ethos*, 1 (1): 53-67.

Clarke, Kevin. 2008. Sternstunde des Belcanto. *Klassik.Com*, http://magazin.klassik.com/konzerte/reviews.cfm?TASK=review&PID=1655 (accessed August 2, 2011).

Coldiron, Margaret. 2004. *Trance and Transformation of the Actor in Japanese Noh and Balinese Masked Dance-Drama*. Lewiston, Queenston, Lampeter: The Edward Mellen Press.

———. 2006. The Actor and the Mask: The Mover Moved. In *Consciousness, Theatre, Literature and the Arts*, ed. Daniel Meyer-Dinkgräfe, 117-123. Newcastle: Cambridge Scholars Publishing.

Collard, Christophe. 2009. Performing Intermediality: On Water Engines, Strange Loops and Transgressive Thought. In *Consciousness, Theatre, Literature and the Arts 2009*, ed. Daniel Meyer-Dinkgräfe, 66-76. Newcastle: Cambridge Scholars Publishing.

Colvin, Claire. 1986. *Plays and Players*. April: 21.

Conde, Natasha. 2007. Nothingness. *Consciousness, Literature and the Arts* 8 (1).

Conquergood, Dwight. 1985. Performing as a Moral Act. *Literature in Performance* 5 (2): 1-13.

Cook, Amy. 2010. *Shakespearean Neuroplay: Reinvigorating the Study of Dramatic Texts and Performance through Cognitive Science*. London: Palgrave MacMillan. (Cognitive Studies in Literature and Performance)

Copley, Antony. 2000. *Gurus and their followers: new religious movements in colonial India*. Oxford: Oxford University Press.

Cornforth, Andy and David Ian Rabey. 1999. Kissing Holes for the Bullets: Consciousness in Directing and Playing Barker's *Uncle Vanya*. *Performing Arts International*, 1 (4): 25-45.

Coward, Harold G. 1980. *The Sphota Theory of Language. A Philosophical Analysis*. Delhi, Varanasi, Patna: Motilal Banarsidass.

Crane, Mary Thomas. 2001. *Shakespeare's Brain. Reading With Cognitive Theory*. Princeton and Oxford: Princeton University Press.

Creely, Edwin. 2007. Operating postmodernly—my intentional postmodern theatre. *Consciousness, Literature and the Arts* 8 (2).

Crouch, Tim. 2005. *An Oak Tree*. London: Oberon.

Curtis, Anthony. 2010. *Mr Maugham at Home*. Not published. Performed at the New End Theatre, London, 23 April to 16 May, 2010. Reviews in *Theatre Record* 2010: 463.

Daboo, Jerri. 2007. The Altering I/Eye: Consciousness, 'Self', and the New Paradigm in Acting. *Consciousness, Literature and the Arts* 8 (3).

Davies, Howard. 1985. Personal interview, tape, 29 March.

De Jongh, Nicholas. 2009. *Plague over England*. London: Samuel French. Performed at the Duchess Theatre, London, 23 February to 16 May, 2009. Reviews in *Theatre Record* 2009: 183f.

Demastes, William. 2002. *Staging Consciousness: Theater and the Materialization of Mind*. Ann Arbour: University of Michigan Press.

diBenedetto, Stephen. 2010. *The Provocation of the Senses in Contemporary Theatre*. London: Routledge.

Dieckman, Suzanne Burgoyne. 1991. A Crucible for Actors: Questions of Directorial Ethics. *Theatre Topics*, 1 (1): 1-12.

Dillbeck Susan Levin, and Michael C. Dillbeck. 1997. Introduction: Twenty-Five Years of Unfolding Knowledge of Pure Consciousness through Maharishi Vedic Science. *Modern Science and Vedic Science* 7 (1): 1-38.

Döring, Ralph. 2011. Grandioser "Lohengrin" "Ein Wunder! Ein Wunder"! *Neue Osnabrücker Zeitung*, July 28, http://www.noz.de/deutschland-und-welt/kultur/56025209/grandioser-lohengrin-ein-wunder-ein-wunder (accessed August 2, 2011);

dpa. 2010a. Gelungene Premiere von Rusalka in Muenchen. *Frankfurter Rundschau*, October 24, http://www.fr-online.de/panorama/gelungene-premiere-von--rusalka--in-muenchen/-/1472782/4770938/-/index.html (accessed August 2, 2011)

dpa. 2010b. Meistersinger mit Samt in der Stimme. *Frankfurter Rundschau* August 3, http://www.fr-online.de/panorama/meistersinger-mit-samt-in-der-stimme/-/1472782/4528114/-/index.html (accessed August 2, 2011)

Drucker, Vanessa. 1981. *No Regrets*. Not published. British Library Playscript 1413.

Duffy, Carol Ann. 2007. *Casanova*. Not published. Performed at the West Yorkshire Playhouse, Leeds, 12 to 29 September, 2007. Reviews in *Theatre Record* 2007: 1072f.

Edmiston, Brian. 2000. Drama as ethical education. *Research in Drama Education* 5 (1): 63-83.

Elliot, N., J. Sundberg, and P. Gramming. 1995. What happens during vocal warm-up? *Journal of Voice* 9: 37-44.

Fahrmair, Andreas. 2009. Das Panoramabild eines Jahrhunderts. *Frankfurter Allgemeine Zeitung*, April 1. http://www.faz.net/s/RubC17179D529AB4E2BBEDB095D7C41F468/Doc~E A876AC4D1B57460FB317B2CF5651CAA6~ATpl~Ecommon~Scontent.htm l (accessed April 21, 2011).

Fairchild, Terry. 2002. *Oedipus Rex:* The Sins of the Father. *Consciousness, Literature and the Arts* 3 (2).

Favorini, Attilio. 2006. The Remembered Present in Samuel Beckett and Gerald Edelman. *Consciousness, Literature and the Arts* 7 (1).

Fisher, Amanda Stuart. 2005. Developing an ethics of practice in applied theatre: Badiou and fidelity to the truth of the event. *Research in Drama Education* 10 (2): 247-252.

Fischer-Lichte, Erika. 2008. *The Transformative Power of Performance: A New Aesthetics*. London: Routledge.

Fitzmaurice, Catherine. 2000. Zeami Breathing. *Consciousness, Literature and the Arts* 1 (1).

Forman, Robert. 2004. *Grassroots Spirituality: What it is, Why it is here, Where is it going*. Exeter: Imprint Academic.

Fountain, Tim. 2008. *Rock*. Not published. Performed at the Oval House, London, 29 May to 21 June, 2008. Reviews in *Theatre Record* 2008: 629f.

Fradkin, A.J., B.J. Gabbe, and P.A. Cameron. 2006. Does warming up prevent injury in sport? The evidence from randomised controlled trials. *Journal of Science and Medicine in Sport* 9: 214-220.

Frayn, Michael. 2008. *Afterlife*, London: Methuen. Performed at the Lyttleton Theatre, Royal National Theatre, London, 10 June to 16 August, 2008. Reviews in *Theatre Record* 2008: 674f.

———.1982. *Noises Off*, London: Methuen.

———.1990. *Look Look*, London: Methuen.

———.1988. *Copenhagen*, London: Methuen.

———.2003. *Democracy*, London: Methuen.

Freeman, John. 2001. Autobiographical Spectatorship. *Consciousness, Literature and the Arts* 2 (2).

Fugard, Athol. 1985. *The Road to Mecca*. London: Faber.

Gabrielsson, Alf. 2010. Strong Experiences with Music. In *Handbook of Music and Emotion. Theory, Research, Applications*, eds. Patrick N Juslin and John A Sloboda, 547-574. Oxford: Oxford University Press.

Gardner, Lyn. 2008. Edinburgh Festival: Surviving Spike. *The Guardian*, August 5. http://www.guardian.co.uk/culture/2008/aug/05/edinburgh.surviving.spike.mi chael.barrymore (accessed 15 August 2010).

———. 2008. Hedda Gabler. *The Guardian*, February 29. http://www.guardian.co.uk/stage/2008/feb/29/theatre1.print. (accessed December 15, 2011).

Geer, Richard Owen. 1993. Dealing with Emotional Hangover: Cool-down and the Performance Cycle in Acting. *Theatre Topics* 3(2): 147-158.

Gems, Pam. 1979. *Piaf.* Oxford: Amber Lane.
————.2006. *Mrs Pat.* London: Oberon. Performed at the Theatre Royal, York, 15 March to 1 April, 2006. Reviews in *Theatre Record* 2006: 331-332.
Geyer, Michael and Charles Bright. 1995. World History in a Global Age. *The American Historical Review* 100 (4): 1034-1060.
Ginsberg, Howard. 2006. *My Matisse.* Not published. Performed at the Jermyn Street Theatre, London, 16 November to 9 December, 2006. Reviews in *Theatre Record* 2006: 1346.
Gish, Allison, Melda Kunduk, Loraine Sims, and Andrew J. McWhorter. 2011.Vocal Warm-Up Practices and Perceptions in Vocalists: A Pilot Survey. *Journal of Voice,* in Press.
Gohlke, Christian. 2009. Wagner's 'Lohengrin' an der Bayerischen Staatsoper. *Klassic.Com*, July 5. http://magazin.klassik.com/konzerte/reviews.cfm?TASK=review&PID=2372 (accessed December 16, 2011).
Goldstein, A. 1980. Thrills in response to music and other stimuli. *Physiological Psychology* 8: 126-129.
Graham, James. 2010. *The Whiskey Taster.* London: Methuen Drama.
Greer, Bonnie. 2008. *Marilyn and Ella.* Not published. Performed at the Theatre Royal Stratford East, London, 21 February to 15 March, 2008. Reviews in *Theatre Record* 2008: 190-1.
Greither, Aloys. 1967. Die Todeskrankheit Mozarts. *Deutsche Medizinische Wochenschrift* 92 (15): 723-726.
Gruber, Gernot. 1985. *Mozart und die Nachwelt.* Salzburg, Wien: Residenz.
Hall, Peter. 1983. *Peter Hall's Diaries: The story of a dramatic battle*, Ed. John Goodwin. London: Hamish Hamilton.
Hammer, Anita. 2010. *Between Play and Prayer: The Variety of Theatricals in Spiritual Performance. Amsterdam: Rodopi.*
Hampton, Christopher. 1983. *Tales from Hollywood.* London: Faber and Faber.
Haney, William S, II. 2008. *Integral Drama: Culture, Consciousness and Identity.* Amsterdam: Rodopi.
————. 2010. Eugène Ionesco's *Rhinoceros*: Defiance vs. Conformism. *Consciousness, Literature and the Arts* 11 (3).
Harmer, Maria. 2010. Johan Bothas Spiritualität. http://oe1.orf.at/artikel/215427 (accessed October 11, 2010).
Harris, Richard. 2008. *Surviving Spike.* Not published. Performed at the Theatre Royal Windsor, 5 to 16 February, 2008. Reviews in *Theatre Record* 2008: 139.
Harrison, John, and Simon Baron-Cohen.1997. *Synaesthesia: Classic and Contemporary Readings.* Cambridge, MA: Blackwell Publishers.
Hartmann, Gabriel. 1992. *Maharishi-Gandharva-Ved. Die Klassische Musik der Vedischen Hochkultur: Eine Einführung in die musiktheoretischen Grundlagen.* Vlodrop: MVU Press.
Harwood, Ronald. 1980. *The Dresser.* Oxford: Amber Lane.
———— .2008. *Collaborations* and *Taking Sides.* London: Faber and Faber. *Collaborations* performed at the Duchess Theatre, London, 27 May to 22 August, 2009. Reviews in *Theatre Record* 2009: 590.
———— .2001. *Mahler's Conversion.* London: Faber and Faber.

Hastings, Michael. 1985. *Tom and Viv*. Harmondsworth: Penguin.
Hazou, Rand. 2010. Dys-appearance and compassion: The body, pain and ethical enactments in Mike Parr's *Close the Concentration Camps* (2002). *Performing Ethos* 1 (2): 153-166.
Hetzler, Eric. 2009. The Actor's Awareness: An Empirical Examination from The Survey of the Actor's Experience. In *Consciousness, Theatre, Literature and the Arts 2009*, ed. Daniel Meyer-Dinkgräfe, 46-65. Newcastle: Cambridge Scholars Publishing.
Hildesheimer, Wolfgang. 1977. *Mozart*. Frankfurt/Main: Suhrkamp.
Hinden, Michael. 1982. When Playwrights Talk to God. Peter Shaffer and the Legacy of O'Neill. *Comparative Drama* 16: 49-63.
Hopkinson, Bill. 2007. Lecoq's Neutral Mask: Performing a Corporeal Model of Consciousness. In *Consciousness, Theatre, Literature and the Arts 2007*, ed. Daniel Meyer-Dinkgräfe, 43-52. Newcastle: Cambridge Scholars Publishing.
Hubbard, E.M. and V.S. Ramachandran. 2003. Refining the Experimental Lever: A Reply to Shanon and Pribram. *Journal of Consciousness Studies* 10 (3): 77-84.
Huber, Werner und Hubert Zapf. 1984. On the Structure of Peter Shaffer's Amadeus. *Modern Drama* 27: 299-313.
Hughes, Dusty. 1986. *Futurists*. London: Faber and Faber.
Huron, David and Elizabeth Hellmuth Margulis. 2010. Musical Expectancy and Thrills. In *Handbook of Music and Emotion. Theory, Research, Applications*, eds. Patrick N Juslin and John A Sloboda, 575-604. Oxford: Oxford University Press.
Hutchins, Arthur. 1976. *Mozart der Mensch*. Baarn.
Hutchinson, Ron. 2007. *Moonlight and Magnolias*. Not published. Performed at the Tricycle Theatre, London, 2 October to 3 November, 2007. Reviews in *Theatre Record* 2007: 111f.
Irler, Klaus. 2010. Das Montagsinterview: Nicht jede Frau will sich das antun. *Taz*. March 7. http://www.taz.de/!49378/ (accessed August 31, 2012).
Isherwood, Charles. 2006. Enter Hedda, Modern Chic but Still Fighting Boredom. *The New York Times*, November 30. http://theater.nytimes.com/2006/11/30/theater/reviews/30hedd.html?pagewanted=print (accessed December 15, 2011).
Jahnas, Maria and Johann. 2011. Wien: Der Rosenkavalier, 15.12.2011. *Der Neue Merker*. http://www.der-neue-merker.eu/wien-staatsoper-der-rosenkavalier-3-vorstellung-der-serie (accessed September 2, 2012).
Jauß, Hans Robert. 1977. *Ästhetische Erfahrung und Literarische Hermeneutik. Band I: Versuche im Feld der ästhetischen Erfahrung*. München: Fink.
jfl. 2007. Klaus Florian Vogt's Splendor - Lohengrin on DVD *Ioanarts*, March 23. http://ionarts.blogspot.com/2007/03/klaus-florian-vogts-splendor-lohengrin.html (accessed August 2, 2011)
Jones, Betty True. 1987. Kathakali Dance Drama: An Historical Perspective. In Bonnie C Wade (ed.), *Performing Arts in India: Essays on Music, Dance and Drama, Asian Music* 18:2, 14-44.
Jones, Kelly. 2007. Between Nature and Eternity: (Present)ing Absence in Theatrical Representations of Shakespeare as the Ghost of Hamlet. *Consciousness, Literature and the Arts* 8 (3).

Jupp, Kenneth. 2006. *Tosca's Kiss*. Not published. Performed at the Orange Tree Theatre, Richmond, 5 May to 3 June, 2006. Reviews in *Theatre Record* 2006: 519.

Keim, Stefan. 2006. Zwischen Schwan und Wahn. *Die Welt*, September 11. http://www.welt.de/print-welt/article151687/Zwischen_Schwan_und _Wahn.html (accessed August 2, 2011).

Kempinski, Tom. 1981. *Duet for One, London*. London: French.

Kingdom, Bob. 2008. *Stan Laurel, Please Stand Up*. Not published. Performed at the Warehouse Croydon, 14 to 30 March, 2008. Reviews in *Theatre Record* 2008: 291.

Kogan, Sam, and Helen Pierpoint. 2006. The Science of Acting and Consciousness. In *Consciousness, Theatre, Literature and the Arts*, ed. Daniel Meyer-Dinkgräfe, 52-59. Newcastle: Cambridge Scholars Publishing.

Kohse, Petra. 2005. Zwei verpasste Chancen, die Geschichte zu verändern. *Frankfurter Rundschau*, October 28. https://www.lustaufkultur.de/kulturkalender/veranstaltungen/presse/Hedda-Gabler-25843.html (accessed December 15, 2011)

Konečni, Vladimir, Amber Brown, and Rebekah A Wanic. 2008. Comparative effects of music and recalled life-events on emotional state. *Psychology of Music* 36 (3): 289-308.

Krause, Peter. 2009. Schwanenritter singt sensationell. *Die Welt* September 9. http://www.welt.de/die-welt/kultur/article4537346/Schwanenritter-singt-sensationell.html (accessed August 2, 2011)

Kröner, Eva. 2011. Vom Sängerknaben zum Dauerdirigenten. *Nordbayerischer Kurier*, August 23. http://www.nordbayerischer-kurier.de/nachrichten/vom _s_ngerknaben_zum_dauerdirigenten_22786 (accessed September 2, 2012).

Kumar, Sanjay 2012. Dramatising an evolving consciousness: theatre with Nithari's children. In *Consciousness, Theatre, Literature and the Arts 2011*, ed. Daniel Meyer-Dinkgräfe, 170-199. Newcastle: Cambridge Scholars Publishing.

Kurtz, Anna K. 2011. *Completing the Circle: The Actor's Cool-Down*. MFA Thesis, Virginia Commonwealth University. Online at https://digarchive.library.vcu.edu/bitstream/handle/10156/3272/Completing% 20the%20Circle-%20The%20Actor%27s%20Cool%20Down.pdf?sequence=1 (accessed November 15, 2011).

Lai, Ming-Yan. 2010. The sexy maid in Indonesian migrant workers' activist theatre: subalternity, performance and witnessing. *Performing Ethos* 1 (1): 21-34.

Laine, Tarja, and Wanda Strauven. 2009. Introduction: The synaesthetic turn. *New Review of Film and Television Studies* 7 (3): 249-255.

Lambert, Hervé Pierre. 2010. New Relations between Literature and *Synaesthesia*. In *Consciousness, Theatre, Literature and the Arts 2009*, ed. Daniel Meyer-Dinkgräfe, 159-169. Newcastle: Cambridge Scholars Publishing.

Lange, Joachim. 2011. Lauter Schwere Fälle. *Frankfurter Rundschau*, March 2, http://www.fr-online.de/kultur/musik/lauter-schwere-faelle/-/1473348/7508344/-/index.html (accessed August 2, 2011)

Larrass, Michael. 2000. The Evolution of Awareness Parallels and Contrasts in the *Bhagavad Gita* and *Macbeth*. *Consciousness, Literature and the Arts* 1 (1).

Lavery, Carl and Ralph Yarrow. 2004. Genet's Sacred Theatre: Practice and Politics. *Consciousness, Literature and the Arts* 5 (1).

Lawrence, Amanda. 2009. *Jiggery Pokery*. Not published. Performed at the Battersea Arts Centre, London, 2 to 19 December, 2009. Reviews in *Theatre Record* 2009: 1290f.

Lewis, David. 2005. *Monkey's Uncle*. Not published. Performed at the Orange Tree Theatre, Richmond, 7 October to 5 November, 2005. Reviews in *Theatre Record* 2005: 1233.

Lierde, Kristiane M. Van, Evelien D'haeseleer, Nele Baudonck, Sofie Claeys, Mark De Bodt, and Mara Behlau. 2011. The Impact of Vocal Warm-Up Exercises on the Objective Vocal Quality in Female Students Training to be Speech Language Pathologists. *Journal of Voice* 25 (3): e115-e121.

Logan, Brian. 2009. Eric Morecambe and Charles Hawtrey: Bring me sunshine … again, *The Guardian*, November 30. http://www.guardian.co.uk/stage/2009/nov/30/eric-morecambe-charles-hawtrey-biography (accessed August 15, 2010).

Luckhurst, Mary. 2010. Ethical stress and performing real people. *Performing Ethos* 1 (2): 135-152.

Luehrs-Kaiser, Kai. 2011. Deutsche Oper Berlin: Klaus Florian Vogt. *Kulturradio rbb*, Berlin, July 9. http://www.kulturradio.de/rezensionen/buehne/2011/Deutsche_Oper_Berlin__Klaus_Florian_Vogt.html (accessed August 2, 2011)

Lundquist, Lars-Olov, Frederik Carlsson, Per Hilmersson, and Patrik N. Juslin. 2009. Emotional response to music: experience, expression, and physiology. *Psychology of Music* 37 (1): 61-90.

Lutterbie, John. 2011. *Toward a General Theory of Acting: Cognitive Science and Performance*. London: Palgrave MacMillan.

MacDonald, Stephen. 1983. *Not About Heroes: The Friendship of Siegfried Sassoon and Wilfred Owen*. London: Faber and Faber.

Madhavan, Arya. 2010. *Kudiyattam Theatre and the Actor's Consciousness*. Amsterdam: Rodopi.

Maharishi Mahesh Yogi. 1969. *On the Bhagavad-Gita. A New Translation and Commentary, Chapters 1 – 6*. Harmondsworth: Penguin.

———. 1997.*Perfection in Education*. Jabalpur: Maharishi Vedic University Press.

Majzels, Ashley. 2008. John Cage's 'Chance' and Richard Foreman's 'Consciousness': Performing the Sublime. *Consciousness, Literature and the Arts* 9 (1).

Malekin, Peter, and Ralph Yarrow. 2000. The Pashyanti Project. *Consciousness, Literature and the Arts* 1 (2).

Malekin, Theo. 2010. *Strindberg and the Quest for Sacred Theatre*. Amsterdam: Rodopi.

Malliou, Paraskevi, Stella Rokka, Anastasia Beneka, George Mavridis and George Godolias. 2007.Reducing risk of injury due to warm up and cool down in dance aerobic instructors. *Journal of Back and Musculoskeletal Rehabilitation* 20: 29–35.

Mandengue, S.H., I. Miladi, D. Bishop, A. Temfemoa, F. Cisse, and S. Ahmaidi. 2009. Methodological approach for determining optimal active warm-up intensity: predictive equations. *Science & Sports* 24: 9–14.

Mangan, Michael. 2007. Conjuring, Consciousness and Magical Thinking. In *Consciousness, Theatre, Literature and the Arts 2007*, ed. Daniel Meyer-Dinkgräfe, 1-20. Newcastle: Cambridge Scholars Publishing.

———. 2007. *Performing Dark Arts: A Cultural History of Conjuring*. Bristol: Intellect.

Mangold, Alex. 2007. The empty "I"— Echoes of Subjectivity in Sarah Kane's *Crave*. In *Consciousness, Theatre, Literature and the Arts 2007*, ed. Daniel Meyer-Dinkgräfe, 116-125. Newcastle: Cambridge Scholars Publishing.

Marriott, Tim. 2005. *Pete 'n' Me*. Not published. Performed at the New End Theatre, London, 5 to 26 February, 2005. Reviews in *Theatre Record* 2005: 170.

Marshall, Anne. 1963. *Hunting the Guru in India*. London: Gollancz.

Martens, Söhnke. 2011. Klaus Florian Vogt. Das Interview: Ein Gefühl von Freiheit. *Das Opernglas*, 07-08. https://archiv.opernglas.de/index.php?sid= u3sdkk25la2g9i8ad8j1lbcp4l4opm41& (accessed August 2, 2011)

Matheopoulos, Helena. 1982. *Maestro: Encounters with Conductors of Today*. London: Hutchinson.

———.1989. *Bravo. The World's Great Male Singers discuss their Roles*. London: Victor Gollancz.

———.1991. *Diva. Great Sopranos and Mezzos discuss their Art*. London: Victor Gollancz.

———. 1998. *Diva: The New Generation. The Sopranos and Mezzos of the Decade discuss their Roles*. London: Little Brown and Company.

———.2000. *Placido Domingo: My Operatic Roles*. London: Little, Brown and Company.

Maxwell, Dominic. 2008. Whatever Happened to the Cotton Dress Girl? at the New End Theatre, NW3. *The Times*, June 17. http://www.thetimes.co.uk/tto/arts/stage/theatre/article1868753.ece (accessed August 15, 2010).

McArdle, W. D., F. I. Katch, and V. L. Katch. 2001. *Exercise Physiology*, 5th ed., Philadelphia, PA: Lippincott Williams & Wilkins.

McConachie, Bruce and Faith Elizabeth Hart. 2006. *Performance and Cognition: Theatre Studies and the Cognitive Turn*. London: Routledge.

McConachie, Bruce. 2008. *Engaging Audiences*: *A Cognitive Approach to Spectating in the Theatre*. London: Palgrave MacMillan. (Cognitive Studies in Literature and Performance)

McCutcheon, Jade Rosina. 2001. Theatre—Re-assessing the Sacred in Actor Training. *Consciousness, Literature and the Arts* 2 (2).

———. 2006. Explorations under (Below) Standing Consciousness: The Actor's Altered State in Performance—Actor as Shaman. In *Consciousness, Theatre, Literature and the Arts*, ed. Daniel Meyer-Dinkgräfe, 27-33. Newcastle: Cambridge Scholars Publishing.

———. 2008. *Awakening the Performing Body*. Amsterdam: Rodopi.

McGuinness, Donna, and Catherine Doody. 2006. The Injuries of Competitive Irish Dancers. *Journal of Dance Medicine&Science* 10 (1,2): 35-39.

McGuiness, Frank. 2010. *Greta Garbo came to Donegal*. Not published. Performed at the Tricycle Theatre, London, January 11 to February 20, 2010. Reviews in *Theatre Record* 2010: 29f.

————.2010. When Greta Garbo came to town. *The Guardian*, January 11. http://www.guardian.co.uk/stage/2010/jan/11/greta-garbo-donegal-frank-mcguinness (accessed August 15, 2010).

McHenry, Monica, Jim Johnson and Brianne Foshea. 2009. The Effect of Specific Versus Combined Warm-up Strategies on the Voice. *Journal of Voice* 23(5): 572-576.

Mende, Hans Jürgen. 2012. Dirigentin Karen Kamensek. *Alpha Forum* January 16. http://www.br.de/fernsehen/br-alpha/sendungen/alpha-forum/karen-kamensek104.html (accessed August 31, 2012).

Meyer-Dinkgräfe, Daniel. 2003. Consciousness, Theatre and Terrorism. *Consciousness, Literature and the Arts* 4 (3)

————. 2005a. *Theatre and Consciousness: Explanatory Scope and Future Potential.* Bristol: Intellect.

————. 2005b. Artaud's mental illness reconsidered. *Studies in Theatre and Performance* 25 (2): 165-168.

————. 2006. Cold Dark Soft Matter Research and Atmosphere in the Theatre. *Body Space Technology* Volume 6, 2006. Online at http://people.brunel.ac.uk/bst/vol0601/home.html

————. 2007. The Body as Consciousness: Concepts and Implications for Actor Training. In *Consciousness, Theatre, Literature and the Arts 2007*, ed. Daniel Meyer-Dinkgräfe, 53-66. Newcastle: Cambridge Scholars Publishing.

————. 2009. Body against Boundaries: Consciousness in Raimund Hoghe's Choreography. In *Consciousness, Theatre, Literature and the Arts 2009*, ed. Daniel Meyer-Dinkgräfe, 155-158. Newcastle: Cambridge Scholars Publishing.

————. 2010. The Ethical Dimension of Theatre. In *Ethical Encounters: Boundaries of Theatre, Performance and Philosophy*, eds. Daniel Meyer-Dinkgräfe and Dan Watt, 135-153. Newcastle: Cambridge Scholars Publishing.

————. 2011. Opera and Spirituality. *Performance and Spirituality* 2 (1):38-59. Online at http://www.utdl.edu/ojs/index.php/pas/article/viewFile/3/3

Moran, Andrew. 2005. *Synaesthesia* and Eating in *The Winter's Tale*. *Religion and the Arts* 9 (1-2): 38-61.

Morgan, Michael. 2006. Creative Chaos in Fitzmaurice Voicework. In *Consciousness, Theatre, Literature and the Arts,* ed. Daniel Meyer-Dinkgräfe, 34-40. Newcastle: Cambridge Scholars Publishing.

Mower, Susan. 2009. Etienne Decroux: A Corporeal Consciousness. *Consciousness, Literature and the Arts* 10 (2).

————. 2010. Peter Brook's Mahabharata: An Intercultural Consciousness. *Consciousness, Literature and the Arts* 11 (2).

Munro, Raymond. 2006. Witness Consciousness and the Acting Process. In *Consciousness, Theatre, Literature and the Arts,* ed. Daniel Meyer-Dinkgräfe, 92-100. Newcastle: Cambridge Scholars Publishing.

Murphy, Gregory. 2005. *The Countess*. Not published. Performed at the Criterion Theatre, London, 7 June to 9 July, 2005. Reviews in *Theatre Record* 2005: 786-9.

Nader, Tony. 1995. *Human Physiology: Expression of Veda and Vedic Literature.* Vlodrop: Maharishi Vedic University.

Nair, Sreenath. 2007. *Restoration of Breath: Consciousness and Performance*.
    Amsterdam: Rodopi
Neki, J.S. 1973. Guru-chela relationships: The possibility of therapeutic paradigm.
    American Journal of Orthopsychiatry 43: 755-66.
————. (1976). The nature of guruship: A psychological perspective. In *The nature of
    guruship*, ed. C.O. Macmullen. Batala: The Christian Institute of Sikh Studies.
Nelson, Richard, with Colin Chambers. 2004. *Tynan*. London: Faber and Faber.
    Performed at the Arts Theatre, London, in a Royal Shakespeare Company
    production, 21 February to 26 March, 2005. Reviews in *Theatre Record* 2005:
    222-224.
Neumann, Carolin. 2011. Eine Frauenquote in der Musik? Unmöglich. *Spiegel
    Online*. February 2.
    http://spiegel.de/politik/deutschland/0,1518,742728,00.html (accessed August
    31, 2012).
Novello, Vincent und Mary. 1959. Eine Wallfahrt zu Mozart: Die Reisetagebücher
    von Vincent und Mary Novello aus dem Jahre 1829. Deutsche Übertragung
    von Ernst Roth. Bonn: Boosey and Hawkes.
Nutten, Laura. 2001. Madness and Signification in *A Mouthful of Birds*.
    Consciousness, Literature and the Arts 2 (3).
O'Brien, Edna. 1981.*Virginia*, London: Hogarth.
Öztürk, Maya N. 2006. Through the Body: Corporeality and Consciousness at the
    Performance Site. In *Consciousness, Theatre, Literature and the Arts*, ed.
    Daniel Meyer-Dinkgräfe, 143-158. Newcastle: Cambridge Scholars
    Publishing.
Osterhammel, Jürgen. 2009. *Die Verwandlung der Welt. Eine Geschichte des 19.
    Jahrhunderts*. München: C.H. Beck.
Owens, Naomi 1987. The Dagar Gharana: A Case Study of Performing Artists. In
    Performing Arts in India: Essays on Music, Dance and Drama, ed. Bonnie C
    Wade. *Asian Music* 18 (2): 158-195.
Padoux, André. 1992. *Vac. The Concept of the Word in Selected Hindu Tantras*.
    Delhi: Sri Satguru Publications.
Panksepp, Jaak. 1995. The emotional sources of "chills" induced by music. *Music
    Perception* 13: 171-207.
Panzarella, Robert. 1980. The phenomenology of aesthetic peak experiences. *Journal
    of Humanistic Psychology* 20 (1): 69-85.
Paumgartner, Rudolf. 1949. *Mozart*. Freiburg & Zürich: Atlantis.
Peterson, Michael. 2007. The Animal Apparatus: From a Theory of Animal Acting to
    an Ethics of Animal Acts. *The Drama Review* 51 (1): 33-48.
Pienaar, Samantha. 2007. Enchanted Bodies: The Contemporary Performer as Urban
    Shaman. In *Consciousness, Theatre, Literature and the Arts 2007*, ed. Daniel
    Meyer-Dinkgräfe, 37-42. Newcastle: Cambridge Scholars Publishing.
Pierce, Jennifer Ewing. 2004. The Actor-Problem: Live and Filmed Performance and
    Classical Cognitivism. *Consciousness, Literature and the Arts* 5 (3).
Pifer, Drury. 2008. *Strindberg in Hollywood*. Not published. Performed at the
    Pentameters Theatre, London, 7 to 24 February, 2008. Reviews in *Theatre
    Record* 2008: 111.
Piper, Frances. 2006. Keeping Mum: Towards a "Voix Maternelle" in Howard
    Barker's *Wounds to the Face*. *Consciousness, Literature and the Arts* 7 (2).

Pitz-Grewenig, Michael. 2012. Reine Poesie. *Klassic.com*. July 26.
http://magazin.klassik.com/konzerte/reviews.cfm?task=review&PID=4510
(accessed September 2, 2012).

Pizzato, Mark. 2011. *Inner Theatres of Good and Evil: The Mind's Staging of Gods, Angels and Devils*. Jefferson: McFarland.

Plater, Alan. 2005. *Sweet William*. Not published. Performed at the Viaduct Theatre, Halifax, 23 to 26 February, 2005. Reviews in *Theatre Record* 2005: 242.

Postlewait, Thomas. 2009. *The Cambridge Introduction to Theatre Historiography*. Cambridge: Cambridge University Press.

Power, Cormac. 2008. *Presence in Play: A Critique of Theories of Presence in the Theatre*. Amsterdam: Rodopi.

Pownall, David. 1983. *Master Class*, London: Faber and Faber.

———. 1985. Interview with the author, March 4.

Pribram, Karl. 2003. Commentary on 'Synaesthesia' by Ramachandran and Hubbard. *Journal of Consciousness Studies* 10 (3): 75-76.

Prickett, Stacey. 2004. Techniques and Institutions: The Transformation of British Dance Tradition through South Asian Dance. *Dance Research* 22(1):1-21.

Prinz, Jesse. 2009. Is Consciousness Embodied? In *The Cambridge Handbook of Situated Cognition*, eds. Philip Robbins and Murat Aydede, 419-436. Cambridge: Cambridge University Press.

Pritchard, Jim. 2012. Bayreuth stalwarts bow out in final Tristan performance. *Seen and Heard International*. August 27. http://www.seenandheard-international.com/2012/08/27/bayreuth-festival-3-bayreuth-stalwarts-bow-out-in-final-tristan-performance/ (accessed September 2, 2012).

Raina, M.K. 2002. *Guru Shishya* relationship in Indian culture: The possibility of a creative resilient framework. *Psychology Developing Societies* 14: 167-198.

Ramachandran, V.S. and E.M.Hubbard. 2001. *Synaesthesia*—Perception, Thought and Language. *Journal of Consciousness Studies* 8 (12): 3-34.

———. 2003. The Phenomenology of *Synaesthesia*. *Journal of Consciousness Studies* 10 (8): 49-57.

Ramsay, Gordon. Robotic Theatre in Extremis. *Consciousness, Literature and the Arts* 4 (2).

Rausch, Angelika. 2009. Klaus Florian Vogt im Interview: Der Heldentenor vom Grünen Hügel. *Domradio.de*, August 13. http://www.domradio.de/aktuell/55844/der-heldentenor-vom-gruenen-huegel.html (accessed August 2, 2011)

Rickard, Nikki S. 2004. Intense emotional responses to music: a test of the physiological arousal hypothesis. *Psychology of Music* 32 (4): 371-388.

Ridout, Nicholas. 2009. *theatre & ethics*, Basingstoke: Palgrave macmillan.

Risi, Clemens. 2010. Oper: Live – Fetishized – Mediatized. Paper presented at the IFTR World Congress, Munich, 30 July.

Robbins, Kenneth. 2003. The Healing Power of Butoh. *Consciousness, Literature and the Arts* 4 (3).

Rolston, Adam. 2009. *A Sentimental Journey*. Not published. Performed at the Mill at Sonning, Reading, 4 March to 19 April, 2009. Reviews in *Theatre Record* 2009: 260.

Runde, Jessica. 2007. Ionesco beyond Absurdism. *Consciousness, Literature and the Arts* 8 (1).

Saint Germain. 2004. *Das Tor zum Goldenen Zeitalter*. Seeon: ChFalk.

Sarngadev. 1984. *Sangita Ratnakara*. Translated and edited by P. Sharma and R. Shringy. Delhi: Motilal Barnasidass.

Saunders, Amanda. 1085. Interview with the author, January 25.

Schechner, Richard. 1985. *Between Theatre and Anthropology*. Philadelphia: University of Pennsylvania Press.

Schiller, Friedrich. 1789/1972. *The Nature and Value of Universal History: An Inaugural Lecture*. History and Theory 11 (3): 321-334.

Schneider, Peter. 2003. Climbing Mount Everest: On Conducting *Die Meistersinger*. In *Wagner's Meistersinger: Performance, History, Representation*, ed. Nicholas Vazsonyi, 23-38. Rochester: University of Rochester Press.

———. 2011a. Die Opernwerkstatt. Der Dirigent Peter Schneider im Gespräch mit Peter Dusek. Aufgneommen am 3 April 2011 im ORF KulturCafe. OE1@ORF May 1.

———. 2011b. Interview by author. Tape recording. Deutsche Oper Berlin, July 9.

Schneider, Uwe. 2006a. Wagner, laut und deutlich. *Klassik.com*. December 3. http://magazin.klassik.com/konzerte/reviews.cfm?TASK=review&PID=1089 (accessed September 2, 2012).

Schneider, Uwe. 2006b. Die Sänger machen die Oper. *Klassik.com*. October 31. http://magazin.klassik.com/konzerte/reviews.cfm?TASK=review&PID=1082 (accessed September 2, 2012).

Schreiber, Wolfgang. 2011. Wagner-Energien: Neuenfels und Nelsons begeistern in Bayreuth mit dem "Lohengrin". July 29, http://www.sueddeutsche.de/Y5338W/126052/Wagner-Energie.html (accessed August 2, 2011).

Sellers-Young, Barbara. 2002. Breath, Perception and Action: The Body and Critical Thinking. *Consciousness, Literature and the Arts* 3 (2).

Seton, Mark Cariston. 2006. 'Post-Dramatic' Stress: Negotiating Vulnerability for Performance. *Being There*. Sydney: University of Sydney.

———.2010. The ethics of embodiment: actor training and habitual vulnerability. *Performing Ethos* 1 (1): 5-20.

Shaffer, Peter. 1980. *Amadeus*. London: Deutsch.

Shankar, Sri Sri` Ravi. 1990. *Bhakti Sutras* http://www.artofliving.org/guru-poornima (accessed August 2, 2011).

Shanon, Benny. 2003. Three Stories Concerning *Synaesthesia*: A commentary on Ramachandran and Hubbard. *Journal of Consciousness Studies* 10 (3): 69-74.

Shaughnessy, Nicola. 2005. Truths and lies: exploring the ethics of performance applications. *Research in Drama Education* 10 (2): 201-212.

Shepherd, Andrew. 2005. *The Trial of Sir Henry Irving (Lately Deceased)*. Not published. Performed at the Courtyard, Covent Garden, London, 11 to 30 October, 2005. Reviews in *Theatre Record* 2005: 1357.

Shepherd, Jack. 2010. *Demi-Monde: The Half World of William Morris*. Not published. Performed at the Riverside Studios, London, 17 February to 17 March, 2010. Reviews in *Theatre Record* 2010: 189.

Sher, Anthony. 2007. *The Giant*, London: Nick Hern. Performed at the Hampstead Theatre, London, 7 November to 1 December, 2007. Reviews in *Theatre Record* 2007: 1351f.

Shiota, Michelle N. and James W. Kalat. 2011. *Emotion*. 2nd edition. Wadsworth.

Sinkovicz, Wilhelm. 2008. Aus Glanz und Wonne kommt er her: Klaus Florian Vogts
umjubeltes Lohengrin-Debüt. *Die Presse*, May 23,
http://diepresse.com/home/kultur/news/385668/Kritik_Staatsoper_Aus-Glanz-
und-Wonne-kommt-er-her?from=suche.intern.portal (accessed August 2,
2011).
———. 2010. Oper: Paris lockt Wagner-Freunde *Die Presse*, September 20,
http://diepresse.com/home/kultur/klassik/595881/Oper_Paris-lockt-
WagnerFreunde?from=simarchiv (accessed August 2, 2011).
Sion, Ioana. 2006. The Shape of the Beckettian Self: *Godot* and the Jungian Mandala.
Consciousness, Literature and the Arts 7 (1).
Skarvellis, Jackie. 2007. *James Dean is Dead [Long Live James Dean]*. Not
published. Performed at the Pentameters Theatre, London, 3 to 30 April, 2007.
Reviews in *Theatre Record* 2007: 382.
Slade, Laurie. 2005. *Joe and I*. Not published. Performed at the King's Head Theatre,
London, 15 November to 18 December, 2005. Reviews in *Theatre Record*
2005: 1516.
Smiles, Roy. 2009. *Kurt and Sid*, London: Oberon. Performed at the Trafalgar Studios
2, London, 24 September to 3 October, 2009. Reviews in *Theatre Record*
2009: 973-4.
———. 2004. *Ying Tong*, London: Oberon. Performed at the New Ambassadors
Theatre, London, 14 February to 19 March, 2005. Reviews in *Theatre Record*
2005:197.
Smith, A.C.H. 1985. Athol Fugard. *Programme Notes for The Road to Mecca*.
London: National Theatre.
Spahn, Claus. 2009. Pausbäckiger Wagner. *Die Zeit*, April 7,
http://www.zeit.de/2009/16/Lohengrin (accessed August 2, 2011).
Spencer, Charles. 2008. Hedda Gabler: Shocking then, shocking now. *The Telegraph*,
February 28,
http://www.telegraph.co.uk/culture/theatre/drama/3671492/Hedda-Gabler-
Shocking-then-shocking-now.html (accessed December 15, 2011).
Stasio, Marilyn. 2006. Hedda Gabler, *Variety*, November 29,
http://www.variety.com/review/VE1117932221?refcatid=33@printerfriendly
=true (accessed December 15, 2011).
Stevenson, Jill. 2010. *Performance, Cognitive Theory, and Devotional Culture:
Sensual Piety in Late Medieval York*. London: Palgrave MacMillan.
Stewart, Brian. 2005. *Marilyn: Case # 81128*. Not published. Performed at Jermyn
Street Theatre, London, 5 to 28 March, 2005. Reviews in *Theatre Record*
2005: 583.
Stokes, John. 2004. "Lion griefs": the Wild Animal Acts as Theatre. *New Theatre
Quarterly* 20 (2): 138-154.
Swann, Julia. N.d. Hedda Gabler. *Birkbeck German Society*,
http://www.selectideas.co.uk/webspacewest/germansoc/reviews/hedda_gabler.
htm (accessed December 15, 2011).
Tomlin, Liz. 2010. A Political Suspension of the Ethical: *To Be Straight With You*
(2007) and *An Evening with Psychosis* (2009). *Performing Ethos* 1 (2): 167-
180.
Thompson, James. 2003. *Applied theatre: bewilderment and beyond*. Bern: Peter
Lang.

Thompson, W. 2006 'Brief one night stand', *Metro*, 27 March.
    http://www.standard.co.uk/arts/theatre/brief-one-night-stand-7387001.html
    (accessed August 15, 2010)
Thomsen, Christian W. und Gabriele Brandstetter. 1982. "Mozart und Shaffers
    Amadeus. *Anglistik und Englischunterricht* 16: 191-210.
Tilmann, Christina. 2005. Die Leiden der jungen H.: Ein Ibsen für heute: Thomas
    Ostermeier triumphiert mit *Hedda Gabler* an der Berliner Schaubühne. *Der
    Tagesspiegel*, October 28. http://tagesspiegel.de/kultur/die-leiden-der-jungen-
    h-/645376.html (accessed December 15, 2011).
Tribble, Evelyn B. 2011. *Cognition in the Globe: Attention and Memory in
    Shakespeare's Theatre*. London: Palgrave MacMillan.
Umlauf, Karsten. 2004. Pancakes und Puccini. *Kultur Joker*. Februar.
    http://www.kulturjoker.de/wp-ebooks/joker-archiv/2004/02-2004.pdf
    (accessed August 31, 2012).+
Venkataraman, Leela. 1994. Transcending the Cultural Divide. *The Drama Review* 38
    (2): 81-88.
Vogt, Klaus Florian. 2008. Interview. *Das Pausenzeichen: Klassikstars im Gespräch*.
    Bayern 4, July 27.
————. 2010a. Interview with Hans Jürgen Mende. *Kultur: Klassik a la carte*. NDR,
    July 26.
    http://www.podcast.de/episode/1690287/Klaus_Florian_Vogt,_Tenor/
    (accessed August 2, 2011)
————. 2010b. Interview with Richard Lorber. *Orfeo, Das Opernstudio* WDR 3. July
    2.
————. 2011a. Interview by author. Tape recording. Deutsche Oper Berlin, July 9.
————. 2011b. Interview by Heino Rindler. *Kulturradio Deutschland*, recorded 9
    July, Berlin, broadcast 21 July 2011.
————.2011c. Interview with Hans Jürgen Mende. *Alpha Forum im BR*, Munich,
    broadcast January 18, 2011, http://www.br-
    online.de/content/cms/Universalseite/2011/07/12/cumulus/BR-online-
    Publikation-ab-10-2010--201958-20110712143517.pdf (accessed August 2,
    2011).
————. 2011d. Interview by Mariana Schroeder. *Wall Street Journal* 19 August.
    http://online.wsj.com/article/SB1000142405311190339290457651005174260
    9530.html#articleTabs%3Darticle. (accessed August 19, 2011).
Voigt, Kerstin. 2011. Zürich: Don Giovanni 9.11.2011. *Der neue Merker*.
    http://www.der-neue-merker.eu/zurich-don-giovanni-am-9-11-2011 (accessed
    September 2, 2012).
————. 2012a. Zürich: Ariadne auf Naxos, 15.2.2012. *Der neue Merker*.
    http://www.der-neue-merker.eu/zurich-ariadne-auf-naxos (accessed
    September 2, 2012).
Wagner, Richard. *Lohengrin*. Synopsis.
    http://www.metoperafamily.org/metopera/history/stories/synopsis.aspx?id=12
    7 (accessed November 12, 2010).
Walsh, Robert. 2009. Can *Synaesthesia* be Cultivated? Indications from Surveys of
    Meditators. *Journal of Consciousness Studies* 16 (4): 81-107.

Ward, Jamie, Daisy Thompson-Lake, Roxanne Ely, and Flora Kaminski. 2008. *Synaesthesia*, creativity and art: What is the link? *British Journal of Psychology* 99: 127-141.

Wardle, Irving. 1986. Wordy Verdi in the stalls. *The Times*, March 20.

Weber, Max. 1964. *The Theory of Social and Economic Organisation.* New York: Free Press.

Weiss, William. 2000. The Ego and the Self in Actor Training. *Consciousness, Literature and the Arts* 1 (1).

————. 2006. How do you apply "spirituality" in actor training? *Consciousness, Literature and the Arts* 7 (3).

Wells, Win.1981. *Gertrude Stein and a Companion.* Not published. British Library Playscript 1621.

Wertenbaker, Timberlake. 2009. *The Line.* London: Faber and Faber. Performed at the Arcola Theatre, London, 23 November to 12 December 2009. Reviews in *Theatre Record* 2009: 1260f.

West, Timothy. 1985. Interview with the author, March 14.

Westecker, Dieter. 1983. Hatten sie wirklich Glück? *Düsseldorfer Nachrichten*, March 28.

White, Hayden. 1990.*The Content of the Form: Narrative Discourse and Historical Representation.* Baltimore: Johns Hopkins University Press.

White, Michael. 2010. Elizabeth picks the wrong man, again, in Covent Garden's new Tannhäuser, *The Telegraph*, December 12. http://blogs.telegraph.co.uk/culture/michaelwhite/100049771/elisabeth-picks-the-wrong-man-again-in-covent-gardens-new-tannhauser/ (accessed December 16, 2011).

Whitnall, Tim. 2009. *Morecambe.* Not published. Performed at the Duchess Theatre, London, 10 December 2009 to 17 January 2010. Reviews in *Theatre Record* 2009: 1324f.

Wilkinson, Tom. 1985. Interview with the author, March 29.

Willner, Monika. 2011. Zwischen Klangrausch und Misstönen. *Westdeutsche Allgemeine Zeitung*, August 1. http://www.derwesten.de/kultur/zwischen-klangrausch-und-misstoenen-id4925051.html (accessed September 2, 2012)

Wilson, J. L. 2005. *Nostalgia: Sanctuary of Meaning*, Cranbury, NJ: Associated University Presses.

Wolf, Matt. 2007. In London, Anthony Sher's 'Giant' fascinates and frustrates. *New York Times*, 13 November. http://www.nytimes.com/2007/11/13/arts/13iht-lon14.4.8314958.html?_r=0 (accessed August 23, 2010).

Woods, Krista, Phillip Bishop and Eric Jones. 2007. Warm-Up and Stretching in the Prevention of Muscular Injury. *Sports Med*, 37 (12): 1089-1099.

Valentine, Elizabeth, Daniel Meyer-Dinkgräfe, Veronika Acs, David Wasley. 2006. Exploratory Investigation of South Indian Techniques and Neurolinguistic Programming as Methods of Reducing Stage Fright in Actors. *Medical Problems of Performing Artists* 21(3): 126-136.

Yarrow, Ralph. 2008. *Sacred Theatre.* Bristol: Intellect.

Zibulski, Axel. 2011. Schwerelos. *Allgemeine Zeitung*, July 29, http://www.allgemeine-zeitung.de/nachrichten/kultur/10995683.htm (accessed August 2, 2011).

Zuccarini, Carlo. 2010. The (lost) vocal object in opera: The voice, the listener and *jouissance*/arousal. *The Erotic: Exploring Critical Issues. 4th Global Conference—Draft Conference Paper.* http://www.inter-disciplinary.net/ci/erotic/er4/zuccarini%20paper.pdf (accessed November 12, 2010).

Index

Lightning Source UK Ltd.
Milton Keynes UK
UKOW040805180413

209410UK00002B/124/P

9 789042 036635